MW01097123

Rookwood Pottery

Rookwood plaque, A.R. Valentien, Seagreen glaze, 8" x 10", mint 25,000-35,000
June 3, 2000 Sold for $45,000

Over Ten Years of Auction Results
1990-2002

A Presentation by Treadway Gallery, Inc. of Cincinnati, Ohio in
Association with the John Toomey Gallery of Oak Park, Illinois

Book design and layout: Carrie White and Dave Warren, Treadway Gallery Inc.

COLLECTOR BOOKS
P.O. Box 3009
Paducah, Kentucky 42002-3009

www.collectorbooks.com

Copyright © 2003 Treadway Gallery, Inc.

The current values in this book should be used only as a guide. They
are not intended to set prices, which vary from one section of the
country to another. Auction prices as well as dealer prices vary greatly
and are affected by condition as well as demand. Neither the authors
nor the publisher assumes responsibility for any losses that might be
incurred as a result of consulting this guide.

Searching For A Publisher?

We are always looking for people knowledgeable within their fields. If
you feel that there is a real need for a book on your collectible subject
and have a large comprehensive collection, contact Collector Books.

Treadway Gallery Inc.
2029 Madison Road
Cincinnati, OH 45208
Phone: 513-321-6742
E-mail: info@treadwaygallery.com
Website: www.treadwaygallery.com

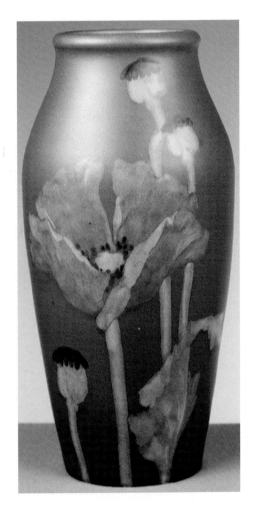

Rookwood vase, poppy decoration,
1901, #192BZ, A.R. Valentien 12"h, mint
7500-10,000
June 4, 1993 Sold for $23,000

Conditions of Sale

The objects in this book were sold following these guidelines.

"**Ceramics** are free of repairs, chips or cracks unless noted in the description of each lot. Our term "mint" refers to the object being in the same condition that it was in when originally produced. Sizes are approximate. Crazing, surface scratches, stilt marks, firing flaws and base flakes will be noted if we feel that they are objectionable. Many pottery makers ground the bottom of their vases causing minute chips or flakes around the bottom. Unless we feel that they are objectionable, they will not be mentioned. Quite often the glaze on pots will run, sometimes reaching the base and being ground off. We will point out anything that we feel to be excessive. When fired in the kiln, pots will sometimes stick to the shelf creating small base chips upon removal. Some framed tiles or plaques may have chips which are hidden by their frames. We will not be responsible for their disclosure. We will mention any of these conditions if we feel that they are objectionable."

Treadway Gallery, Inc.
2029 Madison Rd.
Cincinnati, OH 45208
Voice: 513-321-6742
Fax: 513-871-7722

We want to purchase objects outright or take on consignment for our future auctions. One piece or a collection are of interest. We can arrange delivery or personally pick up objects throughout the world.

We have an established international clientele that we feel is the best in the business. That clientele has enabled us to achieve more world record prices than any of our competitors.

 Expertise - Our expertise in the field of Rookwood objects is second to none. The prices we obtain can attest to that.

 Commission - These terms are flexible for special consignments.

 Payments - Payment is made in 30 business days or less.

 Catalog - Our catalogs are exceptional. Please compare our Rookwood catalog with our competition to judge for yourself. This quality is a key to our success.

 Advertising - We advertise worldwide and maintain the largest and most active mailing list in the industry.

 Photography - Consignors will be pleased to note there is no charge for photography. Our catalogs contain high-quality, professional photographs.

 Estimates - We invite you to bring or send photographs of your property for our estimates. Evaluations of the property can be conducted in your home by contacting Don Treadway at 513-321-6742.

E-mail: info@treadwaygallery.com
Web: www.treadwaygallery.com

1. Rookwood vase, sea green glaze, roses, 1903, shape #80B, S.E. Coyne, 7"h, mint 1500-2000
June 15, 1990 Sold for $1800

2. Rookwood plaque, vellum glaze, sailboats, C. Schmidt, 8"h x 6"w, mint 3000-3500
June 15, 1990 Sold for $3500

3. Rookwood vase, iris glaze, tulips, 1903, #598, S. Sax, drilled, 13.5"h, mint 2500-3000
June 15, 1990 Sold for $2400

4. Rookwood bowl, vellum, cherry blossoms, E.T. Hurley, 1920, #1375, 6"h x 8.5"dia., mint 800-1000
June 15, 1990 Sold for $1000

5. Rookwood vase, vellum, scenic, S.E. Coyne, 1922, #1358F, 6"h, mint 700-900
June 15, 1990 Sold for $1000

6. Rookwood vase, vellum, grasses and palms, E.T. Hurley, 1913, #1124D, 9"h, mint 900-1200
June 15, 1990 Sold for $1300

7. Rookwood plaque, vellum, snow scene, 1915, S.E. Coyne, 9"h x 11"w, mint 2750-3500
June 15, 1990 Sold for $3250

8. Rookwood vase, porcelain glaze, floral design, S. Sax, 1919, #356F, 5.5"h, mint 400-600
June 15, 1990 Sold for $550

9. Rookwood vase, vellum, landscape, E. Diers, 1919, #2103, 5.75"h, mint 700-900
June 15, 1990 Sold for $900

10. Rookwood vase, vellum, landscape, E. Diers, 1915, #939B, 11"h, mint 1200-1500
June 15, 1990 Sold for $2500

11. Rookwood vase, vellum, seascape, E.T. Hurley, 1911, #913D, 7.5"h, mint 900-1200
June 15, 1990 Sold for $650

12. Rookwood vase, porcelain glaze, circular designs, S. Sax, 1924, #2720, 6"h, mint 400-600
June 15, 1990 Sold for $650

13. Rookwood ewer, standard glaze, dogwood design, C.A.B, 1893, #468D, 8"h, mint 350-550
June 15, 1990 Sold for $350

14. Rookwood vase, standard glaze, floral design, J. Swing, 1901, #864, 7"h, mint 400-550
June 15, 1990 Sold for $400

15. Rookwood vase, standard glaze, floral design, L. Fry, 1885, #112, 6"h, mint 700-900
June 15, 1990 Sold for $600

16. Rookwood jug, standard glaze, corn design, A. B. Sprague, 1896, #767, 6"h, mint 450-650
June 15, 1990 Sold for $300

17. Rookwood tankard, standard glaze, swallows, A.R. Valentien, 1893, #286A, 18"h, mint 2000-3000
June 15, 1990 Sold for $1900

18. Rookwood dish, cameo glaze, Mums, A.M. Valentien, 1892, #198, 1.75"h x 7"l, mint 200-300
June 15, 1990 Sold for $180

19. Rookwood vase, standard glaze, floral design, 1901, #498B, E.T. Hurley, 6"h, mint 400-600
June 15, 1990 Sold for $550

20. Rookwood vase, handled, standard glaze, pansies, S. Markland, 1892, #533E, 7"h, mint 400-600
June 15, 1990 Sold for $300

21. Rookwood humidor, standard glaze, tobacco products, 1903, #805, C. Steinle, 6"h, mint 600-750
June 15, 1990 Sold for $850

22. Rookwood vase, iris glaze, flowers, R. Fechheimer, 1903, #905, 10"h, mint 1250-1750
June 15, 1990 Sold for $1300

23. Rookwood coffee pot, cameo glaze, wisteria, G. Young, 1889, #343, 9"h, mint 700-900
June 15, 1990 Sold for $550

24. Rookwood vase, hi-glaze, blossoms and leaves, H.E. Wilcox, 1922, #1926, 6"h, mint 600-800
June 15, 1990 Sold for $500

25. Rookwood vase, sea green, cranes, M.A. Daly, 1899, #787B, 15"h, restored chips 3500-5000
June 15, 1990 Sold for $3000

26. Rookwood vase, iris glaze, cherry blossoms, C.C. Lindeman, 1907, #925E, 6"h, mint 1000-1500
June 15,1990 Sold for $750

27. Rookwood vase, porcelain glaze, vines and flowers, A. Conant, 1918, #292B, 14"h, mint 800-1100
June 15, 1990 Sold for $750

28. Rookwood vase, Chinese plum glaze, white roses, H.E. Wilcox, 1924, #2544, 8"h, mint 700-900
June 15, 1990 Sold for $600

29. Rookwood vase, flaring form on wooden base, metallic rust and gold, #6305, 1932, 6"h, mint 275-350
June 15, 1990 Sold for $325

30. Rookwood vase, squat form, drip glaze, #620, 1951, 7"h x 7"dia., mint 175-250
June 15, 1990 Sold for $200

31. Rookwood vase, flared top, hi-glaze, floral design, L. Epply, 1925, #2240, 6.75"h, mint 450-600
June 15, 1990 Sold for $325

32. Rookwood vase, porcelain glaze, irises, C. Zanetta, date not legible, #2782, 9"h, mint 600-800
June 15, 1990 Sold for $950

33. Rookwood vase, hi-glaze, ribbed, 1933, marked "S," 6"h, mint 300-400
June 15, 1990 Sold for $325

34. Rookwood vase, crystalline drip, 1932, #603C, 7"h, mint 250-350
June 15, 1990 Sold for $210

35. Rookwood vase, porcelain glaze, floral, M.H. McDonald, 1936, #S2132, 12"h, mint 600-800
June 15, 1990 Sold for $600

36. Rookwood vase, drip glaze, 1932, #6315, 6.5"h, mint 250-350
June 15, 1990 Sold for $250

37. Rookwood vase, butterfat glaze, floral, J. Jensen, 1944, no #, 5.5"h, mint 400-600
June 15, 1990 Sold for $325

38. Rookwood vase, porcelain glaze, floral, Shiraya-madani, 1946, #6596, 7.5"h, mint 600-800
June 15, 1990 Sold for $475

39. Rookwood vase, butterfat glaze, birds and flowers, J. Jensen, 1933, #6400, 6"h, mint 700-900
June 15, 1990 Sold for $550

40. Rookwood vase, squeeze bag, L. Holtkamp, #6933, 1950, 70th anniversary mark, 12", mint 450-650
June 15, 1990 Sold for $475

41. Rookwood vase, vellum, carnations, E. Diers, 1907, #907DD, 11"h, mint 600-800
June 15, 1990 Sold for $850

42. Rookwood vase, vellum, sailboats, S.E. Coyne, 1909, #1655D, 10"h, mint 800-1100
June 15, 1990 Sold for $1300

43. Rookwood vase, bisque, flower design, A.R. Valentien, 1884, #162C, 9"h, mint 700-900
June 15, 1990 Sold for $850

44. Rookwood vase, vellum, berries, F. Rothenbush, 1909, #951B, 13"h, mint 700-900
June 15, 1990 Sold for $1100

45. Rookwood vase, vellum, floral design, A. Conant, 1916, 10"h, mint 750-1000
June 15, 1990 Sold for $1200

46. Rookwood vase, bisque, painted flowers, L.A. Fry, 1887, #30B, 12"h, mint 1250-1750
June 15, 1990 Sold for $1300

49. Rookwood jardinere, Limoges style with birds, 1884, attributed to M. Daly, 15"dia. x 11"h, mint 3000-5000
June 15, 1990 Sold for $3500

47. Rookwood vase, decoration of cranes, Shirayamadani, #732B, 1899, 10"h, mint 2000-3000
June 15, 1990 Sold for $3250

48. Rookwood vase, decoration of swallows, C.C. Lindeman, #917B, 1906, 9"h, mint 2000-3000
June 15, 1990 Sold for $1400

50. Rookwood vase, incised design, 1933, W. Rehm, 5"h, mint 500-700
April 5, 1992 Sold for $280

51. Rookwood vase, daffodils, 1937, #6622, Shirayamadani, 4.5"h, mint 1000-1500
April 5, 1992 Sold for $550

52. Rookwood vase, floral design, 1931, #904D, J. Jensen, 9"h, mint 1000-1200
April 5, 1992 Sold for $1300

53. Rookwood vase, daffodils, 1937, #6622, Shirayamadani, 4.5"h, mint 1000-1500
April 5, 1992 Sold for $850

54. Rookwood vase, daffodils, 1933, E.T. Hurley, 8"h, mint 1500-2000
April 5, 1992 Sold for $2200

55. Rookwood vase, silver overlay, 1915, #1369E, C.S. Todd, 8"h, mint 1500-2500
April 5, 1992 Sold for $1600

56. Rookwood vase, floral design, 1927, #130, E. Diers, 7" x 7", mint 700-900
April 5, 1992 Sold for $1100

57. Rookwood vase, berries, 1930, #2885, J. Jensen, 8"h, mint 1000-1500
April 5, 1992 Sold for $850

58. Rookwood vase, iris glaze, floral design, 1901, #808, S. Sax, 7"h, mint 1500-1750
April 5, 1992 Sold for $1500

59. Rookwood vase, iris glaze, poppy design, 1902, #732BB, J. Zettel, 8"h, mint 1500-1750
April 5, 1992 Sold for $1400

60. Rookwood vase, standard glaze, orchids, 1890, #139A, A.R. Valentien, 20", mint 4000-6000
April 5, 1992 Sold for $3750

61. Rookwood vase, standard glaze, roses, 1890, #560A, M.A. Daly, 16"h, mint 2500-3000
April 5, 1992 Sold for $1900

62. Rookwood vase, vellum, landscape, 1923, #900D, E. Diers, 7"h, mint 1000-1500
April 5, 1992 Sold for $1700

63. Rookwood vase, vellum, landscape, 1913, #952F, S.E. Coyne, 7"h, mint 900-1200
April 5, 1992 Sold for $900

64. Rookwood vase, vellum, water lilies, 1913, #988C, E. Diers, 9"h, mint 1000-1500
April 5, 1992 Sold for $1000

65. Rookwood vase, vellum, wisteria, 1927, #977, E. T. Hurley, 11"h, uncrazed, mint 2000-2500
April 5, 1992 Sold for $1800

66. Rookwood vase, vellum, landscape, 1912, #1930, S. Sax, 7"h, mint 1200-1700
April 5, 1992 Sold for $1800

67. Rookwood vase, vellum, lake scene, 1915, #946, L. Asbury, 11"h, hairline in top 700-900
April 5, 1992 Sold for $900

68. Rookwood vase, matt glaze, dogwood, 1940, #2745, Shirayamadani, 9"h, mint 900-1200
April 5, 1992 Sold for $750

69. Rookwood vase, vellum, landscape, 1914, #939D, M.G. Denzler, 7"h, mint 900-1200
April 5, 1992 Sold for $1100

70. Rookwood vase, sea green, butterflies and grass, 1896, #817, L. Asbury, 8"h, mint 3000-3500
April 5, 1992 Sold for $4000

71. Rookwood vase, standard glaze, crayfish, 1894, incised #A5, A.R. Valentien, 6"h, mint 2000-2500
April 5, 1992 Sold for $1900

72. Rookwood cup, standard, Native American, silver overlay, 1898, #810, G. Young, 7" x 5", mint 6000-8000
April 5, 1992 Sold for $4750

73. Rookwood vase, iris glaze, decoration of fish, 1911, #1658E, S.E. Coyne, 9"h, mint 1000-1500
April 5, 1992 Sold for $550

74. Rookwood vase, porcelain glaze, circle design, 1946, #778, E. Barrett, 10"h, mint 800-1100
April 5, 1992 Sold for $700

75. Rookwood vase, porcelain glaze, poppies, 1936, #6614, Shirayamadani, 10"h, mint 1500-2000
April 5, 1992 Sold for $750

76. Rookwood vase, porcelain glaze, poppies, 1936, #6614, Shirayamadani, 10"h, mint 1500-2000
April 5, 1992 Sold for $750

77. Rookwood vase, porcelain glaze, honeysuckle, Shirayamadani, 1922, #1664C, 13"h, mint 3000-4000
April 5, 1992 Sold for $6500

78. Rookwood vase, hi-glaze, floral design, 1933, E.T. Hurley, 5"h, mint 500-700
April 5, 1992 Sold for $500

79. Rookwood vase, hi-glaze, swallows and water lilies, 1946, #6204C, E.T. Hurley, 7"h x 7", mint 1000-1500
April 5, 1992 Sold for $1200

80. Rookwood vase, hi-glaze, daffodils, 1936, S for special piece, M.H. McDonald, 7"h, mint 500-700
April 5, 1992 Sold for $650

81. Rookwood vase, hi-glaze, floral and bird design, 1929, #2313, E.T. Hurley, 10"h, mint 1500-2500
April 5, 1992 Sold for $2000

82. Rookwood vase, Aerial Blue, landscape scene, 1894, #741C, #273, W.P. McDonald, museum numbers, old paper label on side, 5.5"h, mint 4000-5000
April 5, 1992 Sold for $4500

83. Rookwood vase, sea green, peacock feathers, 1908, C. Schmidt, 10"h, mint 5000-7000
April 5, 1992 Sold for $4500

84. Rookwood vase, iris glaze, fish, 1899, #860, E.T. Hurley, museum numbers, 6"h, mint 2000-2500
April 5, 1992 Sold for $2700

85. Rookwood vase, iris glaze, apple blossoms, 1908, #743C, K. Van Horne, 7"h, mint 900-1100
April 5, 1992 Sold for $1000

86. Rookwood vase, vellum, poppies, 1909, #952F, E.N. Lincoln, 6"h, mint 500-700
April 5, 1992 Sold for $500

87. Rookwood vase, hi-glaze, roses, 1900, #614D, W.P. McDonald, 10"h, mint 1000-1500
April 5, 1992 Sold for $1700

88. Rookwood bowl, matt glaze, carnations, 1904, #366Z, S. Toohey, 3"h x 5"w, mint 400-600
April 5, 1992 Sold for $550

89. Rookwood vase, vellum, floral design, 1916, #907D, K. Van Horne, 12"h, mint 900-1200
April 5, 1992 Sold for $1050

90. Rookwood vase, vellum, incised floral design, 1931, #2191, Shirayamadani, 5"h, mint 500-700
April 5, 1992 Sold for $1000

91. Rookwood vase, matt glaze, cherries and leaves, 1926, #1357C, S.E. Coyne, 11"h, mint 700-900
April 5, 1992 Sold for $900

92. Rookwood vase, vellum, sailboat scene, 1913, #932D, S.E. Coyne, 10"h, mint 1700-2200
April 5, 1992 Sold for $2500

93. Rookwood vase, matt glaze, daisies, 1930, #1930, Shirayamadani, 7"h, mint 600-800
April 5, 1992 Sold for $900

94. Rookwood vase, iris glaze, roses, 1902, #745C, E. Diers, 6"h, mint 500-700
April 5, 1992 Sold for $650

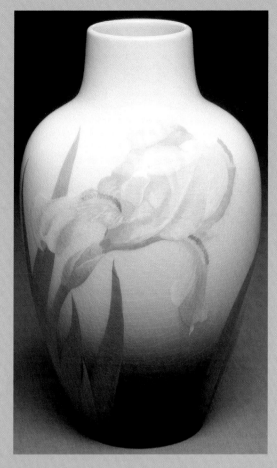

95. Rookwood vase, iris glaze, irises, 1907, #905C, C. Schmidt, 10"h, mint 5000-7000
April 5, 1992 Sold for $5250

96. Rookwood vase, vellum, swallows, 1906, #952B, Shirayamadani, 13"h, mint 6000-8000
April 5, 1992 Sold for $6000

97. Rookwood vase, hi-glaze, frog, A.B. Sprague, 1882, 8"h x 8"w, mint 2500-3500
April 5, 1992 Sold for $1600

98. Rookwood vase, sea green, bronze overlay, lilies, 1900, #901C, E. Diers, 9"h, mint 2000-3000
April 5, 1992 Sold for $1100

99. Rookwood vase, standard glaze, dragon, 1888, #400, Shirayamadani, 7"h x 6"w, mint 2500-3500
April 5, 1992 Sold for $3250

100. Rookwood vase, standard glaze, nude, 1896, #218A, S. Laurence, 12"h, restored 2500-3500
April 5, 1992 Sold for $3500

101. Rookwood vase, standard glaze, cavalier, 1903, #904D, G. Young, marked "after Franz Hals," 8"h, mint 1500-2000
April 5, 1992 Sold for $1300

102. Rookwood mug, standard glaze, ghost, 1899, #830C, H.E. Wilcox, 7"h x 6"w, repaired 2500-3500
April 5, 1992 Sold for $2300

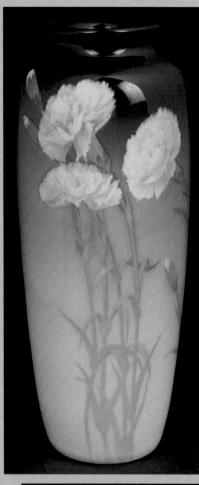

103. Rookwood vase, iris glaze, carnations, 1903, #904B, C. Schmidt, 13"h, mint 8000-10,000
April 5, 1992 Sold for $11,000

104. Rookwood vase, carved vellum, flamingos, 1904, #907C, J.D. Wareham, 14"h, mint 9,000-11,000
April 5, 1992 Sold for $6000

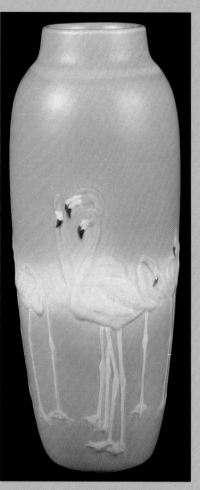

105. Rookwood pitcher, Limoges style, bats, 1883, #200, W.P. McDonald, 8"h, mint 900-1200
April 5, 1992 Sold for $700

106. Rookwood vase, bisque, flowers and leaves, 1887, #238C, M.A. Daly, 11"h, mint 1000-1500
April 5, 1992 Sold for $550

107. Rookwood vase, standard glaze, cavalier, 1903, #917A, G. Young, 12"h, restored hole 1200-1700
April 5, 1992 Sold for $1200

108. Rookwood potpourri, standard glaze, berries, 1889, #232D, H. Wilcox, 5"h x 5", mint 400-600
April 5, 1992 Sold for $550

109. Rookwood vase, standard glaze, daffodils, 1888, #216, Shirayamadani, 13"h, mint 1000-1500
April 5, 1992 Sold for $1600

110. Rookwood pitcher, Limoges style, fisherman, 1882, M.L. Nichols, 10"h, repaired 1500-2500
April 5, 1992 Sold for $1300

111. Rookwood flask, ginger clay body, Oriental figure, 1884, #85, Cranch, 8"h x 5"w, mint 1500-2500
April 5, 1992 Sold for $850

112. Rookwood flask, ginger clay body, men running, 1884, Cranch, 8"h x 5"w, mint 2000-2500
April 5, 1992 Sold for $2500

113. Rookwood vase, standard glaze, floral, 1897, #S1343A, C.A. Baker, 8"h, repaired 900-1200
June 4, 1993 Sold for $800

114. Rookwood vase, bisque, floral, 1886, #162XX, A.R. Valentien, 25"h, restored 4000-5000
June 4, 1993 Sold for $4250

115. Rookwood basket, Limoges style, spiders, feet molded like gargoyle heads, A. Humphreys, 20"w x 9"dia. x 9"h,
restored handles 1500-2500
June 4, 1993 Sold for $425

116. Rookwood vase, standard glaze, chestnuts and leaves, L. Asbury, 1898, #814A, 10"h, mint 600-800
June 4, 1993 Sold for $750

117. Rookwood vase, hi-glaze, flowers, 1926, #906E, Shirayamadani, 5"h, mint 600-800
June 4, 1993 Sold for $1200

118. Rookwood plaque, vellum, landscape, L. Asbury, 1920, 12" x 9", mint 4000-5000
June 4, 1993 Sold for $3250

119. Rookwood plate, hi-glaze, inscription, 1885, #45C, E.P. Cranch, 9"dia., mint 700-900
June 4, 1993 Sold for $300

120. Rookwood mug, standard glaze, corn, 1900, #587C, M. Nourse, 5"h, mint 300-400
June 4, 1993 Sold for $275

121. Rookwood vase, iris glaze, cherry blossoms, 1907, #925E, C.C. Lindeman, 7"h, mint 800-1100
June 4, 1993 Sold for $1200

122. Rookwood vase, matt glaze, flowers and leaves, 1923, L. Abel, #1357D, 9"h, mint 800-1100
June 4, 1993 Sold for $700

123. Rookwood vase, vellum, floral design, no crazing, E. Diers, 1931, #6112, 8"h, mint 2500-3500
June 4, 1993 Sold for $3500

124. Rookwood vase, iris glaze, rooks, C. Schmidt, 1907, #732BB, 9"h, mint 3500-5500
June 4, 1993 Sold for $4250

125. Rookwood vase, porcelain glaze, magnolias, J. Jensen, 1931, #6184C, 10"h, mint 1500-2000
June 4, 1993 Sold for $1500

126. Rookwood coffee pot, standard glaze, wisteria, A. Sprague, 1898, #772, 9"h, mint 600-800
June 4, 1993 Sold for $500

127. Rookwood plaque, vellum, landscape, E. Diers, c.1920s, 9" x 7", original frame, mint 3000-4000
June 4, 1993 Sold for $2700

128. Rookwood bowl, matt glaze, leaves and berries, M. McDonald, 1923, #2739F, 4"dia., mint 250-350
June 4, 1993 Sold for $275

129. Rookwood vase, vellum, floral, 1905, #904C, S. Sax, 12"h, mint 1700-2200
June 4, 1993 Sold for $1500

130. Rookwood vase, decorated porcelain, palm trees, S. Sax, 1929, #2977, 7.5"h, mint 400-600
June 4, 1993 Sold for $3000

131. Rookwood plaque, vellum, landscape, 1921, L. Asbury, 9"h x 5"w, original frame, mint 1750-2750
June 4, 1993 Sold for $2250

132. Rookwood vase, decorated porcelain, A. Conant, 1920, #551, 7"h, no crazing, mint 1000-1500
June 4, 1993 Sold for $3000

133. Rookwood vase, vellum, landscape, 1920, #1920, F. Rothenbush, 10"h, mint 1200-1700
June 4, 1993 Sold for $1700

134. Rookwood vase, vellum, snow scene, 1917, #1357E, S.E. Coyne, 7"h, mint 1200-1700
June 4, 1993 Sold for $1100

135. Rookwood vase, aventurine glaze, floral design, 1920, #942D, W. E. Hentschel, 6"h, mint 700-900
June 4, 1993 Sold for $650

136. Rookwood vase, hi-glaze, abstract design, J. Jensen, 1944, #6315, 6"h, mint 700-900
June 4, 1993 Sold for $1200

137. Rookwood vase, decorated porcelain, stylized fish, J. Jensen, 1943, #6148, 5.5"h, mint 700-900
June 4, 1993 Sold for $400

138. Rookwood vase, hi-glaze, abstract design, 1925, #2825A, L. Epply, 17"h, mint 1200-1700
June 4, 1993 Sold for $1100

139. Rookwood bowl, hi-glaze, floral design, 1933, S for special, L. Epply, 6"w x 3"h, mint 400-600
June 4, 1993 Sold for $350

140. Rookwood vase, matt glaze, berries, 1927, #614E, S.E. Coyne, 9", mint 700-900
June 4, 1993 Sold for $750

141. Rookwood vase, butterfat glaze, circle design, 1929, #2969, W.E. Hentschel, 6"w x 8"h, mint 800-1100
June 4, 1993 Sold for $500

142. Rookwood vase, porcelain glaze, leaves and flowers, J. Jensen, 1943, #356E, 6.5"h, mint 400-600
June 4, 1993 Sold for $450

143. Rookwood vase, matt glaze, flowers, 1922, #1656F, E.N. Lincoln, 6"h, mint 250-350
June 4, 1993 Sold for $300

144. Rookwood candlesticks, Chinese Plum, floral design, S. Sax, 1925, #2598, 10"h, mint 1500-2500
June 4, 1993 Sold for $1300

145. Rookwood vase, vellum, floral design, 1911, #808, E.N. Lincoln, 8"h, minor flake 300-400
June 4, 1993 Sold for $375

146. Rookwood vase, iris glaze, cherry blossoms, C.C. Lindeman, 1907, #925E, 6.5"h, mint 1200-1700
June 4, 1993 Sold for $800

147. Rookwood bowl, iris glaze, fish, 1900, #S1637, J.D. Wareham, 14"d, mint 2000-3000
June 4, 1993 Sold for $1400

148. Rookwood vase, iris glaze, poppies, K. Van Horn, 1908, #938D, 6"h, mint 800-1100
June 4, 1993 Sold for $750

149. Rookwood vase, deep hi-glaze, 1935, probably hand thrown by Menzel, 6"h, mint 150-250
June 4, 1993 Sold for $300

150. Rookwood vase, flowers, L. Epply, 1922, #1667, 11"h, mint 700-900
June 4, 1993 Sold for $900

151. Rookwood vase, beaded hi-glaze, pansies, E.T. Hurley, 1948, 5"w x 7"h, mint 900-1200
June 4, 1993 Sold for $475

152. Rookwood vase, hi-glaze, flowers and leaves, W. Rehm, 1946, #6866, 9"h, mint 400-600
June 4, 1993 Sold for $400

153. Rookwood vase, hi-glaze, leaves, 1944, #6306, J. Jensen, 7"h, mint 500-700
June 4, 1993 Sold for $425

154. Rookwood vase, hi-glaze, cactus, 1942, Shi-rayamadani, #6666, 6.5"h, mint 700-900
June 4, 1993 Sold for $700

155. Rookwood vase, hi-glaze, floral design, 1945, #6863, 4"h, mint 100-150
June 4, 1993 Sold for $110

156. Rookwood vase, matt glaze, floral design, E.N. Lincoln and L. Abel, 1921, #914E, 6"h, mint 300-400
June 4, 1993 Sold for $300

157. Rookwood vase, iris glaze, roses, 1905, #901A, A.R. Valentien, 14"h, mint 2700-3700
June 4, 1993 Sold for $4000

158. Rookwood vase, decorated porcelain, pine cones, L. Asbury, 1917, #703, 5"h, mint 1200-1700
June 4, 1993 Sold for $850

159. Rookwood vase, iris glaze, floral design, 1901, #74SC, R. Fechheimer, 6"h, mint 500-700
June 4, 1993 Sold for $550

160. Rookwood vase, vellum, landscape, 1921, #2101, F. Rothenbush, 7"h, mint 1200-1700
June 4, 1993 Sold for $1100

161. Rookwood candlestick, vellum, dragon, 1909, L. Epply, #922G, 7"h, mint 800-1100
June 4, 1993 Sold for $425

162. Rookwood vase, matt glaze, floral design, 1920, L. Abel, #950C, 11"h, mint 600-800
June 4, 1993 Sold for $700

163. Rookwood vase, vellum, floral, 1906, E. Noo-nan, #969D, 5"h, mint 400-600
June 4, 1993 Sold for $350

164. Rookwood vase, matt glaze, floral design, M.H. McDonald, 1940, #2918E, 7"h, uncrazed, mint 600-800
June 4, 1993 Sold for $650

165. Rookwood vase, vellum, landscape, 1923, #950F, F. Rothenbush, 6"h, mint 1200-1700
June 4, 1993 Sold for $1800

166. Rookwood vase, butterfat glaze, flowers, S. Sax, 1931, #2032C, 12"h, mint 2000-2500
June 4, 1993 Sold for $1700

167. Rookwood vase, hi-glaze, pansies, 1900, #6199F, E.T. Hurley, 4"h, mint 400-600
June 4, 1993 Sold for $1100

168. Rookwood vase, vellum, floral design, 1921, L. Asbury, #732C, 7"h, mint 700-900
June 4, 1993 Sold for $1200

169. Rookwood vase, matt glaze, leaves and berries, 1913, W.E. Hentschel, #534C, 8"h, mint 500-700
June 4, 1993 Sold for $475

170. Rookwood jug, standard glaze, corn, S. Toohey, 1899, #512X, 13"h, mint 1200-1700
June 4, 1993 Sold for $1800

171. Rookwood vase, standard glaze, clover, V.B. Demarest, 1898, #536F, 2"w x 3"h, mint 200-300
June 4, 1993 Sold for $300

172. Rookwood vase, standard glaze, berries, 1902, #625, Van Briggle, 6", mint 350-450
June 4, 1993 Sold for $550

173. Rookwood vase, standard glaze, flowers, 1898, #S1058, S. Toohey, 20"h, mint 2000-3000
June 4, 1993 Sold for $2100

174. Rookwood plate, Limoges style, flowers, 1887, #87, no artist signature, 6"dia., mint 300-500
June 4, 1993 Sold for $200

175. Rookwood vase, standard glaze, nasturtium, 1891, #533C, H.E. Wilcox, 9"h, hairlines 300-400
June 4, 1993 Sold for $300

176. Rookwood vase, standard glaze, dogwood, 1895, #664C, H.R. Strafer, 9"h, mint 800-1100
June 4, 1993 Sold for $1400

177. Rookwood vase, matt glaze, floral, 1919, E.N. Lincoln, #1872, 7"h, mint 400-600
June 4, 1993 Sold for $475

178. Rookwood vase, porcelain glaze, floral, L. Epply, 1929, #6115, 10"h, mint 1200-1700
June 4, 1993 Sold for $950

179. Rookwood vase, vellum, three men in a boat, 1912, #900C, E.T. Hurley, 9"h, mint 1000-1500
June 4, 1993 Sold for $950

180. Rookwood tile, matt glaze, geese, framed in wide dark oak frame, 6"sq., mint 500-700
June 4, 1993 Sold for $650

181. Rookwood vase, iris glaze, dogwood, 1942, E.T. Hurley, #6204F, 4"h, mint 600-800
June 4, 1993 Sold for $900

182. Rookwood vase, standard glaze, poppies, silver overlay, 1892, #612C, C. Steinle, 6"h, flake 2000-3000
June 4, 1993 Sold for $2300

183. Rookwood vase, matt glaze, irises, 1929, #2785, M.H. McDonald, 13"h, mint 1200-1700
June 4, 1993 Sold for $1300

184. Rookwood vase, vellum, floral, M. Denzler, 1916, #1358F, 6"h, mint 500-700
June 4, 1993 Sold for $600

185. Rookwood vase, bisque, bird and reeds, A.M. Bookprinter, 1886, #80B, 6"h, repaired 600-800
June 4, 1993 Sold for $450

186. Rookwood ramekin, cameo glaze, floral, O.G. Reed, 1892, #193, 2"h x 6.5"l, mint 200-300
June 4, 1993 Sold for $150

187. Rookwood bowl, cameo glaze, floral, 1886, #305, 4.5"h, uncrazed, mint 700-900
June 4, 1993 Sold for $275

188. Rookwood ramekin, cameo glaze, floral, E.D. Foertmeyer, 1892, #193, 2"h x 6.5"l, mint 200-300
June 4, 1993 Sold for $175

189. Rookwood bowl, standard glaze, tobacco, 1898, #228B, L.A., 10.5"dia., glaze bubbles 300-500
June 4, 1993 Sold for $300

190. Rookwood vase, standard glaze, cavalier, S. Laurence, 1899, #857, 15"h, restored 2500-3500
June 4, 1993 Sold for $1100

191. Rookwood vase, Limoges style, birds and reeds, M. Daly, 1883, #97, 6.5"h, mint 900-1200
June 4, 1993 Sold for $550

192. Rookwood dish, Limoges style, birds, 1882, #222, initials M.H.P., 8.5"dia., mint 400-600
June 4, 1993 Sold for $175

193. Mary Louise McLaughlin vase, floral, L. McLaughlin, 1880, #9D, 7"h, mint 800-1100
June 4, 1993 Sold for $350

194. Rookwood vase, vellum, design of trees, 1931, #2721, E.T. Hurley, 6"h, mint 1000-1500
June 4, 1993 Sold for $1400

195. Rookwood vase, vellum, stylized flowers, 1923, L. Asbury, #357F, 6"h, mint 600-800
June 4, 1993 Sold for $700

196. Rookwood ewer, matt glaze, flowers, 1889, #451, H.E. Wilcox, 5"h x 4"h, mint 600-800
June 4, 1993 Sold for $425

197. Rookwood plaque, vellum, landscape, S. Sax, 1900, 4" x 8", mint 2750-3750
June 4, 1993 Sold for $2400

198. Rookwood vase, standard glaze, test piece, floral design, #115, 3"h, chips 200-300
June 4, 1993 Sold for $100

199. Rookwood box, standard glaze, nasturtiums, 1894, #601C, M. Nourse, 6"w x 2"h, mint 600-800
June 4, 1993 Sold for $800

200. Rookwood vase, vellum, floral, 1909, E. Diers, #935E, 7"h, mint 700-900
June 4, 1993 Sold for $650

201. Rookwood vase, vellum, landscape, C. Schmidt, 1919, #907B, 18"h, mint 9000-12,000
June 4, 1993 Sold for $14,000

202. Rookwood vase, vellum, landscape, F. Rothenbush, 1928, #614B, 7"w x 15"h, mint 6000-8000
June 4, 1993 Sold for $7000

203. Rookwood vase, matt glaze, flowers, birds, J. Jensen, 1930, #6165, 10.5"w x 6"h, mint 1000-1500
June 4, 1993 Sold for $600

204. Rookwood pitcher, standard glaze, corn, 1893, #668, M.L. Perkins, 6" x 5", mint 500-700
June 4, 1993 Sold for $1100

205. Rookwood vase, vellum, landscape, 1921, #907C, Ed Diers, 15"h, minute chip 1500-2000
June 4, 1993 Sold for $1900

206. Rookwood vase, hi-glaze, leaf design, 1946, #6914, K. Ley, 6"h, mint 600-800
June 4, 1993 Sold for $500

207. Rookwood vase, matt glaze, carved flowers, 1905, #1126C, S.E. Coyne, 9"h, mint 900-1200
June 4, 1993 Sold for $750

208. Rookwood vase, oxblood glaze, 1932, 5"h, mint 200-300
June 4, 1993 Sold for $250

209. Rookwood vase, vellum, stylized trees, 1922, L. Asbury, #922D, 8"h, mint 900-1200
June 4, 1993 Sold for $1300

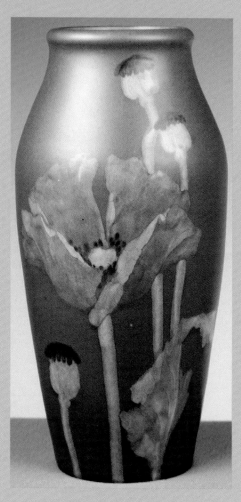

210. Rookwood vase, matt glaze, poppy design, 1901, #192BZ, A.R. Valentien 12"h, mint 7500-10,000
June 4, 1993 Sold for $23,000

211. Rookwood vase, vellum, fish, E.T. Hurley, 1906, #946, 11"h, mint 5000-7000
June 4, 1993 Sold for $4500

212. Rookwood vase, vellum, daisies, F. Rothenbush, 1907, #951D, 9"h, mint 600-800
June 4, 1993 Sold for $850

213. Rookwood vase, hi-glaze, fish and birds, J. Jensen, 1944, #2720, 6"h, mint 600-800
June 4, 1993 Sold for $650

214. Rookwood pitcher, standard glaze, dog, 1896, #259B, McDonald, 9"h, restored 1200-1500
June 4, 1993 Sold for $900

215. Rookwood vase, oxblood glaze, R.E. Menzel, 1947, marked S for special, 4.5"h, mint 200-300
June 4, 1993 Sold for $500

216. Rookwood vase, vellum, landscape, 1913, E.T. Hurley, 13"h, drilled base 1000-1500
June 4, 1993 Sold for $750

217. Rookwood vase, hi-glaze, 1929, #6041, L. Epply, 6"h, mint 500-700
June 4, 1993 Sold for $450

218. Rookwood vase, standard glaze, silver overlay, flowers, 1894, #162D, S. Markland, 5"h, mint 1200-1700
June 4, 1993 Sold for $1200

219. Rookwood ewer, standard glaze, mums, E.T. Hurley, 1898, #781B, 12"h, mint 600-800
June 4, 1993 Sold for $900

220. Rookwood vase, vellum, birds, E. Diers, 1912, #1369C, 11"h, mint 2500-3500
June 4, 1993 Sold for $3750

221. Rookwood vase, decorated porcelain, birds, E.T. Hurley, 1924, #2245, 8"h, mint 3000-4000
June 4, 1993 Sold for $5000

222. Rookwood vase, vellum, scenic, 1918, #1369C, F. Rothenbush, 11"h, mint 2500-3500
June 4, 1993 Sold for $1500

223. Rookwood vase, hi-glaze, incised linear design, 1931, #6231, 5"h, mint 150-250
June 4, 1993 Sold for $260

224. Rookwood vase, standard glaze, nasturtiums, 1898, A.D. Sehon, #504E, 7"h, mint 400-600
June 4, 1993 Sold for $400

225. Rookwood vase, iris glaze, blossoms, 1910, #1656D, L. Asbury, 9"h, no crazing, mint 1700-2200
June 4, 1993 Sold for $1,200

226. Rookwood vase, standard glaze, ibis, 1893, B. Horsfall, #533E, 7"h, mint 1200-1700
June 4, 1993 Sold for $2,000

227. Rookwood paperweight, rook, hi-glaze, 1924, #1623, 4"w x 3"h, mint 300-500
June 4, 1993 Sold for $600

228. Rookwood vase, Chinese Plum, magnolias, S. Sax, 1926, #2918B, 12"h, mint 2500-3500
June 4, 1993 Sold for $6,500

229. Rookwood vase, matt glaze, flowers, K. Jones, 1930, #6198F, 5"h, mint 300-400
June 4, 1993 Sold for $500

230. Rookwood vase, matt glaze, stylized leaves, 1928, #2918E, E. Barrett, 7"h, mint 400-600
June 4, 1993 Sold for $500

231. Rookwood vase, iris glaze, flowers, 1900, C.A. Baker, #744C, 7"h, mint 900-1200
June 4, 1993 Sold for $950

232. Rookwood ewer, standard glaze, iris, 1894, #611D, E.D. Foertmeyer, 10"h, mint 600-800
June 4, 1993 Sold for $650

233. Rookwood vase, vellum, landscape, 1920, #892B, E.T. Hurley, 11"h, mint 2500-3500 June 4, 1993 Sold for $2200

234. Rookwood vase, vellum, cherry blossoms, L. Asbury, 1934, #977, 11"h, mint 3500-4500 June 4, 1993 Sold for $3500

235. Rookwood vase, vellum, landscape, 1914, F. Rothenbush, #170, 12"h, mint 2500-3500 June 4, 1993 Sold for $3750

236. Rookwood vase, hi-glaze, cherries, 1928, #6042, L. Epply, 6"h, mint 300-500 June 4, 1993 Sold for $350

237. Rookwood vase, crystalline glaze, flaring flattened form, 1932, #6314, 8"h, mint 200-300 June 4, 1993 Sold for $150

238. Rookwood vase, hi-glaze, grapes, 1928, #1642, 6"w x 6"h, mint 150-250 June 4, 1993 Sold for $125

239. Rookwood vase, matt glaze, stylized flowers, 1924, #2785, E. Barrett, 13"h, mint 800-1100 June 4, 1993 Sold for $800

240. Rookwood bowl, lilies, 1945, #6343, 6"w x 4"h, mint 150-250 June 4, 1993 Sold for $125

241. Rookwood vase, butterfat glaze, floral design, 1930, #2246C, L. Epply, 9"w x 14"h, mint 2500-3500 June 4, 1993 Sold for $1600

242. Rookwood vase, hi-glaze, fish, 1944, #2193, J. Jensen, 6"w x 5"h, mint 500-700 June 4, 1993 Sold for $400

243. Rookwood vase, matt glaze, flowers, S.E. Coyne, 1928, #6005C, 13"h, mint 800-1100 June 4, 1993 Sold for $700

244. Rookwood vase, aventurine glaze, inscription, one of a kind piece dated 1941, 6"h, mint 200-250 June 4, 1993 Sold for $150

245. Rookwood vase, hi-glaze, bird, 1946, #6816A, C. Zanetta, 10"w x 8"h, mint 400-600 June 4, 1993 Sold for $475

246. Rookwood vase, vellum, palm trees, 1917, #900D, A. Craven, 7"h, mint 1000-1500
June 4, 1993 Sold for $2300

247. Rookwood vase, standard glaze, lilies, E. Noonan, 1905, #924, 6"h, mint 350-450
June 4, 1993 Sold for $500

248. Rookwood vase, goldstone glaze, 1932, #6315, 7"h, mint 250-350
June 4, 1993 Sold for $425

249. Rookwood vase, matt glaze, blossoms, 1885, #139B, A.R. Valentien, 13"h, mint 2000-2500
June 4, 1993 Sold for $1000

250. Rookwood bowl, vellum, roses, 1913, #2038, S.E. Coyne, 5"h, mint 400-600
June 4, 1993 Sold for $500

251. Rookwood vase, matt glaze, stylized floral design, 1918, E.N. Lincoln, #904E, 7"h, mint 500-700
June 4, 1993 Sold for $450

252. Rookwood vase, hi-glaze, cameo style bird, 1943, #2724, E. Barrett, 6"h, mint 700-900
June 4, 1993 Sold for $650

253. Rookwood vase, matt glaze, pinecones, 1920, E.N. Lincoln, #2100, 5"h, mint 400-600
June 4, 1993 Sold for $400

254. Rookwood vase, vellum, landscape, 1915, #1126C, L. Asbury, 9"h, mint 1500-2000
June 4, 1993 Sold for $1300

255. Rookwood ewer, standard glaze, silver overlay, floral, 1898, #537F, S. Markland, 7"h, mint 3000-4000
June 4, 1993 Sold for $1500

256. Rookwood lamp base, matt glaze, wisteria, 1904, #583Z, Shirayamadani, 15"h, restored 1500-2000
June 4, 1993 Sold for $1000

257. Rookwood vase, matt glaze, flowers, 1928, #6041, L. Abel, 6"h, mint 400-600
June 4, 1993 Sold for $325

258. Rookwood vase, butterfat glaze, flowers, 1944, shape# legible, J. Jensen, 6"h, mint 500-700
June 4, 1993 Sold for $400

259. Rookwood vase, standard glaze, leaves, S.E. Coyne, 1904, #907DD, 10"h, tiny flake 300-500
June 4, 1993 Sold for $350

260. Rookwood mug, standard glaze, boy, 1890, #328B, A.M. Valentien, 6"h, mint 1000-1500 June 4, 1993 Sold for $850

261. Rookwood vase, matt glaze, floral design, 1926, #2900, M.H. McDonald, 10"h, drill hole 500-700 June 4, 1993 Sold for $550

262. Rookwood bowl, matt glaze, floral and leaf design, 1916, C.S. Todd, #923, 2"h, mint 400-600 June 4, 1993 Sold for $475

263. Rookwood vase, vellum, landscape, 1915, #951D, L. Epply, 10"h, mint 1200-1700 June 4, 1993 Sold for $1400

264. Rookwood vase, crystalline glaze, ferns, 1930, E. Barrett, 14"h, bottom drilled 700-900 June 4, 1993 Sold for $1000

265. Rookwood vase, matt glaze, floral design, 1913, C.S. Todd, #1843, 5"h, mint 300-500 June 4, 1993 Sold for $300

266. Rookwood pitcher, Limoges style, floral, 1882, A.R. Valentien, anchor mark, #2457, 8"h, mint 1000-1500 June 4, 1993 Sold for $1200

267. Rookwood vase, matt glaze, daffodils, M.H. McDonald, 1926, #1920, 9"h, mint 800-1100 June 4, 1993 Sold for $1100

268. Rookwood vase, matt glaze, flowers, C.S. Todd, 1913, #975D, 7"h, mint 600-800 June 4, 1993 Sold for $475

269. Rookwood vase, matt glaze, reminiscent of designs of Henry Van de Velde, 1913, #1660C, 11"h, mint 300-400 June 4, 1993 Sold for $475

270. Rookwood tray, copper overlay, mistletoe, Shirayamadani, 1901, #2672, 5"dia., mint 1200-1700 June 4, 1993 Sold for $1400

271. Rookwood lamp base, matt glaze, berries, Shirayamadani, 1903, #583Z, 14"h, mint 2500-3500 June 4, 1993 Sold for $1500

272. Rookwood vase, vellum, cyclamens, 1912, S. Sax, #926C, 9"h, mint 1500-2000 June 4, 1993 Sold for $1700

273. Rookwood vase, standard glaze, poppy, silver overlay, K. Hickman, 1897, #79D, 7"h, mint 2500-3500 June 4, 1993 Sold for $1900

274. Rookwood vase, iris glaze, wisteria, 1911, E.T. Hurley, #1369E, 7"h, thin glaze at rim 1000-1500 June 4, 1993 Sold for $600

275. Rookwood dish, bisque, hi-glaze interior, 1900, #279C, H. Altman, 4"w, mint 150-250
June 4, 1993 Sold for $120

276. Rookwood pitcher, Tiger Eye, spider mums, 1886, #292, M.A. Daly, 10"h, repaired 400-600
June 4, 1993 Sold for $290

277. Rookwood jug, bisque, floral design, 1883, #61, H. Wenderoth, 5"h, mint 300-400
June 4, 1993 Sold for $210

278. Rookwood dish, standard glaze, strawberries, 1891, #451, M. Nourse, 8"w, mint 300-500
June 4, 1993 Sold for $200

279. Rookwood pitcher, standard glaze, goldenrod, F. Rothenbush, 1899, #772, 9"h, flake 400-600
June 4, 1993 Sold for $1500

280. Rookwood vase, standard glaze, ghost, 1899, #830C, H.E. Wilcox, 7"h, repaired handle 2500-3500
June 4, 1993 Sold for $3500

281. Rookwood ashtray, standard glaze, 1894, #714, O.G. Reed, 9"l x 4"w, repaired 250-350
June 4, 1993 Sold for $275

282. Rookwood vase, standard glaze, silver overlay, roses, A. Sprague, 1892, #557, 10"h, mint 3700-4700
June 4, 1993 Sold for $5000

283. Rookwood ewer, bisque, Virginia creeper, 1882, H. Wenderoth, 7"h, mint 400-600
June 4, 1993 Sold for $300

284. Rookwood vase, standard glaze, daisies, 1904, #938D, S. Coyne, 6"h, mint 300-400
June 4, 1993 Sold for $425

285. Rookwood vase, matt glaze, leaf design, 1912, C.S. Todd, #77A, 8"h, mint 400-600
June 4, 1993 Sold for $1000

286. Rookwood vase, hi-glaze, birds and flowers, 1933, #6400, J. Jensen, 6"h, mint 900-1200
June 4, 1993 Sold for $950

287. Rookwood plaque, vellum, landscape, S.E. Coyne, 1914, 9"h, mint 3000-4000
June 4, 1993 Sold for $5000

288. Rookwood bowl, hi-glaze, roses, 1920, #1929, S. Sax, 7"w, mint 1000-1500
June 4, 1993 Sold for $1500

289. Rookwood mug, standard glaze, boy, 1890, #328B, A.M. Valentien, 6"h, mint 1000-1500
June 4, 1993 Sold for $425

290. Rookwood vase, hi-glaze, doves and vines, 1946, #4260, #6919, K. Ley, 12"h, mint 1000-1500
June 4, 1993 Sold for $1000

291. Rookwood ewer, Limoges style, bird and bamboo, #56, 1883, H. Horton, 6"h, mint 600-800
June 4, 1993 Sold for $400

292. Rookwood vase, standard glaze, portrait, B. Horsfall, 1894, #707A, 8"h, mint 3500-4500
June 4, 1993 Sold for $2500

293. Rookwood vase, standard glaze, elk, 1900, #821B, E.T. Hurley, 12"h, line in the bottom 1200-1700
June 4, 1993 Sold for $900

294. Rookwood covered jar, Limoges style, birds, 1885, #142C, M.A. Daly, 6"h, repaired 500-700
June 4, 1993 Sold for $350

295. Rookwood vase, standard glaze, fish, Shirayamadani, 1897, #659B, 8"h, mint 2000-3000
June 4, 1993 Sold for $1600

296. Rookwood vase, hi-glaze, floral design, S. Sax, 1920, #356F, 6"h, mint 800-1100
June 4, 1993 Sold for $1900

297. Rookwood vase, Chinese Plum, flowers, 1924, #2544, H.E. Wilcox, 8"h, mint 1000-1500
June 4, 1993 Sold for $950

298. Rookwood vase, standard glaze, silver overlay, poppies, 1903, #901BB, E.N. Lincoln, 10"h, mint 3000-4000
June 4, 1993 Sold for $4000

299. Rookwood vase, matt glaze, floral, E. Barrett, 1924, #2078, 5" x 6", mint 400-600
June 4, 1993 Sold for $325

300. Rookwood vase, hi-glaze, flowers, 1930, W.E. Hentschel, #6185D, 9"h, mint 800-1100
June 4, 1993 Sold for $400

301. Rookwood plaque, vellum, landscape, L. Asbury, 1920s, plaque of 8" x 10", mint 2750-3750 June 4, 1993 Sold for $2800

302. Rookwood box, cigarette lighter and ashtray, hi-glaze, dogs, F. King, 1946, 6"w x 2"h, mint 500-700
June 4, 1993 Sold for $550

303. Rookwood vase, hi-glaze, fish, J. Jensen, 1943, #6036, 6"w x 6"h, mint 700-900
June 4, 1993 Sold for $450

304. Rookwood pitcher, standard glaze, chestnuts, A.B. Sprague, 1889, #525, 7"h x 6"w, mint 600-800
June 4, 1993 Sold for $750

305. Rookwood vase, vellum, landscape, 1910, #1883D, E.T. Hurley, 1910, 9"h, mint 1500-2500
June 4, 1993 Sold for $1100

306. Rookwood plaque, vellum, landscape, 1923, F. Rothenbush, 9"h, mint 2000-3000
June 4, 1993 Sold for $1800

307. Rookwood vase, vellum, landscape, 1918, #907C, E. Diers, 15"h, professionally restored 2000-3000
June 4, 1993 Sold for $1300

308. Rookwood vase, iris glaze, lilies, 1898, #765C, J.D. Wareham, 10.5"h, mint 1500-2500
June 4, 1993 Sold for $1900

309. Rookwood plaque, vellum, landscape, F. Rothenbush, c.1920, 4" x 8", mint 1700-2200
June 4, 1993 Sold for $1600

310. Rookwood vase, vellum, harbor scene, C. Schmidt, 1920, #2039C, 12"h, repaired 2200-2700
June 4, 1993 Sold for $2200

311. Rookwood jug, standard glaze, berries, E. Felten, 1897, #767, 7"h, minute chip 350-450
June 4, 1993 Sold for $600

312. Rookwood vase, standard glaze, violets,M. Fogelsong, 1898, #568C, 7"h, mint 400-600
June 4, 1993 Sold for $300

313. Rookwood bowl, standard glaze, daisies, O.G. Reed, 1894, #45D, 4"h x 7"w, mint 300-400
June 4, 1993 Sold for $325

314. Rookwood ewer, standard glaze, flowers, M. Daly, 1888, #262, 12"h, mint 1500-2000
June 4, 1993 Sold for $1650

315. Rookwood vase, standard glaze, poppies, 1902, #787B, C. Baker, 15"h, mint 2500-3500
June 4, 1993 Sold for $3250

316. Rookwood vase, standard glaze, berries, C. Steinle, 1891, #503A, 5"h, mint 1200-1700
June 4, 1993 Sold for $1750

317. Rookwood vase, standard glaze, wild roses, Shirayamadani, 1889, #506, 13"h, mint 1500-2500
June 4, 1993 Sold for $3300

318. Rookwood vase, standard glaze, birds, F. Rothenbush, 1896, #712, 5"h, mint 900-1200
June 4, 1993 Sold for $425

319. Rookwood jug, standard glaze, corn, S. Toohey, 1898, #512A, 10"h, mint 700-900
June 4, 1993 Sold for $1000

320. Rookwood vase, standard glaze, grapes, L. Asbury, 1899, #830E, 5"h, mint 300-500
June 4, 1993 Sold for $400

321. Rookwood vase, standard glaze, Native American, 1899, G. Young, #797, 7"h, fine line 2500-3500
June 4, 1993 Sold for $1500

322. Rookwood ewer, standard glaze, tulips, 1893, #387C, H.E. Wilcox, 10.5"h, mint 700-900
June 4, 1993 Sold for $650

323. Rookwood vase, standard glaze, holly, 1892, W.P. McDonald, #557, 9"h, mint 500-700
June 4, 1993 Sold for $475

324. Rookwood vase, standard glaze, fruit, 1893, #589C, A.R. Valentien, 13"h, mint 900-1200
June 4, 1993 Sold for $1300

325. Rookwood vase, standard glaze, papoose, G. Young, 1901, #830E, 5"h, mint 3000-5000
June 4, 1993 Sold for $5500

326. Rookwood vase, standard glaze, flowers, 1903, #900C, L. Asbury, 7.5"h, mint 400-600
June 4, 1993 Sold for $650

327. Rookwood mug, standard glaze, corn, 1899, #587B, C. Steinle, 6"h, mint 400-600
June 4, 1993 Sold for $625

328. Rookwood pitcher, standard glaze, mistletoe, 1902, V.B. Demarest, #818, 7"h, mint 400-500
June 4, 1993 Sold for $325

329. Rookwood vase, matt glaze, the three wise men, 1944, #6869, W. Rehm, 9"h, mint 1000-1500
June 4, 1993 Sold for $750

330. Rookwood vase, standard glaze, carnations, silver overlay, #720C, J. Zettel, 1894, 4"h, mint 3500-4500
June 4, 1993 Sold for $1800

331. Rookwood plaque, vellum, landscape, L. Asbury, 1920, 14" x 9", mint 4000-5000
June 4, 1993 Sold for $3750

332. Rookwood vase, aventurine glaze, leaf design, 1937, #6622, 4"h, mint 250-350
June 4, 1993 Sold for $300

333. Rookwood vase, hi-glaze, abstract designs, 1930, #1844, L. Epply, 5"w x 4"h, mint 400-600
June 4, 1993 Sold for $425

334. Rookwood vase, matt glaze, berries and leaves, J. Jensen, 1930, #2885, 8"h, mint 1000-1500
June 4, 1993 Sold for $850

335. Rookwood vase, vellum, floral design, F. Rothenbush, 1907, #939C, 8"h, mint 900-1100
June 4, 1993 Sold for $1200

336. Rookwood vase, vellum, landscape,
C. Schmidt, 1919, #1358B, 14"h,
mint 5000-7000
June 4, 1993 Sold for $6000

337. Rookwood vase, iris glaze, wisteria,
C. Schmidt, 1906, #907D, 11"h,
mint 5000-7000
June 4, 1993 Sold for $8000

338. Rookwood box, Limoges style, swallows and reeds, 1882, A.R. Valentien, 7"h,
mint 1200-1700
June 4, 1993 Sold for $1100

339. Rookwood vase, vellum, landscape,
1915, #1065B, L. Asbury, 11"h,
mint 1700-2500
June 4, 1993 Sold for $1600

340. Rookwood dish, Limoges style, bat,
1883, M. Rettig, 5"w x 2"h, mint 300-500
June 4, 1993 Sold for $190

341. Rookwood vase, Limoges style, butterfly and tree, 1885, #238, A.R. Valentien,
17"h, mint 2500-3500
June 4, 1993 Sold for $1700

342. Rookwood vase, vellum, dragonflies,
S.E. Coyne, 1906, #1356D, 9"h,
mint 2000-3000
June 4, 1993 Sold for $1500

343. Rookwood vase, drip hi-glaze, 1954,
R. Menzel, 5"h, mint 200-300
June 4, 1993 Sold for $210

344. Rookwood vase, matt glaze, wisteria,
1886, L. Fry, #30B, 11"h, mint 1700-2200
June 4, 1993 Sold for $1200

345. Rookwood urn, matt glaze, abstract design, W. Hentschel, 1926, #2818, 18"h, mint 2500-3500 June 4, 1993 Sold for $1700

346. Rookwood urn, matt glaze, abstract design, W. Hentschel, 1926, #2818, 18"h, mint 2500-3500 June 4, 1993 Sold for $1700

347. Rookwood vase, standard glaze, geese, 1892, #598C, 6"h, mint 1000-1500 June 4, 1993 Sold for $475

348. Rookwood vase, matt glaze, floral design, C. Klinger, 1925, #2735, 8"h, mint 400-600 June 4, 1993 Sold for $400

349. Rookwood vase, standard glaze, flowers, 1894, #708C, J. Zettel, 4"dia., mint 200-300 June 4, 1993 Sold for $275

350. Rookwood vase, iris glaze, flowers, 1901, #900C, C. Baker, 8"h, mint 900-1200 June 4, 1993 Sold for $1000

351. Rookwood plaque, vellum, landscape, K. Van Horne, 1917, 9"h x 11"w, mint 3500-4500 June 4, 1993 Sold for $3500

352. Rookwood jug, Limoges style, birds, 1884, initials KB, #122, not signed, 12"h, mint 300-500 June 4, 1993 Sold for $300

353. Rookwood vase, hi-glaze, 1932, #6319D, 5"w x 5"h, mint 250-350 June 4, 1993 Sold for $225

354. Rookwood vase, hi-glaze, cherry blossoms, S. Sax, 1924, #1833, 7"h, mint 800-1100 June 4, 1993 Sold for $425

355. Rookwood vase, matt glaze, flowers, 1907, O.G. Reed, #881F, 3"h, mint 300-500 June 4, 1993 Sold for $375

356. Rookwood vase, matt glaze, tulips, 1934, J. Jensen, 6"h, mint 800-1100 June 4, 1993 Sold for $600

357. Rookwood vase, hi-glaze, houses, 1951, J. Jensen, #6292C, 8"h, mint 800-1100
June 4, 1993 Sold for $800

358. Rookwood cup and saucer, cameo glaze, floral, 1887, #208, G. Young, cup 3"h, mint 300-500
June 4, 1993 Sold for $375

359. Rookwood vase, matt glaze, floral design, 1917, C.J. McLaughlin, #938D, 7"h, mint 500-700
June 4, 1993 Sold for $550

360. Rookwood vase, butterfat glaze, flowers, 1928, #654D, D. Workum, 5"h, mint 600-800
June 4, 1993 Sold for $550

361. Rookwood vase, vellum, landscape, E.T. Hurley, 1912, #1358D, 13"h, mint 2200-2700
June 4, 1993 Sold for $1400

362. Rookwood dish, hi-glaze, fish, M. Rettig, 1884, #53, 5"w, mint 300-500
June 4, 1993 Sold for $140

363. Rookwood vase, matt glaze, floral design, W.E. Hentschel, 1914, #130, 7"h, mint 700-900
June 4, 1993 Sold for $650

364. Rookwood dish, Limoges style, butterflies, 1883, #140, H. Horton, 6"dia., mint 300-500
June 4, 1993 Sold for $260

365. Rookwood jug, standard glaze, berries, L. Asbury, 1896, #961, 8"h, minute flake 500-750
June 4, 1993 Sold for $1100

366. Rookwood vase, hi-glaze, fruit and leaves, A. Conant, 1916, #2305, 9"h, mint 1000-1500
June 4, 1993 Sold for $1300

367. Rookwood vase, goldstone glaze, 1930, #6142, 4"h, mint 250-350
June 4, 1993 Sold for $350

368. Rookwood vase, matt glaze, flowers and leaves, 1930, #2720, K. Jones, 6"h, mint 350-550
June 4, 1993 Sold for $600

369. Rookwood plaque, vellum, landscape, C. Schmidt, 1900s, 9" x 11", original frame, mint 5000-7000
June 4, 1993 Sold for $3500

370. Rookwood box, matt glaze, flowers, M.H. McDonald & L. Abel, 1931, #6238, 4"h, mint 500-700
June 4, 1993 Sold for $350

371. Rookwood bowl, standard glaze, turtle and crab, 1889, #59C, 9"w x 3"h, mint 900-1200
June 4, 1993 Sold for $425

372. Rookwood dish, matt glaze, dragon, Shirayamadani, 1907, #1080E, 3"w, mint 250-350
June 4, 1993 Sold for $475

373. Rookwood vase, vellum, floral design, F. Rothenbush, 1906, #900G, 7"h, mint 1000-1250
June 4, 1993 Sold for $1300

374. Rookwood vase, vellum, blueberries, 1907, #935E, L. Epply, 7"h, mint 700-900
June 4, 1993 Sold for $600

375. Rookwood vase, matt glaze, iris, 1894, #589F, no artist signature, 7"h, mint 500-700
June 4, 1993 Sold for $650

376. Rookwood vase, standard glaze, berry design, 1903, #915F, artist C.F.B., 5"h, mint 300-400
June 4, 1993 Sold for $375

377. Rookwood vase, standard glaze, roses, 1889, #463B, M.A. Daly, 19"h, mint 2500-3500
June 4, 1993 Sold for $3250

378. Rookwood vase, standard glaze, daffodils, silver overlay, 1894, #162D, J. Zettel, 5"h, mint 2750-3500
June 4, 1993 Sold for $2800

379. Rookwood vase, matt glaze, floral design, 1919, E.N. Lincoln, #1828, 5"h, mint 400-600
June 4, 1993 Sold for $400

380. Rookwood vase, sage clay, matt glaze, floral, #238C, A.M. Bookprinter, 1887, 11"h, mint 1000-1500
June 4, 1993 Sold for $550

381. Rookwood vase, vellum, floral, 1914, E. Diers, #1278E, 9"h, mint 700-900
June 4, 1993 Sold for $900

382. Rookwood vase, hi-glaze, birds, animals, 1920, #900E, W.E. Hentschel, 7"h, mint 600-800
June 4, 1993 Sold for $650

383. Rookwood vase, matt glaze, flowers and leaves, 1922, V. Tischler, #614E, 7"h, mint 500-700
June 4, 1993 Sold for $600

384. Rookwood plaque, vellum, landscape, L. Asbury, 1916, 9"h, original frame, mint 3500-4500
June 4, 1993 Sold for $4,500

385. Rookwood jar, vellum, floral design, 1920, L. Asbury, #1321E, 4"h, mint 400-600
June 4, 1993 Sold for $550

386. Rookwood vase, standard glaze, clover, silver overlay, J. Zettel, 1892, #584C, 5"h, mint 2500-3500
June 4, 1993 Sold for $2,100

387. Rookwood vase, matt glaze, leaves and berries, 1936, M.H. McDonald, #6578, 7"h, mint 800-1100
June 4, 1993 Sold for $650

388. Rookwood vase, goldstone glaze, bird and butterflies, 1933, #6350, 5"h, mint 150-250
June 4, 1993 Sold for $270

389. Rookwood vase, dull finish, flowers, H.E. Wilcox, 1887, #238C, 10"h, mint 800-1100
June 4, 1993 Sold for $550

390. Rookwood vase, matt glaze, wisteria, M. McDonald, 1926, #2039D, 9"h, mint 600-800 June 4, 1993 Sold for $650

391. Rookwood vase, matt glaze, poppies, 1928, S.E. Coyne, #6005F, 6"h, mint 700-900 June 4, 1993 Sold for $600

392. Rookwood vase, standard glaze, a flower, 1887, #76, A.M. Bookprinter, 2.5"h, mint 300-400 June 4, 1993 Sold for $175

393. Rookwood vase, standard glaze, cavalier, G. Young, 1902, #907D, 11"h, mint 2500-3500 June 4, 1993 Sold for $900

394. Rookwood vase, lustre glaze, geometric design, 1915, #2182, S. Sax, 5"h, mint 250-350 June 4, 1993 Sold for $400

395. Rookwood vase, vellum, landscape, 1919, #1356B, F. Rothenbush, 14"h, restored 2000-2500 June 4, 1993 Sold for $1500

396. Rookwood vase, vellum, floral design, 1929, #912, F. Rothenbush, 7"h, mint 700-900 June 4, 1993 Sold for $650

397. Rookwood vase, decorated porcelain, roses, E.T. Hurley, 1926, #654C, 5.5"h, mint 600-800 June 4, 1993 Sold for $1300

398. Rookwood vase, iris glaze, leaves, 1906, #935C, S.E. Coyne, 9"h, mint 1500-2000 June 4, 1993 Sold for $1900

399. Rookwood ewer, standard glaze, floral, silver overlay, 1902, #639C, H. Altman, 10"h, mint 3500-4500 June 4, 1993 Sold for $2,100

400. Rookwood vase, vellum, landscape, 1909, #1818, L. Asbury, 8", mint 1500-2500 June 4, 1993 Sold for $1,400

401. Rookwood Faience tile, matt glaze, ship, 12", c.1905, mint 1200-1700 June 4, 1993 Sold for $1,100

402. Rookwood vase, matt glaze, floral design, 1920, E.N. Lincoln, #1780, 7", mint 600-800 June 4, 1993 Sold for $425

403. Rookwood box, hi-glaze, floral, 1924, #2793, W.E. Hentschel, 6"w, mint 300-400 June 4, 1993 Sold for $240

404. Rookwood vase, matt glaze, flowers, C. Covalenco, 1924, #2738, 7" x 5", mint 400-600 June 4, 1993 Sold for $300

405. Rookwood vase, porcelain glaze, tulips, 1948, #6895, J. Jensen, 7"h, mint 700-900 June 4, 1993 Sold for $1,100

406. Rookwood vase, vellum, floral, E. McDermott, 1916, #913D, 8"h, mint 600-800 June 4, 1993 Sold for $700

407. Rookwood vase, porcelain, birds and flowers, 1944, #778, E. Barrett, 10"h, mint 700-900 June 4, 1993 Sold for $600

408. Rookwood vase, matt glaze, flowers, 1915, C.S. Todd, #2039D, 9.5"h, mint 400-600
June 4, 1993 Sold for $475

409. Rookwood vase, matt glaze, flowers, 1930, W. Rehm, #914E, 6"h, mint 500-700
June 4, 1993 Sold for $425

410. Rookwood vase, porcelain, flowers, 1948, #2785, E. Barrett, 13"h, mint 1000-1500
June 4, 1993 Sold for $1000

411. Rookwood vase, matt glaze, blueberries, E.N. Lincoln, 1922, #1779, 7"h, mint 600-800
June 4, 1993 Sold for $500

412. Rookwood tray, hi-glaze, magnolias, 1946, #6927, J. Jensen, 9"w x 12"l x 2"h, mint 500-700
June 4, 1993 Sold for $375

413. Rookwood vase, matt glaze, peacock feathers, 1920, #1356B, E.N. Lincoln, 14"h, drilled 700-900
June 4, 1993 Sold for $750

414. Rookwood vase, hi-glaze, flowers, E. Barrett, 1946, #6359, uncrazed, 7.5"h, mint 400-600
June 4, 1993 Sold for $500

415. Rookwood vase, hi-glaze, floral design, not signed, 1945, #6632, 5"h, mint 200-300
June 4, 1993 Sold for $250

416. Rookwood vase, hi-glaze, 1952, L. Holtkamp, #7099, 13"h, mint 500-800
June 4, 1993 Sold for $650

417. Rookwood vase, hi-glaze, square design, L. Holtkamp, 1953, 9"h, mint 400-600
June 4, 1993 Sold for $500

418. Rookwood vase, iris glaze, mistletoe, 1901, R. Fechheimer, #809E, 6.5"h, mint 700-900
June 4, 1993 Sold for $600

419. Rookwood plaque, vellum, landscape, E.T. Hurley, c.1920s, 5.5" x 9.5", mint 2500-3500
June 4, 1993 Sold for $2200

420. Rookwood vase, standard glaze, bleeding hearts, 1901, F. Vreeland, #913, 6"h, mint 300-500
June 4, 1993 Sold for $550

421. Rookwood plaque, vellum, harbor scene, C. Schmidt, 1920s, 15"w x 10", mint 6500-8500
June 4, 1993 Sold for $8500

422. Rookwood chamberstick, standard glaze, insects, 1898, #627, F. Rothenbush, 8"l x 4"h, mint 1000-1500
June 4, 1993 Sold for $800

423. Rookwood vase, standard glaze, roses, silver overlay, 1896, S. Markland, #30E, 6"h, mint 2500-3500
June 4, 1993 Sold for $1600

424. Rookwood plaque, vellum, scenic, F. Rothenbush, 1920, 5.5" x 9.5", mint 2200-2700
June 4, 1993 Sold for $1800

425. Rookwood vase, iris glaze, floral design, 1903, #860, R. Fechheimer, 6"h, mint 600-800
June 4, 1993 Sold for $800

426. Rookwood vase, iris glaze, flowers, C.C. Lindeman, 1904, #614E, 8"h, mint 1500-2000
June 4, 1993 Sold for $1700

427. Rookwood vase, hi-glaze, Venetian boat scene, C. Schmidt, 1923, #357F, 6"h, mint 900-1200
June 4, 1993 Sold for $750

428. Rookwood vase, decorated porcelain, birds, J. Jensen, 1948, #6873, 12"h, uncrazed, mint 2500-3500
June 4, 1993 Sold for $3500

429. Rookwood humidor, Chinese Plum, peacock feathers, S. Sax, 1926, #2622, 9"h, mint 1500-2500
June 4, 1993 Sold for $1400

430. Rookwood vase, matt glaze, flowers, 1923, L. Abel, #931, 5" x 5", mint 400-600
June 4, 1993 Sold for $450

431. Rookwood jar, vellum, daisies, 1907, E.N. Lincoln, #622C, trial 1889, 4"h, mint 500-700
June 4, 1993 Sold for $600

432. Rookwood vase, hi-glaze, fish, J. Jensen, 1933, 6"h, mint 1000-1500
June 4, 1993 Sold for $1100

433. Rookwood vase, vellum, scenic, 1914, #1023C, F. Rothenbush, 10"h, mint 1700-2200
June 4, 1993 Sold for $2200

434. Rookwood vase, iris glaze, poppies, I. Bishop, 1908, #1357D, 9"h, mint 1200-1700
June 4, 1993 Sold for $1500

435. Rookwood vase, crystalline glaze, 1932, #6317F, 4"h, mint 200-300
June 4, 1993 Sold for $250

436. Rookwood vase, vellum, floral, 1938, E. T. Hurley, #6199D, 5" x 6", mint 700-900
June 4, 1993 Sold for $700

437. Rookwood vase, sea green, poppies, E.N. Lincoln, 1905, #907DD, 9"h, mint 3000-4000
June 4, 1993 Sold for $5500

438. Rookwood vase, sea green, tiger lilies, 1901, #946C, S. Toohey, 9"h, mint 2500-3500
June 4, 1993 Sold for $3750

439. Rookwood vase, sea green, bats, E.T. Hurley, 1900, #77C, 5"h, mint 1000-1500
June 4, 1993 Sold for $1800

440. Rookwood vase, sea green, birds, 1899, #787C, S. Toohey, 12"h, restored 4000-6000
June 4, 1993 Sold for $3000

441. Rookwood vase, sea green, water lilies, E.T. Hurley, 1900, #732BB, 8"h, mint 2000-2500
June 4, 1993 Sold for $2500

442. Rookwood vase, sea green, rook, Shirayamadani, 1895, #496A, 12"h, repair 2000-3000
June 4, 1993 Sold for $1500

443. Rookwood vase, sea green, floral, S.E. Coyne, 1901, #920, 5"h, mint 1000-1500
June 4, 1993 Sold for $1500

444. Rookwood vase, goldstone glaze, 1932, #6316, 4"w x 4"h, mint 350-500
June 4, 1993 Sold for $375

445. Rookwood pitcher, cameo glaze, lilies, 1888, #246, A. Van Briggle, 9"h, mint 1000-1500
June 4, 1993 Sold for $650

446. Rookwood bowl, sage clay body, a fish, 1885, W.P. McDonald, 7"dia., mint 600-800
June 4, 1993 Sold for $400

447. Rookwood jug, Limoges style, birds, 1884, initials KB, #122, 12"h, mint 300-500
June 4, 1993 Sold for $350

448. Rookwood vase, standard glaze, daisies, 1900, #913, I. Bishop, 6"h, mint 300-500
June 4, 1993 Sold for $400

449. Rookwood vase, Limoges glaze, birds, M.A. Daly, 1882, anchor mark, 8"h, mint 1200-1500
June 4, 1993 Sold for $650

450. Rookwood pitcher, standard glaze, holly, 1896, #774, M.L. Perkins, 6"h, mint 350-450
June 4, 1993 Sold for $250

451. Rookwood jug, Limoges style, birds, 1883, A.R. Valentien, 5"h, mint 300-500
June 4, 1993 Sold for $425

452. Rookwood vase, dull finish, flowers, 1887, #238C, M. A. Daly, 11"h, mint 1000-1500
June 4, 1993 Sold for $650

453. Rookwood vase, hi-glaze, floral design, M.A. Daly, 1887, #271, 8"h, mint 750-1000
June 4, 1993 Sold for $600

454. Rookwood vase, Iris glaze, orchids, S.E. Coyne, 1907, #925C, 9.5"h, hairline 600-800
June 10, 1994 Sold for $900

455. Rookwood vase, Iris glaze, lilies, S. Sax, 1906, #941C, 9.5"h, mint 2500-3500
June 10, 1994 Sold for $2200

456. Rookwood vase, Iris glaze, magnolias, S. Sax, 1903, #909, 10"h, mint 2500-3500
June 10, 1994 Sold for $2600

457. Rookwood vase, hi-glaze, hydrangeas, Shirayamadani, 1928, #614C, 13"h, mint 7000-9000
June 10, 1994 Sold for $9500

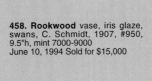

458. Rookwood vase, iris glaze, swans, C. Schmidt, 1907, #950, 9.5"h, mint 7000-9000
June 10, 1994 Sold for $15,000

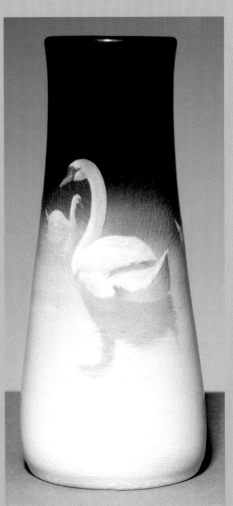

459. **Rookwood** vase, vellum, floral, L. Asbury, 1922, #1697P, 8.5"h, mint 2000-2500
June 10, 1994 Sold for $1800

460. **Rookwood** vase, vellum, floral, L. Asbury, 1930, #6206D, 7.5"h, mint 2500-3500
June 10, 1994 Sold for $2600

461. **Rookwood** vase, vellum, floral, E. Diers, 1932, #1369E, 7.5"h, mint 2000-2500
June 10, 1994 Sold for $1700

462. **Rookwood** vase, Iris glaze, dragonflies, C. Schmidt, 1906, #909BB, 10"h, mint 10,000-15,000
June 4, 1993 Sold for $14,000

463. **Rookwood** vase, Iris glaze, poppies, C. Schmidt, 1908, #614B, 15"h, mint 10,000-15,000
June 4, 1993 Sold for $11,000

464. Rookwood vase, vellum, dogwood, E. Diers, 1905, #951, 7"h, mint 600-800
June 10, 1994 Sold for $900

465. Rookwood vase, vellum, daisies, K. Van Horne, 1913, #2070, 8"h, mint 700-900
June 10, 1994 Sold for $800

466. Rookwood vase, vellum, blossoms, H. Wilcox, 1923, #614E, 8.5"h, mint 1000-1500
June 10, 1994 Sold for $1100

467. Rookwood vase, vellum, violets, E. Diers, 1907, #30E, 8"h, mint 700-900
June 10, 1994 Sold for $900

468. Rookwood vase, vellum, dogwood, E.F. McDermott, 1913, #732C, 7"h, mint 500-700
June 10, 1994 Sold for $500

469. Rookwood vase, vellum, landscape, 1924, #1918, F. Rothenbush, 9"h, mint 2500-3500
June 4, 1993 Sold for $2300

470. Rookwood vase, standard glaze, carnations, silver overlay, 1893, #614E, E. Felten, 8"h, mint 6000-8000
June 4, 1993 Sold for $8500

471. Rookwood vase, vellum, deer, Shirayamadani, 1908, #952D, 9"h, mint 4000-6000
June 4, 1993 Sold for $3500

472. Rookwood vase, matt glaze, floral design, E. Barrett, 1925, #614F, 7"h, mint 300-500
June 10, 1994 Sold for $300

473. Rookwood vase, matt glaze, leaves and berries, V. Tischler, 1922, #356E, 6.5"h, mint 800-1100
June 10, 1994 Sold for $850

474. Rookwood vase, matt glaze, floral design, J. Jensen, 1930, #2969, 7.5"h, mint 800-1100
June 10, 1994 Sold for $900

475. Rookwood vase, matt glaze, leaves and blooms, C.S. Todd, 1921, #900D, 7"h, mint 800-1000
June 10, 1994 Sold for $600

476. Rookwood vase, vellum, floral design, L. Holtkamp, 1942, 8"h, mint 700-900
June 10, 1994 Sold for $600

477. Rookwood vase, vellum, floral, L. Asbury, 1930, uncrazed, #1065B, 11"h, mint 3500-4500
June 4, 1993 Sold for $4500

478. Rookwood vase, matt glaze, berries, 1903, Shirayamadani, #584Z, 14"h, mint 4000-5000
June 4, 1993 Sold for $2300

479. Rookwood vase, matt glaze, irises, J. Jensen, 1930, #6181C, 7"w x 9"h, mint 1200-1700
June 4, 1993 Sold for $1100

480. Rookwood vase, standard glaze, nasturtiums, M. Daly, 1882, #612A, 8"h, mint 2000-2500
June 10, 1994 Sold for $2300

481. Rookwood vase, standard glaze, puff balls, A. Valentien, 1890, #330W, 14.5"h, mint 2000-3000
June 10, 1994 Sold for $1700

482. Rookwood vase, standard glaze, dogwood, A. Valentien, 1889, 10"h, mint 1500-2000
June 10, 1994 Sold for $1000

483. Rookwood mug, standard glaze, clover, signature illegible, 1890s, #328S, 6"h, mint 300-400
June 10, 1994 Sold for $225

484. Rookwood vase, standard glaze, floral design, J. Zettel, 1894, #763C, 5.5"h, mint 600-800
June 10, 1994 Sold for $450

485. Rookwood ewer, standard glaze, flowers and leaves, silver overlay, line to spout 1500-2500
June 10, 1994 Sold for $1500

486. Rookwood vase, standard glaze, berries, Dibowski, 1893, #442C, 6.5"h, mint 700-900
June 10, 1994 Sold for $1100

487. Rookwood ewer, standard glaze, flowers, not signed, 1889, #40W, 5.5"h, tiny flakes 250-350
June 10, 1994 Sold for $240

488. Rookwood vase, standard glaze, palm, A.M. Valentien, 1898, #556B, 13.5"h, mint 900-1200
June 10, 1994 Sold for $650

489. Rookwood vase, standard glaze, shells, Shirayamadani, 1891, #42W, 7.5"h, mint 1500-2000
June 10, 1994 Sold for $950

490. Rookwood vase, standard glaze, fish, Shirayamadani, 1895, #S1173, 10"h, mint 3000-4000
June 10, 1994 Sold for $7000

491. Rookwood vase, aventurine glaze, 1916, #821F, X1637X, 5"h, mint 200-300
June 10, 1994 Sold for $275

492. Rookwood candlestick, Tiger Eye, wild rose, 1889, #508, H. Wilcox, 6"h, mint 300-400
June 10, 1994 Sold for $240

493. Rookwood vase, Tiger Eye, impressed Rookwood, 1885, #1726, 8.5"h, mint 900-1200
June 10, 1994 Sold for $800

494. Rookwood ewer, early standard glaze, mums, S. Toohey, 1890, #433, 7"h, mint 600-800
June 10, 1994 Sold for $450

495. Rookwood vase, Tiger Eye, 1887, #533, 7"h, mint 700-900
June 10, 1994 Sold for $700

496. Rookwood pitcher, Tiger Eye, lily design, 1886, #230, A.R. Valentien, 5"h, mint 500-700
June 10, 1994 Sold for $325

497. **Rookwood** vase, Iris glaze,
leaves, S. Sax, 1902, #922D, 7"h,
mint 1000-1500
June 10, 1994 Sold for $1800

498. **Rookwood** vase, Iris glaze, dogwood, C. Baker, 1902, #S1717, 6"h,
mint 900-1200
June 10, 1994 Sold for $1100

499. **Rookwood** vase, Iris glaze with
crocuses, E. Diers, 1903, #614F, 6"h,
mint 1000-1500
June 10, 1994 Sold for $1100

500. **Rookwood** vase, Iris glaze, flowers, F. Rothenbusch, 1905, #913D,
7"h, mint 1000-1500
June 10, 1994 Sold for $1600

501. **Rookwood** vase, Iris glaze, oak
leaves, K. Van Horne, 1909, #1278E,
7"h, mint 800-1100
June 10, 1994 Sold for $950

502. **Rookwood** plaque, vellum, landscape,
L. Asbury, 1920, 8"w x 6"h, mint 2000-3000
June 10, 1994 Sold for $2850

503. **Rookwood** plaque, vellum, trees, F.
Rothenbusch, 1916, 8"w x 10"h,
mint 2000-3000
June 10, 1994 Sold for $2500

504. **Rookwood** plaque, vellum, landscape,
F. Rothenbusch, 8"w x 6"h, mint 2000-3000
June 10, 1994 Sold for $2800

505. **Rookwood** vase, Iris glaze,
grasshopper, S. Toohey, 1899, #604F,
3"h, mint 800-1100
June 10, 1994 Sold for $1100

506. **Rookwood** vase, Ariel Blue, lilies,
Shirayamadani, 1895, #483, 6"h,
mint 1500-2500
June 10, 1994 Sold for $2600

507. **Rookwood** vase, Iris glaze,
daisies, E. Noonan, 1909, #901D, 7.5"h,
mint 1200-1700
June 10, 1994 Sold for $3200

508. **Rookwood** vase, Iris glaze, pansies, S. Sax, 1902, #741C, 5.5"h,
mint 900-1200
June 10, 1994 Sold for $1400

509. **Rookwood** vase, Iris glaze, snap-
dragons, C. Schmidt, 1904, #654E,
3.5"h, mint 1000-1500
June 10, 1994 Sold for $1600

510. Rookwood vase, hi-glaze, berries, F. Rothenbusch, 1924, #1325, 5.5"h, mint 900-1200
June 10, 1994 Sold for $900

511. Rookwood vase, hi-glaze, birds and leaves, geometric, A. Conant, 1919, #2120, 7"h, mint 1200-1700
June 10, 1994 Sold for $900

512. Rookwood vase, hi-glaze, birds, A. Conant, 1919, #2, 6"h, mint 1000-1500
June 10, 1994 Sold for $950

513. Rookwood vase, hi-glaze, flowers, P. Conant, 1917, #2061P, 7"h, mint 800-1100
June 10, 1994 Sold for $900

514. Rookwood vase, hi-glaze, floral design, L. Holtkamp, 1953, 6.5"h, mint 600-800
June 10, 1994 Sold for $350

515. Rookwood plaque, vellum, landscape, E.T. Hurley, 4.5"w x 7.5"h, mint 1500-2000
June 10, 1994 Sold for $1400

516. Rookwood plaque, vellum, landscape, unsigned, 1918, 8"w x 5.5"h, mint 2700-3700
June 10, 1994 Sold for $3750

517. Rookwood plaque, vellum, landscape, F. Rothenbusch, 5"w x 8"h, mint 2200-2700
June 10, 1994 Sold for $2000

518. Rookwood vase, vellum, landscape, E.T. Hurley, 1942, #2721, 6.25"h, repair 600-800
June 10, 1994 Sold for $600

519. Rookwood vase, vellum, landscape, E.F. McDermott, 1915, #924, 6"h, mint 900-1200
June 10, 1994 Sold for $900

520. Rookwood vase, vellum, landscape, L. Epply, 1910, #1659, 7.5"h, mint 1200-1700
June 10, 1994 Sold for $1200

521. Rookwood vase, vellum, landscape, E. Diers, 1918, #913E, 6.5"h, mint 1000-1500
June 10, 1994 Sold for $1000

522. Rookwood vase, vellum, landscape, 1921, F. Rothenbusch, #913F, 5.5"h, mint 1000-1500
June 10, 1994 Sold for $800

523. Rookwood vase, vellum, poppies, 1905, M. Nourse, #905D, 8"h, mint 2500-3500
June 4, 1993 Sold for $2500

524. Rookwood vase, iris glaze, dragon, O.G. Reed, 1897, #743C, 7"h, mint 2000-3000
June 4, 1993 Sold for $1600

525. Rookwood vase, iris glaze, poppies, A.R. Valentien, 1898, #821C, 10"h, mint 3000-4000
June 4, 1993 Sold for $4500

526. Rookwood vase, vellum, Queen Anne's lace, L. Asbury, 1911, #900A, 13"h, mint 2500-3500
June 10, 1994 Sold for $2500

527. Rookwood vase, vellum, blossoms, applied silver, E.T. Hurley, 1912, #379D, 10.5"h, repair 2500-3500
June 10, 1994 Sold for $1900

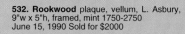

532. Rookwood plaque, vellum, L. Asbury, 9"w x 5"h, framed, mint 1750-2750
June 15, 1990 Sold for $2000

528. Rookwood vase, matt glaze, sea horses, S. Toohey, 1907, #950F, 6"h, mint 800-1100
June 4, 1993 Sold for $650

529. Rookwood vase, matt, floral, Shirayamadani, 1904, #1064, 4"h, mint 1200-1700
June 4, 1993 Sold for $1300

530. Rookwood vase, matt glaze, violets, C.A. Baker, 1901, #743C, 7"h, mint 2000-3000
June 4, 1993 Sold for $1300

531. Rookwood vase, matt, mistletoe, 1901, J.D. Wareham, #922E, 6"h, mint 3000-4000
June 4, 1993 Sold for $2700

533. Rookwood vase, iris glaze, C. Schmidt, 1904, #932C, 12"h, mint 6000-8000
June 10, 1994 Sold for $4750

534. Rookwood vase, iris glaze, iris blooms, C. Schmidt, 1910, 1856D, 8.5"h, mint 2500-3500
June 10, 1994 Sold for $2600

535. Rookwood vase, hi-glaze, pussy willows, S. Sax, 1920, #2040E, 7.5"h, mint 700-900
June 4, 1993 Sold for $750

536. Rookwood vase, hi-glaze, flowers, 1920, #356F, A. Conant, 5.5"h, mint 700-900
June 4, 1993 Sold for $550

537. Rookwood vase, hi-glaze, landscape, A. Conant, 1919, #2499A, 19"h, mint 2500-3500
June 4, 1993 Sold for $3500

538. Rookwood vase, hi-glaze, pelicans, 1934, J. Jensen, 6"h, mint 600-800
June 4, 1993 Sold for $600

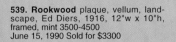

539. Rookwood plaque, vellum, landscape, Ed Diers, 1916, 12"w x 10"h, framed, mint 3500-4500
June 15, 1990 Sold for $3300

540. Rookwood vase, iris glaze, poppies, 1903, #S1750, C. Schmidt, 16"h, mint 10,000-15,000
April 5, 1992 Sold for $6500

541. Rookwood vase, sea green, geese, 1899, #531C, C.A. Baker, 11"h, mint 9,000-12,000
April 5, 1992 Sold for $9000

542. Rookwood vase, matt glaze,
daisies, Shirayamadani, 1938, 6"h,
mint 900-1100
June 10, 1994 Sold for $950

543. Rookwood vase, matt glaze, floral,
Shirayamadani, 1939, #614D, 10"h,
mint 2500-3500
June 10, 1994 Sold for $3250

544. Rookwood vase, matt glaze, lilies
and buds, Shirayamadani, 1943, #935D,
8"h, mint 1200-1700
June 10, 1994 Sold for $1400

545. Rookwood vase, standard glaze, holly, silver
overlay, A. Sprague, 1893, #542, 8.5"h,
mint 3000-4000
June 4, 1993 Sold for $2800

546. Rookwood plaque, vellum, harbor scene, C.
Schmidt, 1918, 9.5" x 14.5", mint 6500-8500
June 4, 1993 Sold for $7000

547. Rookwood vase, vellum, floral, E. Diers, 1913,
#1638B, 14"h, mint 2200-2700
June 4, 1993 Sold for $1800

548. Rookwood vase, standard glaze, wild roses, C.
Baker, 1898, #611D, 8"h, mint 400-600
June 4, 1993 Sold for $750

549. Rookwood pitcher, standard glaze, daffodils,
1890, no number, no signature, 10"h, mint 600-800
June 4, 1993 Sold for $875

550. Rookwood vase, hi-glaze, plums, 1944, #6877, J. Jensen, 7.5"h, mint 1200-1700
June 10, 1994 Sold for $1100

551. Rookwood vase, hi-glaze, roses and leaves, J. Jensen, 1943, #S2130, 6"h, mint 1200-1700
June 10, 1994 Sold for $1700

552. Rookwood vase, hi-glaze, apples, J. Jensen, 1946, #6940, #8708, 9.5"h, mint 1500-2500
June 10, 1994 Sold for $1500

553. Rookwood vase, matt glaze, bouquets, 1934, #6428, McDonald, 8"h, mint 1200-1700
June 4, 1993 Sold for $1400

554. Rookwood plaque, vellum, landscape, E.T. Hurley, 1939, 7" x 11", mint 3500-4500
June 4, 1993 Sold for $3250

555. Rookwood vase, matt glaze, flowers, H.E. Wilcox, 1906, #950B, 12"h, mint 1200-1700
June 4, 1993 Sold for $1900

556. Rookwood plaque, vellum, landscape, E.T. Hurley, 1912, 6" x 8" plaque, mint 2750-3750
June 4, 1993 Sold for $2800

557. Rookwood vase, vellum, scenic, 1918, #1278E, S.E. Coyne, 9"h, mint 1700-2200
June 4, 1993 Sold for $2100

558. Rookwood vase, vellum, tropical birds, E.T. Hurley, 1907, #939C, 8.5"h, mint 2500-3500 June 10, 1994 Sold for $3500

559. Rookwood vase, vellum, Canadian geese, Shirayamadani, 1909, #1659D, 9"h, mint 3000-4000 June 10, 1994 Sold for $3500

560. Rookwood vase, standard glaze, floral, K. Hickman, 1897, #792, 7.5"h, mint 400-600 June 10, 1994 Sold for $375

561. Rookwood vase, standard glaze, floral, C. Steinle, 1901, #533F, 5"h, mint 350-450 June 10, 1994 Sold for $250

562. Rookwood ewer, standard glaze, dogwood, A.D. Sehon, 1898, #715DD, 6"h, mint 500-700 June 10, 1994 Sold for $600

563. Rookwood vase, standard glaze, flowers, E.N. Lincoln, 1894, #667, 6.5"h, mint 400-600 June 10, 1994 Sold for $400

564. Rookwood vase, standard glaze, floral, S. Markland, 1894, #743C, W, 7"h, mint 600-800 June 10, 1994 Sold for $450

565. Rookwood vase, vellum, Venetian harbor, C. Schmidt, 1925, #1358E, 7.5"h, mint 400-600
June 10, 1995 Sold for $3000

566. Rookwood vase, vellum, landscape, E. T. Hurley, 1917, #1555E, 8.5"h, mint 1500-2000
June 10, 1995 Sold for $2300

567. Rookwood vase, vellum, Venetian harbor, C. Schmidt, 1926, #954, 5"h, mint 2500-3500
June 10, 1995 Sold for $3000

568. Rookwood vase, vellum, landscape, F. Rothenbusch, 1930, #2544, 8"h, mint 1000-1500
June 10, 1995 Sold for $950

569. Rookwood vase, vellum, Venetian boats, S. Sax, 1912, #1873, 5.5"h, mint 1000-1500
June 10, 1995 Sold for $800

570. Rookwood plaque, vellum, landscape, E.T. Hurley, 8.5"w x 6.5"h, mint 3500-4500
June 10, 1995 Sold for $4250

571. Rookwood vase, vellum, Venetian harbor, S.E. Coyne, 1909, #614E, 8.5"h, mint 1700-2200
June 10, 1995 Sold for $2500

572. Rookwood vase, hi-glaze, fish, Shirayamadani, 1930, #6091, 11"h, mint 1500-2500
June 10, 1995 Sold for $2800

573. Rookwood vase, hi-glaze, birds, A. Conant, 1922, #2523, 17.5"h, filled drill hole 5000-7000
June 10, 1995 Sold for $2500

574. Rookwood vase, hi-glaze, tropical birds, E.T. Hurley, 1924, #2785, 13"h, mint 3000-4000
June 10, 1995 Sold for $3500

575. Rookwood vase, vellum, blossoms and buds, H.E. Wilcox, 1926, #1358 F, 6"h, mint 700-900
June 1, 1996 Sold for $550

576. Rookwood vase, vellum, blossoms, F. Rothenbusch, 1929, #915E, 6"h, mint 1000-1500
June 1, 1996 Sold for $1200

577. Rookwood vase, vellum, blossoms, E.T. Hurley, 1924, #2544, 8"h, mint 1200-1700
June 1, 1996 Sold for $1400

578. Rookwood vase, vellum, stylized daisies, K. Ley, 1955, #2724, 6"h, mint 800-1100
June 1, 1996 Sold for $1200

579. Rookwood vase, vellum, vines, F. Rothenbusch, 1925, #1356F, 6"h, mint 1000-1500
June 1, 1996 Sold for $1900

580. Rookwood vase, Limoges style, roses, A.R. Valentien, 1882, 11"h, mint 2000-3000 June 10, 1994 Sold for $1600

581. Rookwood vase, dull finish, floral, E.D. Foertmeyer, 1890, #552, W, 9"h, mint 1000-1500 June 10, 1994 Sold for $1800

582. Rookwood vase, Limoges style, butterfly, 1885, #238, A.R. Valentien, 17"h, mint 2500-3500 June 10, 1994 Sold for $2000

583. Rookwood vase, iris glaze, tulips, F. Rothenbusch, 1902, #925C, 9"h, mint 3000-4000 June 10, 1995 Sold for $2100

584. Rookwood vase, iris glaze, cherry blossoms, 1911, S.E. Coyne, #900C, 9"h, mint 1200-1700 June 10, 1995 Sold for $1800

585. Rookwood vase, iris glaze, mushrooms, C. Schmidt, 1903, #917B, 9"h, repair 3500-4500 June 10, 1995 Sold for $1400

586. Rookwood vase, hi-glaze, abstract wisteria, E.T. Hurley, 1923, #1929, 4"h, mint 800-1100
June 10, 1994 Sold for $650

587. Rookwood vase, hi-glaze, birds and wisteria, E.T. Hurley, 1926, #2746, 9.5"h, mint 2500-3500
June 10, 1994 Sold for $2500

588. Rookwood vase, hi-glaze, floral design, E.T. Hurley, 1949, #2154C, 12"h, mint 1200-1700
June 10, 1994 Sold for $1800

589. Rookwood vases, pair, hi-glaze, stylized deer, J.D. Wareham, 1952, 8.5"h, mint 2000-3000
June 10, 1994 Sold for $1500

590. Rookwood vase, porcelain glaze, stylized deer, J. Jensen, 1945, #922D, 7.5"h, mint 1200-1700
June 10, 1994 Sold for $1100

591. Rookwood vase, hi-glaze, hibiscus, E. Barrett, 1944, #3214, 12.5"h, mint 1200-1700
June 10, 1994 Sold for $1100

592. Rookwood vase, standard glaze, geese, M. Daly, 1898, #664, 11"h, minor scratches 3500-4500
June 10, 1995 Sold for $13,750

593. Rookwood jug, standard glaze, silver overlay, M. Daly, 1891, #S976, 6.5"h, mint 3500-4500
June 10, 1995 Sold for $6000

594. Rookwood vase, matt glaze, grapes, R. Fechheimer, 1904, #30EZV, 4"h, mint 400-600
June 10, 1994 Sold for $400

595. Rookwood vase, matt glaze, Art Nouveau, E.N. Lincoln, 1918, 6.5"h, mint 500-700
June 10, 1994 Sold for $550

596. Rookwood jar, matt glaze, Arts & Crafts style, W. Hentschel, 1910, #996, 8.5"h, mint 800-1100
June 10, 1994 Sold for $800

597. Rookwood vase, matt glaze, geometric design, O.G. Reed, 1904, #30F2, 4"h, mint 250-350
June 10, 1994 Sold for $350

598. Rookwood handled vessel, matt glaze, irises, A. Pons, 1907, #1014D, 7"h, mint 500-700
June 10, 1994 Sold for $400

599. Rookwood vase, matt glaze, flowers, S. Sax, 1904, #969C, 6"h, mint 500-700
June 10, 1994 Sold for $600

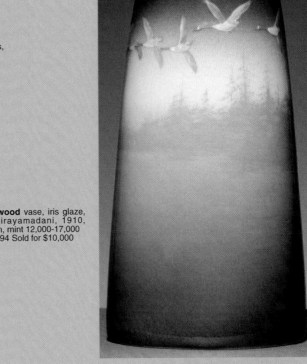

600. Rookwood vase, vellum, flamingos, Shirayamadani, 1907, #1369D, 9"h, mint 7000-9000
June 10, 1994 Sold for $6000

601. Rookwood vase, iris glaze, geese, Shirayamadani, 1910, #1654D, 9"h, mint 12,000-17,000
June 10, 1994 Sold for $10,000

602. Rookwood vase, hi-glaze, elderberry vine, Shirayamadani, 1927, #913D, 8"h, mint 1500-2500
June 10, 1994 Sold for $2600

603. Rookwood vase, hi-glaze, floral, H.E. Wilcox, 1924, #614B, 15"h, mint 2000-3000
June 10, 1994 Sold for $2000

604. Rookwood bowl, hi-glaze, flowers, L. Epply, 1923, #923, 2.5"h, mint 800-1100
June 10, 1994 Sold for $850

605. Rookwood vase, hi-glaze, abstract circles, L. Epply, 1921, #778, 10"h, mint 800-1100
June 10, 1994 Sold for $450

606. Rookwood vase, Chinese Plum, flowers, Shirayamadani, 1925, #2719, 6.5"h, mint 1000-1500
June 10, 1994 Sold for $1100

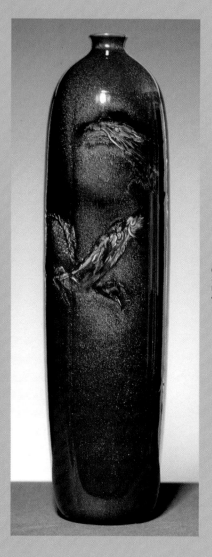

607. **Rookwood** vase, Tiger Eye, serpents,
Shirayamadani, 1893, #644, 18.5"h,
mint 10,000-15,000
June 10, 1994 Sold for $10,000

608. **Rookwood** vase, hi-glaze, poppies and wheat, Shirayamadani, 1927, #1369D, 9"h, mint 8000-11,000
June 10, 1994 Sold for $9500

609. **Rookwood** vases, pair, hi-glaze, flowers, J.
Jensen, 1945, #6644, 6.5"h, both mint 900-1200
June 10, 1994 Sold for $800

610. **Rookwood** vase, hi-glaze, chrysanthemums and
butterflies, A. Conant, 7.5"h, restored 600-900
June 10, 1994 Sold for $1100

611. **Rookwood** bowl, hi-glaze, blossoms, S. Sax, 1921,
#2287, 8"dia. x 4"h, mint 800-1100
June 10, 1994 Sold for $1000

612. **Rookwood** vase, hi-glaze, lilies, M.H. McDonald,
1941, #6578, 8"h, mint 800-1100
June 10, 1994 Sold for $850

613. **Rookwood** vase, hi-glaze, tulips, Shirayamadani,
1945, #6666, 6"h, factory chip 800-1100
June 10, 1994 Sold for $650

614. Rookwood plaque, vellum, landscape, E.T. Hurley, 1947, 14" x 12", mint 6000-8000
June 10, 1994 Sold for $4750

615. Rookwood vase, standard glaze, berries and leaves, G. Young, 1889, #535E, 7"h, mint 400-500
June 10, 1994 Sold for $350

616. Rookwood vase, standard glaze, floral, W. Klemm, 1901, #725C, 67"h, mint 400-600
June 10, 1994 Sold for $350

617. Rookwood bowl, standard, ram's horn, A.M. Valentien, 1892, #360W, 11"dia., flake 500-700
June 10, 1994 Sold for $200

618. Rookwood vase, standard glaze, dogwood, E.N. Lincoln, 1904, #913D, 7"h, mint 500-700
June 10, 1994 Sold for $400

619. Rookwood pitcher, standard glaze, flowers, E.B.I. Cranch, 1895, #552, 7.5"h, mint 500-700
June 10, 1994 Sold for $450

620. Rookwood plaque, matt glaze, two rooks, S. Toohey, early 1900s, 8"w x 6"h, mint 6000-8000
June 7, 1997 Sold for $17,000

621. Rookwood teapot, standard glaze, floral, O.G. Reed, 1893, #528W, 10"h, mint 600-800
June 10, 1994 Sold for $550

622. Rookwood ewer, standard glaze, floral, S. Toohey, 1894, #468CC, 8"h, mint 600-800
June 10, 1994 Sold for $450

623. Rookwood pitcher, standard glaze, floral, M. Daly, 1887, 10"h, mint 900-1200
June 10, 1994 Sold for $200

624. Rookwood ewer, standard glaze, rose, A. Van Briggle, 1889, #S871, 7.5"h, mint 1000-1500
June 10, 1994 Sold for $650

625. Rookwood ewer, standard glaze, dogwood, C. Baker, 1894, #719, 9.5"h, mint 700-900
June 10, 1994 Sold for $600

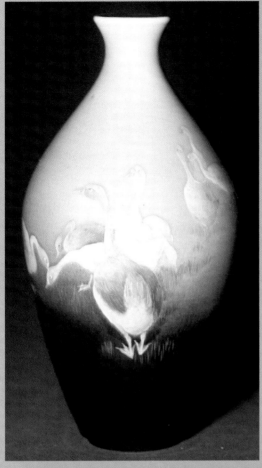

626. Rookwood vase, sea green glaze, geese, A. Valentien, 1896, #745A, 11"h, repair 5000-7500
June 10, 1995 Sold for $4000

627. Rookwood vase, floral, standard glaze, Shirayamadani, 1888, #714S, 17.5"h, mint 4000-5000
June 10, 1995 Sold for $16,000

628. Rookwood vase, hi-glaze, violets, Shiraya-madani, 1945, #6183F, 4.5"h, mint 500-700
June 10, 1995 Sold for $1300

629. Rookwood vase, hi-glaze, pansies, E.T. Hurley, 7"h, mint 900-1200
June 10, 1995 Sold for $700

630. Rookwood vase, butterfat glaze, vines, M.H. McDonald, 1936, #S2139, 12"h, mint 1500-2500
June 10, 1995 Sold for $1100

631. Rookwood vase, hi-glaze, forsythia, M.H. McDonald, 1943, #6620, 4"h, mint 500-700
June 10, 1995 Sold for $375

632. Rookwood vase, hi-glaze, floral, E. Barrett, 1945, #6878, 6"h, mint 600-800
June 10, 1995 Sold for $425

633. Rookwood vase, hi-glaze, floral, Shiraya-madani, 1925, #2719, 6.5"h, mint 1200-1700
June 10, 1995 Sold for $1800

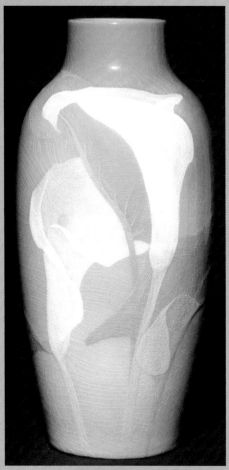

634. Rookwood vase, Iris glaze, lily, S. Sax, 1903, #940B, 13"h, mint 10,000-15,000
June 10, 1995 Sold for $6000

635. Rookwood vase, Black Iris glaze, water lilies, C. Schmidt, 1908, #1278D, 10"h, mint 12,000-17,000
June 10, 1995 Sold for $37,000

636. Rookwood vase, matt glaze, stylized floral, E. Barrett, 1924, #2672, 8"h, mint 600-800
June 10, 1995 Sold for $650

637. Rookwood vase, matt glaze, blossoms, J.W. Pullman, 1930, #6200D, 6"dia. x 7"h, mint 600-800
June 10, 1995 Sold for $600

638. Rookwood vase, matt glaze, floral, D. Workum, 1928, 5"h, mint 600-800
June 10, 1995 Sold for $500

639. Rookwood vase, matt glaze, blossoms, C. Covalenco, 1925, #614B, 15"h, mint 1700-2700
June 10, 1995 Sold for $1800

640. Rookwood vase, matt glaze, blossoms, M.H. McDonald, 1926, #2672, 8"h, mint 600-800
June 10, 1995 Sold for $600

641. Rookwood vase, matt glaze, floral designs, Shirayamadani, 1937, #2932, 14"h, mint 3000-4000
June 10, 1995 Sold for $5500

642. Rookwood vase, standard glaze, portrait, O. Reed, 1898, #830D, 6.5"h, hairlines 2000-3000
June 10, 1995 Sold for $1300

643. Rookwood vase, standard glaze, nymphs, Shirayamadani, 1896, #659B, 8"h, crack 1200-1700
June 10, 1995 Sold for $850

644. Rookwood vase, standard glaze, portrait, S. Laurence 1896, #659C, 6"h, repair 2500-3500
June 10, 1995 Sold for $1800

645. Rookwood vase, matt glaze, dragonflies, S.E. Coyne, 1905, #942C, 6.5"h, mint 1200-1700
June 10, 1995 Sold for $1200

646. Rookwood vase, matt glaze, geometric, W. Hentschel, 1913, #1064, 5"h, mint 700-900
June 10, 1995 Sold for $750

647. Rookwood vase, matt glaze, rays of sun, W.E. Hentschel, 1912, #11, 9"dia., mint 1200-1700
June 10, 1995 Sold for $900

648. Rookwood dish, matt glaze, lizard, Shirayamadani, 1903, #630Z, 3.5"dia., mint 900-1200
June 10, 1995 Sold for $475

649. Rookwood vase, matt glaze, blossoms, C.S. Todd, 1908, #950F, 6.5"h, mint 500-700
June 10, 1995 Sold for $475

650. Rookwood vase, matt glaze, lilies, C. Duell, 1904, #969E, 4"h, mint 500-700
June 10, 1995 Sold for $700

651. Rookwood vase, standard glaze, tulips, H. Altman, 1901, #901D, 7.5"h, mint 450-650
June 10, 1995 Sold for $450

652. Rookwood vase, standard glaze, blueberries, R. Fechheimer, 1900, #743C, 7"h, mint 450-650
June 10, 1995 Sold for $750

653. Rookwood vase, standard glaze, dogwood, silver overlay, Shirayamadani, 1892, #628C, 10"w, minor silver loss 4000-6000
June 10, 1995 Sold for $3250

654. Rookwood vase, standard glaze, berries, C. Steinle, 1896, #763C, 5.5"h, mint 450-650
June 10, 1995 Sold for $425

655. Rookwood vase, standard glaze, poppies, C.C. Lindeman, 1899, #568C, 7"h, mint 550-750
June 10, 1995 Sold for $950

656. Rookwood vase, standard glaze, magnolias, J. Swing, 1903, #922D, 7"h, mint 450-650
June 10, 1995 Sold for $425

657. Rookwood vase, standard glaze, roses, A.B. Sprague, 1898, #484D, 7"h, mint 1500-2000
June 10, 1995 Sold for $850

658. Rookwood vase, standard glaze, geometric design, M.L. Perkins, 1909, 8.5"dia., mint 500-700
June 10, 1995 Sold for $400

659. Rookwood ewer, standard glaze, blossoms, A.M. Valentien, 1891, #387 C, 11"h, mint 700-900
June 10, 1995 Sold for $500

660. Rookwood vase, standard glaze, pansies, E. Diers, 1901, #927, 7"h, mint 500-700
June 10, 1995 Sold for $900

661. Rookwood vase, hi-glaze, fish, J. Jensen, 1945, #C184E, 7"h, mint 900-1200
June 10, 1995 Sold for $600

662. Rookwood vase, hi-glaze, deer, J. Jensen, 1931, #900C, 8.5"h, mint 2000-3000
June 10, 1995 Sold for $4500

663. Rookwood bowl, hi-glaze, stylized figures, J. Jensen, 1946, #2813C, 13.5"dia., mint 2000-3000
June 10, 1995 Sold for $1000

664. Rookwood vase, hi-glaze, stylized nudes, J. Jensen, 1931, #904D, 8.5"h, mint 3500-4500
June 10, 1995 Sold for $2000

665. Rookwood vase, matt glaze, stylized fish, J. Jensen, 1945, #6194D, 6"h, mint 1000-1500
June 10, 1995 Sold for $950

666. Rookwood vase, standard glaze, thistle, L. Asbury, 1901, #901C, 8.5"h, mint 600-800
June 10, 1995 Sold for $500

667. Rookwood vase, standard glaze, roses, J. Zettel, 1895, 7.5"h, mint 800-1100
June 10, 1995 Sold for $600

668. Rookwood vase, standard glaze, vines, A.R. Valentien, 1890, #402X, 9.5"h, mint 2000-3000
June 10, 1995 Sold for $2500

669. Rookwood vase, standard glaze, dogwood, M. Daly, 1890, #486W, 10"h, mint 900-1200
June 10, 1995 Sold for $1500

670. Rookwood vase, standard glaze, poppies, A.B. Sprague, 1900, #902D, 7"h, mint 800-1100
June 10, 1995 Sold for $1100

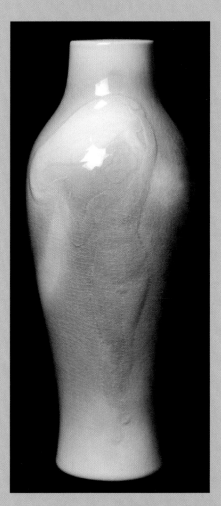

671. Rookwood vase, iris glaze, nude, S. Laurence, 1901, #879C, 12"h, mint 9000-12,000
June 10, 1995 Sold for $8500

672. Rookwood vase, standard glaze, orchids, A.R. Valentien, 1898, 20"h, repaired 7500-10,000
June 10, 1995 Sold for $8500

673. Rookwood vase, vellum, landscape, L. Epply, 1915, #808, 8"h, mint 1200-1700
June 10, 1995 Sold for $1900

674. Rookwood vase, vellum, landscape, F. Rothenbusch, 1923, #1045, 5.5"h, mint 1200-1700
June 10, 1995 Sold for $900

675. Rookwood plaque, vellum, landscape, F. Rothenbusch, 1921, 11.5"w x 8.5"h, flaw 3000-4000
June 10, 1995 Sold for $2400

676. Rookwood vase, vellum, landscape, E.F. McDermott, 1919, #1873, 5.5"h, mint 1000-1500
June 10, 1995 Sold for $1000

677. Rookwood vase, vellum, landscape, E.F. McDermott, 1918, #1369E, 7.5"h, mint 1500-2500
June 10, 1995 Sold for $1900

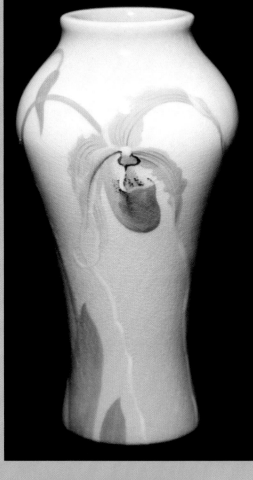

678. Rookwood vase, iris glaze, peonies, S. Sax, 1904, #S1761, 11.5"dia. x 12"h, mint 12,000-17,000
June 10, 1995 Sold for $20,000

679. Rookwood vase, iris glaze, orchids, A.R. Valentien, 1902, #909B, 12"h, mint 8000-11,000
June 10, 1995 Sold for $9000

680. Rookwood vase, vellum, landscape, Shi-rayamadani, 1909, #1655E, 8"h, mint 1500-2500
June 10, 1995 Sold for $2700

681. Edward Diers, mixed media, landscape, signed, 9.5"w x 7.5"h, excellent condition 600-800
June 10, 1995 Sold for $500

682. Rookwood vase, vellum, landscape, E. Diers, 1915, #2032C, 12"h, mint 3000-4000
June 10, 1995 Sold for $2300

683. Rookwood vase, vellum, geese, Shiraya-madani, 1909, #852E, 7.5"h, mint 2500-3000
June 10, 1995 Sold for $2700

684. Rookwood plaque, vellum, landscape, F. Rothenbusch, 1914, 5"w x 8"h, mint 2500-3500
June 10, 1995 Sold for $2400

685. Rookwood plaque, vellum, landscape, E. Diers, 1927, 7.5"w x 5"h, mint 2700-3250
June 10, 1995 Sold for $4500

686. Rookwood plaque, vellum, landscape, E. McDermott, 1916, 5"w x 9"h, mint 2700-3250
June 10, 1995 Sold for $3500

687. Rookwood vase, iris glaze, blossoms, A.R. Valentien, 1900, #907E, 8.5"h, mint 2000-3000
June 10, 1995 Sold for $1500

688. Rookwood vase, iris glaze, daffodils, C. Steinle, 1906, #901D, 7"h, mint 900-1200
June 10, 1995 Sold for $1000

689. Rookwood vase, iris glaze, rose blossoms, F. Rothenbusch, 1909, #950C, 10"h, mint 2500-3500
June 10, 1995 Sold for $2500

690. Rookwood vase, iris glaze, thistle blossoms, L. Asbury, 1911, #1655E, 8"h, mint 1700-2200
June 10, 1995 Sold for $2000

691. Rookwood vase, iris glaze, autumn leaves, L. Asbury, 1904, #900C, 8"h, mint 1200-1700
June 10, 1995 Sold for $1600

692. Rookwood plaque, vellum, landscape, E.T. Hurley, 7.5"w x 3.5"h, mint 2500-3500
June 10, 1995 Sold for $2700

693. Rookwood plaque, vellum, landscape, E.T. Hurley, 11.5"w x 8.5"h, mint 6000-8000
June 10, 1995 Sold for $4000

694. Rookwood plaque, vellum, landscape, S. Sax, 7.5"w x 3.5"h, mint 3000-4000
June 10, 1995 Sold for $2500

695. Rookwood vase, iris glaze, blossoms, R. Fechheimer, 1902, #909C, 9"h, mint 1700-2500
June 10, 1995 Sold for $1900

696. Rookwood vase, iris glaze, blossoms, H.E. Wilcox, 1900, #905E, 6.5"h, mint 1200-1700
June 10, 1995 Sold for $1800

697. Rookwood vase, iris glaze, dogwood, S. Sax, 1906, #925C, 9.5"h, mint 3000-3500
June 10, 1995 Sold for $3500

698. Rookwood vase, iris glaze, dandelions, I. Bishop, 1903, #926E, 6"h, mint 800-1100
June 10, 1995 Sold for $950

699. Rookwood vase, iris glaze, underwater design, 1911, S.E. Coyne, #1781, 6"h, mint 2000-2500
June 10, 1995 Sold for $1800

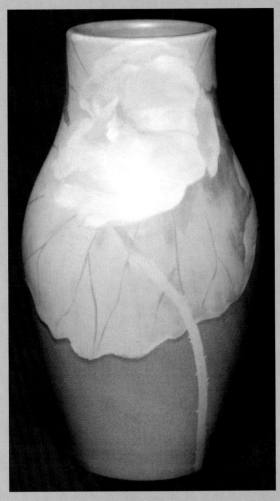

701. Rookwood vase, Chinese Plum, blossoms, H.E. Wilcox, 1926, #2825A, 16.5"h, mint 5000-7000
June 10, 1995 Sold for $18,000

702. Rookwood vase, Chinese Plum, bleeding hearts, Shirayamadani, 1926, 10"h, mint 3500-5500
June 10, 1995 Sold for $7000

700. Rookwood vase, matt glaze, poppies, H. Wilcox, 1901, #198BZ, 11"h, mint 10,000-15,000
June 10, 1995 Sold for $9000

703. Rookwood vase, standard glaze, tulips, M. Daly, 1902, #900B, 10"h, mint 900-1200
June 10, 1995 Sold for $1100

704. Rookwood mug, standard glaze, Native American, E. R. Felten, #587B, 5.5"h, mint 2500-3500
June 10, 1995 Sold for $600

705. Rookwood pitcher, standard glaze, portrait, G. Young, 1899, #656, 9.5"h, minute flakes 4000-6000
June 10, 1995 Sold for $1500

706. Rookwood mug, standard glaze, portrait, A. D. Sehon, 1900, #587B, 5.5"h, mint 2500-3500
June 10, 1995 Sold for $1600

707. Rookwood vase, standard glaze, roses, S. Toohey, 1902, #900E, 10"h, mint 900-1200
June 10, 1995 Sold for $1500

708. Rookwood vase, iris glaze, peacock feathers, C. Schmidt, 1907, #899B, 9.5"h, mint 6000-8000
June 10, 1995 Sold for $6500

709. Rookwood vase, iris glaze, peacock feather, C. Schmidt, 1911, #604F, 3.5"h, mint 1000-2000
June 10, 1995 Sold for $2400

710. Rookwood vase, iris glaze, birch trees, E.T. Hurley, 1945, #6197C, 5053, 8.5"h, mint 4000-6000
June 10, 1995 Sold for $6500

711. Rookwood pitcher, standard glaze, blossoms, H. Wilcox, 1888, #458, 4.5"h, mint 300-500
June 10, 1995 Sold for $375

712. Rookwood ewer, standard glaze, blossoms, H.E. Wilcox, 1888, #433, 6.5"h, mint 600-800
June 10, 1995 Sold for $600

713. Rookwood vase, standard glaze, silver overlay, berries, E.N. Lincoln, 1893, #533E, 7"h, mint 3000-4000
June 10, 1995 Sold for $3000

714. Rookwood vase, standard glaze, elk, E.T. Hurley, 1900, #392C, 9"h, mint 1500-2000
June 10, 1995 Sold for $1700

715. Rookwood vase, standard glaze, silver overlay, holly, K. Hickman, 1895, #504E, 8"h, mint 3000-4000
June 10, 1995 Sold for $2300

716. Rookwood ewer, standard glaze, holly, L. Lindeman, 1900, #462D, 6.5"h, mint 500-700
June 10, 1995 Sold for $400

717. Rookwood vase, standard glaze, berries, E.N. Lincoln, 1893, #312, 4.5"h, mint 350-550
June 10, 1995 Sold for $425

718. Rookwood vase, standard glaze, maple leaves, C. Steinle, 1904, #927E, 6.5"h, mint 550-750
June 10, 1995 Sold for $950

719. Rookwood vase, standard glaze, silver overlay, blossoms, K. Matchette, 1893, #536E, 3"h, mint 1500-2500
June 10, 1995 Sold for $850

720. Rookwood vase, standard glaze, palm, M. Daly, 1898, #S1411C, 14"h, mint 2000-2500
June 10, 1995 Sold for $2100

721. Rookwood potpourri, standard glaze, pansies, M. Nourse, 1894, #601C, 5.5"dia. x 1.5"h, mint 600-800
June 10, 1995 Sold for $650

722. Rookwood vase, standard glaze, leaves and berries, S. Toohey, 1893, #604D, 6.5"h, mint 450-550
June 10, 1995 Sold for $800

723. Rookwood vase, matt glaze, blossoms and buds, M.H. McDonald, 1937, #6629, 6"h, mint 700-900
June 10, 1995 Sold for $500

724. Rookwood vase, vellum, rose, K. Ley, 1945, 8"h, mint 700-900
June 10, 1995 Sold for $700

725. Rookwood vase, vellum, floral, birds, S. Sax, 1917, #814A, 14"h, mint 3000-4000
June 10, 1995 Sold for $4000

726. Rookwood vase, matt glaze, blossoms, M.H. McDonald, 1939, #6315, 6.5"h, mint 800-1100
June 10, 1995 Sold for $650

727. Rookwood vase, vellum, blossoms and buds, E. Diers, 1926, #1357D, 9"h, mint 1000-1500
June 10, 1995 Sold for $1600

728. Rookwood vase, vellum, blossoms, L. Asbury, 1925, #402, 6"h, mint 800-1100
June 10, 1995 Sold for $650

729. Rookwood ewer, standard glaze, blossoms, A.R. Valentien, 1888, #101A, 11.5"h, mint 1200-1700
June 10, 1995 Sold for $750

730. Rookwood plaque, standard glaze, cavalier, #X294, 9"w x 13"h, mint 5500-7500
June 10, 1995 Sold for $3750

731. Rookwood ewer, standard glaze, oak leaves, A.M. Valentien, 1896, #803B, 12.5"h, mint 1200-1700
June 10, 1995 Sold for $800

732. Rookwood vase, vellum, blossoms, F. Rothenbusch, 1925, #2720, 6.5"h, mint 800-1100
June 10, 1995 Sold for $900

733. Rookwood vase, vellum, stylized blossom, E. Diers, 1923, #913F, 5.5"h, mint 900-1200
June 10, 1995 Sold for $900

734. Rookwood vase, vellum, hanging blossoms, F. Rothenbusch, 1925, #2745, 9.5"h, mint 2000-3000
June 10, 1995 Sold for $2000

735. Rookwood vase, vellum, pansy blossoms, E. Diers, 1931, #3587D, 5.5"h, mint 900-1200
June 10, 1995 Sold for $900

736. Rookwood vase, vellum, wisteria blossoms, E. Diers, 1931, #1369F, 6"h, mint 1200-1700
June 10, 1995 Sold for $1200

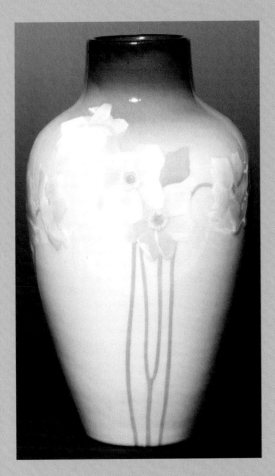

737. Rookwood vase, iris glaze, daffodils, S. Sax, 1908, #905C, 10"h, mint 6000-8000
June 10, 1995 Sold for $8000

738. Rookwood vase, iris glaze, frog, Shirayamadani, 1895, #S1464, 10.5"h, restoration 6500-8500
June 1, 1996 Sold for $4250

739. Rookwood vase, vellum, blossoms, E.T. Hurley, 1918, #932E, 8"h, mint 500-700
June 10, 1995 Sold for $425

740. Rookwood vase, vellum, blossoms, C.J. McLaughlin, 1916, #1918, 9"h, mint 1000-1500
June 10, 1995 Sold for $800

741. Rookwood vase, vellum, blossoms, E.T. Hurley, 1917, #2245, 8"h, minute flake 800-1100
June 10, 1995 Sold for $1000

742. Rookwood vase, vellum, blossoms, E.T. Hurley, 1910, #750C, 5.5"h, mint 500-700
June 10, 1995 Sold for $700

743. Rookwood vase, vellum, blossoms, E.T. Hurley, 1917, #922C, 9.5"h, mint 600-800
June 10, 1995 Sold for $1000

744. Rookwood vase, vellum, blossoms, C.J. McLaughlin, 1916, 9"dia. x 6"h, mint 900-1200
June 10, 1995 Sold for $750

745. Rookwood vase, vellum, stylized blossoms, L. Asbury, 1917, #2039D, 9.5"h, mint 700-900
June 10, 1995 Sold for $900

746. Rookwood vase, vellum, buckeye leaves, K. Van Horne, 1911, #1872, 8"h, mint 500-700
June 10, 1995 Sold for $375

747. Rookwood floor vase, carved hi-glaze, archer, W. Hentschel, #307GY, 26"h, chips 7500-10,000
June 10, 1995 Sold for $12,000

748. Rookwood vase, iris glaze, iris blossoms, Chas. Schmidt, 1910, #901C, 14"h, mint 20,000-25,000
June 10, 1995 Sold for $29,000

749. Rookwood vase, hi-glaze, berries, A. Conant, 1919, #233, 8"h, mint 1000-1500
June 10, 1995 Sold for $1000

750. Rookwood vase, hi-glaze, birds, S. Sax, 1917, #2065, 7.5"h, mint 1700-2200
June 10, 1995 Sold for $1700

751. Rookwood vase, hi-glaze, blossoms, M.H. McDonald, 1939, #902D, 7.5"h, mint 900-1200
June 10, 1995 Sold for $800

752. Rookwood vase, hi-glaze, magnolias, L. Holtkamp, 1949, #2984A, 16"h, mint 1200-1700
June 10, 1995 Sold for $900

753. Rookwood vase, hi-glaze, jonquils, Shirayamadani, 1926, #494B, 5"h, mint 1500-2000
June 10, 1995 Sold for $3250

754. Rookwood vase, hi-glaze, blossoms, L. Holtkamp, 1946, #2781, 7"h, mint 400-600
June 10, 1995 Sold for $450

755. Rookwood vase, hi-glaze, blossoms, W.E. Hentschel, 1920, #943E, 7"h, mint 900-1200
June 10, 1995 Sold for $1000

756. Rookwood vase, Black Opal, feathers, S. Sax, 1928, #2933, 12"h, mint 6000-8000
June 1, 1996 Sold for $8000

757. Rookwood vase, standard glaze, pinecones, Shirayamadani, 1898, #S1405C, 13"h, mint 7000-9000
June 1, 1996 Sold for $9000

758. Rookwood vase, sea green glaze, frog, O.G. Reed, 1898, #816E, 6"h, mint 1500-2000
June 1, 1996 Sold for $3,000

759. Rookwood mug, iris glaze, frog, J.D. Wareham, 1897, #S1337, 4.5"h, base chip 2000-2500
June 1, 1996 Sold for $1,500

760. Rookwood vase, sea green glaze, floral, E.N. Lincoln, 1905, #951E, 6.5"h, mint 1700-2200
June 1, 1996 Sold for $3,750

761. Rookwood vase, sea green glaze, floral, L.E. Lindeman, 1901, #536E, 3"h, mint 1000-1500
June 1, 1996 Sold for $950

762. Rookwood vase, iris glaze, floral design, C.A. Baker, 1896, #792E, 6"h, mint 1000-1500
June 1, 1996 Sold for $900

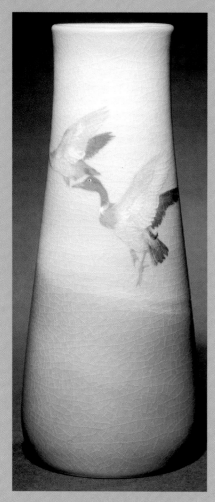

763. Rookwood vase, vellum, ducks, Shirayamadani, 1907, #950C, 10.5"h, mint 6000-8000
June 1, 1996 Sold for $4000

764. Rookwood vase, iris glaze, floral design, A.R. Valentien, 1903, #940B, 12.5"h, mint 7000-9000
June 1, 1996 Sold for $7500

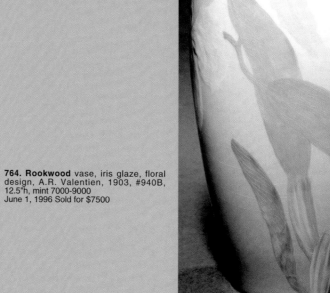

765. Rookwood vase, vellum, bamboo, L. Epply, 1908, #1124E, 7"h, mint 900-1200
June 1, 1996 Sold for $1500

766. Rookwood vase, vellum, blossoms, unknown artist, 1917, #943E, 7.5"h, mint 800-1100
June 1, 1996 Sold for $1200

767. Rookwood vase, vellum, blossoms and buds, E. Diers, 1913, #950D, 9.5"h, mint 900-1200
June 1, 1996 Sold for $850

768. Rookwood vase, vellum, blossoms, F. Rothenbusch, 1906, #900D, 7"h, mint 1000-1500
June 1, 1996 Sold for $1000

769. Rookwood vase, vellum, blossoms, E.N. Lincoln, 1908, #1278 E, 7.5"h, mint 800-1100
June 1, 1996 Sold for $700

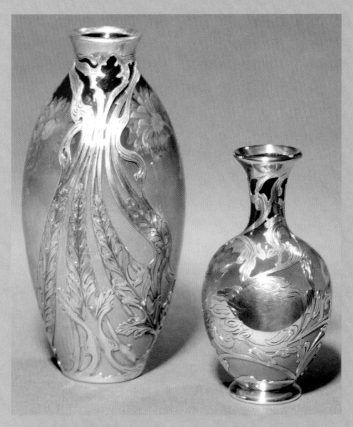

770. Rookwood vase, standard glaze, silver overlay, floral, E. Diers, 1901, #442, 7.5"h, mint 4000-6000
June 1, 1996 Sold for $3750

771. Rookwood vase, standard glaze, silver overlay, floral, M.A. Daly, 1898, #732B, 511.5"h, repaired 2500-3500
June 1, 1996 Sold for $2900

772. Rookwood vase, standard glaze, silver overlay, floral, M. Nourse, 1903, #926A, 13"h, mint 7500-9500
June 1, 1996 Sold for $5500

773. Rookwood vase, iris glaze, jonquils, I. Bishop, 1907, #952, 6"h, mint 800-1100
June 1, 1996 Sold for $950

774. Rookwood vase, iris glaze, roses, S. Sax, 1906, #913 C, 8"h, nicely restored 1000-1500
June 1, 1996 Sold for $1,300

775. Rookwood vase, iris glaze, blossoms, J.D. Wareham, 1898, #821 C, 10"h, tight line 1000-1500
June 1, 1996 Sold for $800

776. Rookwood vase, iris glaze, iris, L. Lindeman, 1903, #922D, 7"h, mint 900-1200
June 1, 1996 Sold for $900

777. Rookwood vase, iris glaze, apple blossoms, S.E. Coyne, 1905, #906E, 4.5"h, mint 700-900
June 1, 1996 Sold for $1,100

778. Rookwood vase, standard glaze, swallows, Shiraya-madani, 1899, #787C, 11"h, mint 8000-11,000
June 1, 1996 Sold for $7000

779. Rookwood vase, sea green glaze, seagulls, E.T. Hurley, 1901, #922C, 8"h, mint 4000-6000
June 1, 1996 Sold for $4750

780. Rookwood vase, sea green glaze, fish, E.T. Hurley, 1903, #982F, 6"h, mint 1500-2000
June 1, 1996 Sold for $4000

781. Rookwood vase, iris glaze, floral design, C.C. Lindeman, 1908, #941, 8"h, mint 1200-1700
June 1, 1996 Sold for $1200

782. Rookwood vase, iris glaze, floral design, I. Bishop, 1904, #926, 7"h, mint 1200-1500
June 1, 1996 Sold for $1000

783. Rookwood vase, iris glaze, roses, S.E. Coyne, 1907, #935C, 9"h, mint 2500-3500
June 1, 1996 Sold for $1500

784. Rookwood vase, iris glaze, berries, C.C. Lindeman, 1906, 9355, 6"h, mint 1000-1500
June 1, 1996 Sold for $800

785. Rookwood vase, iris glaze, daisies, initialed, 1905, #951D, 8.5"h, mint 1200-1700
June 1, 1996 Sold for $1200

786. Rookwood vase, vellum, landscape F. Rothenbusch, 1923, #356E, 6.5"h, mint .1700-2200
June 1, 1996 Sold for $1300

787. Rookwood plaque, vellum, landscape, S. Sax, 1916, 9"w x 7"h, mint 4000-5000
June 1, 1996 Sold for $4250

788. Rookwood vase, vellum, landscape, S.E. Coyne, 1912, #568C, 7.5"h, mint 2000-2500
June 1, 1996 Sold for $1100

789. Rookwood vase, matt glaze, floral design, C. Covalenco, 1924, #2724, 6"h, mint 400-600
June 1, 1996 Sold for $550

790. Rookwood vase, matt glaze, floral design, E.N. Lincoln, 1922, #2062, 6.5"h, mint 550-750
June 1, 1996 Sold for $550

791. Rookwood vase, matt glaze, floral design, L. Epply, 1933, S, 8"h, mint 500-700
June 1, 1996 Sold for $600

792. Rookwood vase, matt glaze, floral design, E. Barrett, 1925, #25445F, 7"h, chip to base 250-350
June 1, 1996 Sold for $200

793. Rookwood vase, matt glaze, orchids, Shiraya-madani, 1945, #6869, 9"h, mint 2000-3000
June 1, 1996 Sold for $2100

794. Rookwood vase, matt glaze, berries and leaves, S.E. Coyne, 1926, #30E, 9"h, mint 700-900
June 1, 1996 Sold for $750

795. Rookwood vase, matt glaze, floral design, E.N. Lincoln, 1918, #1679, 7"h, mint 500-700
June 1, 1996 Sold for $700

796. Rookwood vase, matt glaze, floral design, C.S. Todd, 1922, #1343, 5"h, mint 600-800
June 1, 1996 Sold for $750

797. Rookwood plaque, vellum, landscape, E.T. Hurley, 8"w x 6"h, mint 2000-3000
June 1, 1996 Sold for $2100

798. Rookwood vase, vellum, snow scene, S. Sax, 1910, #952E, 7.5"h, mint 2500-3500
June 1, 1996 Sold for $4000

799. Rookwood plaque, vellum, landscape, F. Rothenbusch, 7.5"w x 5.5"h, mint 2000-3000
June 1, 1996 Sold for $2000

800. Rookwood vase, matt glaze, berries, E. Lincoln, 1921, #912, 6"h, mint 700-900
June 1, 1996 Sold for $750

801. Rookwood vase, matt glaze, blossoms, V. Tischler, 1923, #2545C, 11"h, mint 1000-1500
June 1, 1996 Sold for $550

802. Rookwood potpourri jar, matt glaze, blossoms, E. Barrett, 1925, #1321E, 4"h, mint 500-700
June 1, 1996 Sold for $700

803. Rookwood vase, matt glaze, berries, E.N. Lincoln, 1928, #2996, 9"h, mint 800-1100
June 1, 1996 Sold for $850

804. Rookwood covered jar, matt glaze, blossoms, E.N. Lincoln, 1922, #478, 5"dia. x 5"h, mint 600-800
June 1, 1996 Sold for $400

805. Rookwood vase, matt glaze, blossoms, C. Todd, 1921, #949D, 9.5"h, mint 1000-1500
June 1, 1996 Sold for $1300

806. Rookwood vase, matt glaze, blossoms, D. Workum, 1927, #2831, 6"h, mint 700-900
June 1, 1996 Sold for $800

807. Rookwood ewer, standard glaze, maple leaves, C. Steinle, 1897, #754, 7"h, mint 500-700
June 1, 1996 Sold for $375

808. Rookwood vase, standard glaze, blossoms, S. Toohey, 1898, #611C, 9"h, line under rim 300-400
June 1, 1996 Sold for $325

809. Rookwood vase, standard glaze, daffodils, C. Lindeman, 1900, 5.5"h, mint 500-700
June 1, 1996 Sold for $850

810. Rookwood vase, standard glaze roses, A. Van Briggle, 1889, #490C, 8.5"dia. x 8"h, minor scratches 1200-1700
June 1, 1996 Sold for $650

811. Rookwood vase, standard glaze, pine branches, S. Toohey, 1892, #606B, 9"h, mint 600-800
June 1, 1996 Sold for $375

812. Rookwood ewer, standard glaze, trumpet blossoms, E.N. Lincoln, 1893, #495C, 5"h, mint 500-700
June 1, 1996 Sold for $425

813. Rookwood vase, standard glaze, floral design, initials I.C., # illegible, 6"h, mint 400-600
June 1, 1996 Sold for $250

814. Rookwood ewer, standard glaze, fruit, 1892, #537F, 6.5"h, repair to spout 300-400
June 1, 1996 Sold for $140

815. Rookwood plaque, standard glaze, monks, M. Daly, 1894, 12"w x 9.5"h, restored 4000-6000
June 1, 1996 Sold for $4250

816. Rookwood vase, standard glaze, lily of the valley, I. Bishop, 1905, #605 E, 5"h, mint 400-600
June 1, 1996 Sold for $750

817. Rookwood vase, standard glaze, leaves, initialed by artist, 1899, #614F, 6"h, mint 400-600
June 1, 1996 Sold for $425

818. Rookwood ewer, standard glaze, berries, J.E. Zettel, 1896, #657C, 8.5"h, hidden chip 500-700
June 1, 1996 Sold for $260

819. Rookwood vase, standard glaze, floral design, E.B.I. Cranch, 1895, #741C, 5.5"h, mint 500-600
June 1, 1996 Sold for $450

820. Rookwood vase, standard glaze, berries, F. Rothenbusch, 1900, #906, 4"h, mint 300-500
June 1, 1996 Sold for $375

821. Rookwood ewer, standard glaze, floral design, C.A. Baker, 1894, #740W, 8.5"h, mint 800-1000
June 1, 1996 Sold for $700

822. Rookwood vase, standard glaze, rushes, M. Daly, 1899, #792C, 11"h, repair 800-1100
June 1, 1996 Sold for $800

823. Rookwood sugar and creamer, standard glaze, leaves, A. Sprague, 1890, #330S, both 3"h, mint 400-600
June 1, 1996 Sold for $325

824. Rookwood vase, standard glaze, blossoms, M.A. Daly, 1886, #189Y, 8"dia. x 7.5"h, mint 1000-1500
June 1, 1996 Sold for $600

825. Rookwood vase, standard glaze, blossoms, W.P. McDonald, 1899, #553C, 12"h, mint 1000-1500
June 1, 1996 Sold for $650

826. Rookwood ewer, standard glaze, floral design, S. Toohey, 1888, #410W, 9.5"h, mint 700-900
June 1, 1996 Sold for $425

827. Rookwood vase, standard glaze, blossoms, E.N. Lincoln, 1903, 915 E, 5.5"h, mint 350-550
June 1, 1996 Sold for $350

828. Rookwood vase, standard glaze, leaves, I. Bishop, 1900, #568E, 4.5"h, mint 350-450
June 1, 1996 Sold for $450

829. Rookwood vase, standard glaze, dogwood, A.D. Sehon, #S1442, 9.5"h, mint 700-900
June 1, 1996 Sold for $850

830. Rookwood plaque, two tiles, standard glaze, goat, children, fawns and lamb, B. Horsfall, 20.5"w x 7.5"h, chips restored 9,000-12,000
June 1, 1996 Sold for $8500

831. Rookwood vase, standard glaze, berries, C. Steinle, 1894, #687, 5"dia. x 2"h, mint 400-600
June 1, 1996 Sold for $325

832. Rookwood dish, standard glaze, mice, A. Van Briggle, 1888, #59P, 7"dia. x 1"h, mint 500-700
June 1, 1996 Sold for $550

833. Rookwood vase, standard glaze, floral design, J. Zettel, 1898, #605, 5"h, hairline 250-350
June 1, 1996 Sold for $210

834. Rookwood vase, standard glaze, clover, A.M. Valentien, 1892, #533C, 9"h, mint 600-800
June 1, 1996 Sold for $400

835. Rookwood vase, standard glaze, blossoms, A. Sprague, 1889, #395 S, 4"h, mint 300-400
June 1, 1996 Sold for $375

836. Rookwood vase, vellum, landscape, E.F. McDermott, 1920, #808 V, 8"h, mint 2000-2500 June 1, 1996 Sold for $1400

837. Rookwood vase, vellum, landscape, F. Rothenbusch, 1923, #839B, 9.5"h, mint 2500-3500 June 1, 1996 Sold for $1500

838. Rookwood vase, vellum, landscape, F. Rothenbusch, 1923, #1358E, 7"h, mint 2500-3250 June 1, 1996 Sold for $2000

839. Rookwood vase, vellum, snow scene, L. Asbury, 1914, #925C, 11"h, mint 2500-3500 June 1, 1996 Sold for $3000

840. Rookwood plaque, vellum, harbor at dusk, S. Sax, 1912, 10.5"w x 8"h, mint 5000-6000 June 1, 1996 Sold for $3750

841. Rookwood vase, vellum, landscape, E. Diers, 1916, #1664D, 11"h, mint 2500-3500 June 1, 1996 Sold for $2400

842. Rookwood vase, green vellum, trees and boats S.E. Coyne, 1909, #1369E, 7.5"h, mint 2000-3000
June 1, 1996 Sold for $2000

843. Rookwood vase, vellum, landscape, S.E. Coyne, 1917, #892B, 11"h, mint 2500-3500
June 1, 1996 Sold for $2300

844. Rookwood vase, vellum, landscape, E. Diers, 1921, #907F, 8"h, hard to find, repair to rim 1000-1500
June 1, 1996 Sold for $750

845. Rookwood vase, vellum, flamingos, Shirayamadani, 1907, #1369D, 9"h, mint 4500-6500
June 1, 1996 Sold for $6500

846. Rookwood plaque, vellum, landscape, E.T. Hurley, 1914, 12"w x 9"h, mint 5000-7000
June 1, 1996 Sold for $6000

847. Rookwood vase, vellum, landscape, S. Sax, 1915, #988D, 7"h, mint 1200-1700
June 1, 1996 Sold for $1600

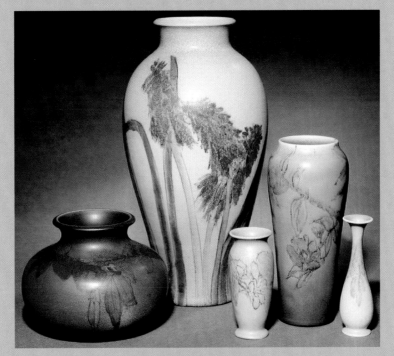

848. Rookwood vase, matt glaze, floral design, E.N. Lincoln, 1926, #2822, 7"h, mint 800-1100
June 1, 1996 Sold for $800

849. Rookwood vase, matt glaze, floral design, E.N. Lincoln, 1928, #6079, 18.5"h, mint 2500-3000
June 1, 1996 Sold for $2100

850. Rookwood vase, matt glaze, blossoms, S.E. Coyne, 1928, #2721, 6.5"h, small chip 400-600
June 1, 1996 Sold for $325

851. Rookwood vase, matt glaze, floral design, E. Barrett, 1924, #2039C, 11.5"h, mint 700-900
June 1, 1996 Sold for $650

852. Rookwood vase, matt glaze, floral design, S.E. Coyne, 1929, #2545F, 7"h, mint 450-650
June 1, 1996 Sold for $375

853. Rookwood vase, matt glaze, blossoms, C. Covalenco, 1925, #1045, 5.5"h, mint 600-800
June 1, 1996 Sold for $600

854. Rookwood vase, matt glaze, berries, C.S. Todd, 1914, #826D, 7"h, mint 500-700
June 1, 1996 Sold for $475

855. Rookwood vase, matt glaze, berries, S.E. Coyne, 1926, #926C, 9"h, mint 700-900
June 1, 1996 Sold for $900

856. Rookwood vase, matt glaze, floral design, M.H. McDonald, 1928, #2785, 12.5"h, mint 1500-2500
June 1, 1996 Sold for $1500

857. Rookwood vase, matt glaze, abstract design, C.S. Todd, 1919, #2082V, 4"h, hairline 300-400
June 1, 1996 Sold for $200

858. Rookwood vase, matt glaze, blossoms, M.H. McDonald, 1926, #926C, 9"h, mint 700-900
June 1, 1996 Sold for $600

859. Rookwood vase, matt glaze, blossoms, L. Abel, 1923, #363, 6.5"h, rim repaired 300-400
June 1, 1996 Sold for $250

860. Rookwood vase, vellum, harbor scene, C. Schmidt, 1922, #1930, 7"h, mint 3000-3500
June 1, 1996 Sold for $3750

861. Rookwood plaque, vellum, landscape, E.T. Hurley, 1945, 10"w x 12"h, mint 4000-5000
June 1, 1996 Sold for $5500

862. Rookwood vase, vellum, seascape, E.T. Hurley, 1943, #932E, 8"h, mint 3000-3500
June 1, 1996 Sold for $2000

863. Rookwood vase, hi-glaze, floral design, J. Jensen, 1948, #6920, 12"h, repaired 900-1200
June 1, 1996 Sold for $800

864. Rookwood vase, hi-glaze, berries, Shirayamadani, 1925, #2720, 6.5"h, mint 1500-2000
June 1, 1996 Sold for $2800

865. Rookwood vase, hi-glaze, magnolias, L. Holtkamp, 1950, #2964A, 16"h, repaired 900-1200
June 1, 1996 Sold for $600

866. Rookwood vase, hi-glaze, floral design, K. Ley, 1945, #6199F, 4277, 5"dia. x 4"h, mint 500-700
June 1, 1996 Sold for $375

867. Rookwood vase, hi-glaze, stylized landscape, A. Conant, 1919, #2040E, 7.5"h, mint 3000-4000
June 1, 1996 Sold for $2500

868. Rookwood vase, hi-glaze, wheat and leaves, M.H. McDonald, 1939, #9358, 11.5"h, mint 800-1100
June 1, 1996 Sold for $1000

869. Rookwood vase, iris glaze, pinecones, L. Asbury, 1906, #935C, W, 9"h, line at top 700-900
June 1, 1996 Sold for $425

870. Rookwood vase, iris glaze, violets, R. Fechheimer, 1901, #614F, 6.5"h, mint 900-1200
June 1, 1996 Sold for $400

871. Rookwood vase, iris glaze, orchid design, C. Schmidt, 1903, #907D, 10.5"h, hairlines 1500-2000
June 1, 1996 Sold for $1700

872. Rookwood vase, iris glaze, dogwood, C.A. Baker, 1901, #30E, 8"h, mint 900-1200
June 1, 1996 Sold for $2000

873. Rookwood vase, iris glaze, crows, K. Van Horne, 1907, #900DW, 6.5"h, hairlines 1000-1500
June 1, 1996 Sold for $1500

874. Rookwood vase, vellum, Queen Anne's lace, S. Sax, 1910, #1655E, 8"h, mint 1000-1500
June 1, 1996 Sold for $1900

875. Rookwood vase, vellum, blossoms, F. Rothenbusch, 1928, #356 D, 8.5"h, flake 500-700
June 1, 1996 Sold for $450

876. Rookwood plaque, vellum, landscape, E. Diers, 1915, 10.5"w x 8"h, mint 4000-5000
June 1, 1996 Sold for $5000

877. Rookwood vase, vellum, floral design, E.T. Hurley, 1911, #170V, 11.5"h, line to top 400-600
June 1, 1996 Sold for $475

878. Rookwood vase, vellum, jonquils, M.H. McDonald, 1920, #915E, 6"h, mint 800-1100
June 1, 1996 Sold for $950

879. Rookwood vase, iris glaze, blossoms, L. Lindeman, 1904, #939C, W, 8"h, bruise 600-800
June 1, 1996 Sold for $425

880. Rookwood vase, sea green glaze, blossoms, M. Mitchell, 1901, #921, 6"h, restored top 800-1100
June 1, 1996 Sold for $400

881. Rookwood vase, iris glaze, mushrooms, Chs. Schmidt, 1907, #925C, 9"h, hairlines 1500-2000
June 1, 1996 Sold for $1700

882. Rookwood vase, iris glaze, crocus, F. Rothenbusch, 1904, #935D, 7.5"h, mint 1500-2000
June 1, 1996 Sold for $2000

883. Rookwood vase, sea green glaze, carp, E.T. Hurley, 1898, #744C, 7.25"h, restored 1200-1700
June 1, 1996 Sold for $1500

884. Rookwood vase, matt glaze, blossoms and buds, K. Shirayamadani, 1936, 6"h, mint 800-1100
June 1, 1996 Sold for $800

885. Rookwood vase, matt glaze, blossoms and buds, K. Shirayamadani, 1933, 7.5"h, mint 900-1200
June 1, 1996 Sold for $1200

886. Rookwood plaque, vellum, landscape, S.E. Coyne, 8.5"w x 4.5"h, mint 3000-4000
June 1, 1996 Sold for $3000

887. Rookwood vase, matt glaze, irises, K. Shirayamadani, 1938, 7"h, mint 1500-2500
June 1, 1996 Sold for $2200

888. Rookwood vase, matt glaze, blossoms, W. Hentschel, 1921, #2191, 5.5"h, mint 500-700
June 1, 1996 Sold for $900

889. Rookwood vase, iris glaze, harbor scene, L. Asbury, 1911, #907E, 8.5"h, tight hairlines 1000-1500
June 1, 1996 Sold for $900

890. Rookwood vase, iris glaze, floral design, C. Steinle, 1906, #935, 6"h, mint 900-1200
June 1, 1996 Sold for $700

891. Rookwood vase, iris glaze, rose, A.R. Valentien, 1902, #904B, 14"h, line 1500-2000
June 1, 1996 Sold for $1200

892. Rookwood vase, iris glaze, clover, O. Reed, 1902, #919, 4"h, mint 600-800
June 1, 1996 Sold for $475

893. Rookwood vase, iris glaze, floral design, J.E. Zettel, 1902, #937, 9"h, mint 1000-1500
June 1, 1996 Sold for $800

894. Rookwood vase, vellum, mistletoe, H.M. Lyons, 1913, #913, 6"h, mint 700-900
June 1, 1996 Sold for $475

895. Rookwood vase, vellum, blossoms, M.H. McDonald, 1917, #1927, 4"h, mint 800-1100
June 1, 1996 Sold for $950

896. Rookwood vase, vellum, blossoms, L. Asbury, 1930, #80C, 7"h, mint 1200-1700
June 1, 1996 Sold for $850

897. Rookwood vase, vellum, floral design, E.T. Hurley, 1944, #6199F, 5"dia. x 4"h, mint 700-900
June 1, 1996 Sold for $800

898. Rookwood vase, vellum, blossoms and buds, E. Diers, 1925, #1356F, 6"h, mint 1000-1500
June 1, 1996 Sold for $1500

899. Rookwood vase, hi-glaze, blossoms, plumes and swirls, L. Epply, 1929, #914E, 5.5"h, mint 700-900
June 1, 1996 Sold for $750

900. Rookwood vase, hi-glaze, blossoms, Shiraya-madani, 1928, #2831, 5.5"h, mint 1500-2000
June 1, 1996 Sold for $1600

901. Rookwood vase, hi-glaze, landscape, M. H. McDonald, 1940, #614D, 10.5"h, hole filled 1200-1700
June 1, 1996 Sold for $1400

902. Rookwood vase, hi-glaze, geometric design, S. Sax, 1930, #6143, 4"h, mint 500-700
June 1, 1996 Sold for $900

903. Rookwood vase, hi-glaze, floral design, M. H. McDonald, 1940, #2918E, 6.5"h, mint 700-900
June 1, 1996 Sold for $600

904. Rookwood vase, hi-glaze, sailboats, birds and water, W. Rehm, 1943, #6194F, 5"h, mint 500-700
June 1, 1996 Sold for $300

905. Rookwood vase, hi-glaze, blossoms, W. E. Hentschel, 1922, #1348, 3.5"h, mint 700-900
June 1, 1996 Sold for $300

906. Rookwood vase, hi-glaze, iris blossoms, Shiraya-madani, 1946, #6314, 7.5"h, mint 900-1200
June 1, 1996 Sold for $900

907. Rookwood vase, hi-glaze, sailing ships, W. Rehm, 1954, #6869, 9"h, mint 1000-1500
June 1, 1996 Sold for $850

908. Rookwood vase, hi-glaze, lily blossoms and buds, L. Holtkamp, 1945, #6163E, 4.5"h, mint 400-600
June 1, 1996 Sold for $260

909. Rookwood jug, hi-glaze, blossoms, L. Epply, 1926, #2974, 8.5"h, mint 1000-1500
June 1, 1996 Sold for $750

910. Rookwood vase, hi-glaze, stylized design, W.E. Hentschel, 1921, #214 C, 3"h, mint 300-400
June 1, 1996 Sold for $290

911. Rookwood vase, iris glaze, poppies, C. Steinle, 1911, #943E, 7"h, mint 900-1200
June 7, 1997 Sold for $1200

912. Rookwood vase, iris glaze, jonquil, S.E. Coyne, 1901, #562, 10"h, mint 2750-3250
June 7, 1997 Sold for $2900

913. Rookwood vase, iris glaze, underwater scene, E.T. Hurley, 1903, #745C, 5.5"h,
mint 1000-1500
June 7, 1997 Sold for $850

914. Rookwood vase, iris glaze, blossoms, I. Bishop, 1906, #951E, 7"h, mint 800-1100
June 7, 1997 Sold for $650

915. Rookwood vase, hi-glaze, bird and floral design, J. Jensen, 1945, #6640, 6.5"h, mint 1200-1700
June 1, 1996 Sold for $1300

916. Rookwood vase, iris glaze, roses, Jensen, 1946, #6359, 7.5"h, mint 500-700
June 1, 1996 Sold for $600

917. Rookwood vase, hi-glaze, stylized blossoms, S. Sax, 1922, #2634, 10"h, grinding chip 800-1100
June 1, 1996 Sold for $1100

918. Rookwood vase, hi-glaze, swans and blossoms, J. Jensen, 1934, #2783, 9.5"h, mint 1200-1700
June 1, 1996 Sold for $1800

919. Rookwood vase, hi-glaze, grape design, L. Epply, 1931, #6184E, 7"h, mint 600-800
June 1, 1996 Sold for $850

920. Rookwood vase, hi-glaze, blossoms, W.E. Hentschel, 1931, #2032D, 9.5"h, mint 1200-1700
June 1, 1996 Sold for $1100

921. Rookwood vase, hi-glaze, blossoms, aventurine glaze, S. Sax, 1922, #1873, 5.5"h, restored 700-900
June 1, 1996 Sold for $300

922. Rookwood vase, hi-glaze, chrysanthemum, H. Wilcox, 1929, #2984, 16"h, line to body 1500-2500
June 1, 1996 Sold for $2700

923. Rookwood vase, Chinese Plum, blossoms, H. Wilcox, 1927, #2308, 7"h, mint 1000-1500
June 1, 1996 Sold for $1600

924. Rookwood vase, hi-glaze, blossoms, C. Stegner, 1946, #775, 10"h, mint 900-1200
June 1, 1996 Sold for $850

925. Rookwood vase, matt glaze, stylized floral design, C.S. Todd, 1920, #654C, 5.5"h, mint 400-500
June 1, 1996 Sold for $475

926. Rookwood vase, matt glaze, blossoms, M.H. McDonald, 1928, #1357E, 7.5"h, mint 500-700
June 1, 1996 Sold for $550

927. Rookwood bowl, matt glaze, hibiscus, S.E. Coyne, 1925, #1929, 6.5"dia. x 4.5"h, mint 500-700
June 1, 1996 Sold for $550

928. Rookwood vase, inlaid matt glaze, berries and leaves, C.S. Todd, 1920, #942C, 7.5", mint 700-900
June 1, 1996 Sold for $550

929. Rookwood bowl, matt glaze, blossoms, W.E. Hentschel, 1910, #1348, 6"dia. x 3.5"h, mint 400-600
June 1, 1996 Sold for $425

930. Rookwood vase, matt glaze, blossoms, K. Jones, 1925, #402, 6"h, mint 500-700
June 1, 1996 Sold for $800

931. Rookwood vase, matt glaze, zigzag design, E. Barrett, 1931, #6148, 5.5"h, mint 400-600
June 1, 1996 Sold for $700

932. Rookwood vase, matt glaze, flowers, S.E. Coyne, 1931, #914E, 5"h, mint 500-600
June 1, 1996 Sold for $500

933. Rookwood vase, standard glaze, clover, C. Steinle, 1905, #935E, 6.5"h, mint 450-650
June 1, 1996 Sold for $375

934. Rookwood vase, standard glaze, tulips, G. Hall, 1904, #932E, 7.5"h, mint 500-700
June 1, 1996 Sold for $850

935. Rookwood vase, standard glaze, clover, C.C. Lindeman, 1904, #917E, 5.5"h, mint 350-550
June 1, 1996 Sold for $325

936. Rookwood vase, standard glaze, lily blossoms, O. Reed, 1900, #803A, 15"h, mint 1200-1700
June 1, 1996 Sold for $1000

937. Rookwood basket, standard glaze, blossoms, signed illegibly, 1891, #406W, 6.5"l x 4.5"h, mint 300-500
June 1, 1996 Sold for $260

938. Rookwood vase, standard glaze, blossoms, A.B. Sprague, 1892, #S993W, 9"h, mint 500-700
June 1, 1996 Sold for $350

939. Rookwood vase, standard glaze, tulips, E. Diers, 1898, #337, 6.5"h, mint 500-700
June 1, 1996 Sold for $475

940. Rookwood vase, vellum, stylized blossoms, K. Van Horne, 1914, #1663, V, 9"h, mint 500-700
June 1, 1996 Sold for $650

941. Rookwood vase, vellum, floral design, E. Diers, 1912, #1843, 5"h, mint 400-600
June 1, 1996 Sold for $450

942. Rookwood vase, vellum, blue jays and flowers, L. Epply, 1917, #703, 5.5"h, mint 900-1200
June 1, 1996 Sold for $850

943. Rookwood plaque, vellum, trees, Hurley, 1945, 10"w x 12"h, mint 4000-5000
June 1, 1996 Sold for $4000

944. Rookwood vase, vellum, blossoms, Hurley, 1927, #494B, 5"h, mint 600-800
June 1, 1996 Sold for $550

945. Rookwood vase, vellum, floral design, S. Sax, 1905, 6"h, tight line 250-350
June 1, 1996 Sold for $250

946. Rookwood vase, vellum, floral design, E. Diers, 1914, #295D, 9"h, mint 900-1200
June 1, 1996 Sold for $800

947. Rookwood set, standard glaze, silver overlay, portraits, B. Horsfall, 1894, #259B on pitcher, #259E on mugs, pitcher 8"h, mugs 4.5"h, hairlines to one mug 22,000-27,000
June 1, 1996 Sold for $29,000

948. Rookwood plaque, matt glaze, landscape, 1904, 12"sq., mint 2700-3700
June 1, 1996 Sold for $3750

949. Rookwood vase, matt glaze, floral design, C.S. Todd, 1912, #1816, 8"h, mint 600-800
June 1, 1996 Sold for $850

950. Rookwood vase, matt glaze, stylized waves, O.G. Reed, 1903, #40DZ, 6.5"h, mint 1200-1700
June 1, 1996 Sold for $1400

951. Rookwood vase, matt glaze, acorns and leaves, S.E. Coyne, 1904, #922, 5.5"h, mint 600-800
June 1, 1996 Sold for $600

952. Rookwood plaque, matt glaze, seascape, 1904, 8"w x 12"h, mint 2200-3200
June 1, 1996 Sold for $3500

953. Rookwood vase, matt glaze, geometric design, A.M. Valentien, markings obscured, 7"w, mint 600-800
June 1, 1996 Sold for $600

954. Rookwood covered jar, hi-glaze, tropical birds, E.T. Hurley, 1924, #2301E, 9.5"h, mint 2000-3000
June 1, 1996 Sold for $1800

955. Rookwood vase, hi-glaze, tropical birds, E.T. Hurley, 1924, #2785, 13"h, mint 2500-3500
June 1, 1996 Sold for $2200

956. Rookwood covered jar, hi-glaze, tropical birds, E.T. Hurley, 1924, #2301E, 9.5"h, mint 2000-3000
June 1, 1996 Sold for $1900

957. Rookwood vase, standard and Tiger Eye, plums, A.R. Valentien, 1891, #589C, 12.5"h, mint 1000-1500
June 1, 1996 Sold for $750

958. Rookwood pitcher, standard glaze, floral, 1886, #259, 8.5"h, mint 500-700
June 1, 1996 Sold for $350

959. Rookwood vase, standard glaze, pinecones, M. Daly, 1902, #907B, 17"h, scratch, line 1500-2000
June 1, 1996 Sold for $1400

960. Rookwood vase, standard glaze, floral design, A.R. Valentien, 1886, #162A, 12"h, hairline 900-1200
June 1, 1996 Sold for $400

961. Rookwood vase, standard glaze, floral design, S. Sax, 1899, #611, 8"h, mint 600-800
June 1, 1996 Sold for $500

962. Rookwood vase, Tiger Eye, blossoms, A.R. Valentien, 1889, #216R, 13.5"h, mint 1500-2500
June 1, 1996 Sold for $950

963. Rookwood vase, Tiger Eye, floral design, M. Daly, 1886, #39B, 13.5"h, mint 1500-2500
June 1, 1996 Sold for $950

964. Rookwood vase, Tiger Eye, S. Toohey, 1899, #792C, 11.5"h, chip 1000-1500
June 1, 1996 Sold for $900

965. Rookwood vase, hi-glaze, orchids, Shirayamadani, 1930, #1065B, 10.5"h, filled drill hole in base 2500-3500
June 1, 1996 Sold for $1200

966. Rookwood vase, hi-glaze, flowers, Shirayamadani, 1939, #6735, 7"h, mint 2000-3000
June 1, 1996 Sold for $1400

967. Rookwood vase, hi-glaze, floral design, C.S. Todd, 1920, #2368, 16.5"h, restored 1500-2000
June 1, 1996 Sold for $2400

968. Rookwood vase, hi-glaze, fish, J. Jensen, 1934, S, 5"h, mint 1000-1500
June 1, 1996 Sold for $1900

969. Rookwood vase, hi-glaze, floral design, Shirayamadani, 1922, #295C, 11"h, mint 4000-5000
June 1, 1996 Sold for $550

970. **Rookwood** vase, sea green glaze, floral design, S. Toohey, 1902, #932D, 8.5"h, mint 3000-4000
June 1, 1996 Sold for $2500

971. **Rookwood** vase, sea green, roses, C.A. Baker, 1903, #926 C, 8.5"h, repair 1500-2000
June 1, 1996 Sold for $1600

972. **Rookwood** vase, iris glaze, leaves, S.E. Coyne, 1908, #905D, 8"h, mint 2000-2500
June 1, 1996 Sold for $2500

973. **Rookwood** vase, vellum, fish, E.T. Hurley, 1904, 8"h, hairline 800-1100
June 1, 1996 Sold for $600

974. **Rookwood** vase, vellum, floral design, E.T. Hurley, 1927, 419, 8.5"h, mint 800-1100
June 1, 1996 Sold for $900

975. **Rookwood** plaque, vellum, landscape, L. Epply, 1914, 5"w x 9"h, mint 2200-2700
June 1, 1996 Sold for $1500

976. **Rookwood** vase, vellum, floral design, E. Noonan, 1907, #932F, 6.5"h, mint 500-700
June 1, 1996 Sold for $375

977. **Rookwood** vase, vellum, grapes, S.E. Coyne, 1915, #614D, 11"h, mint 1500-2000
June 1, 1996 Sold for $1500

978. **Rookwood** vase, vellum, tropical birds, E.T. Hurley, 1907, #905D, 8.5"h, repair 2000-2500
June 1, 1996 Sold for $1500

979. Rookwood vase, matt glaze, floral design, Shiraya-madani, 1935, #892C, 9"h, mint 2500-3500
June 1, 1996 Sold for $2000

980. Rookwood vase, matt glaze, fruit, M.H. McDonald, 1929, #2933, 12"h, mint 3500-4500
June 1, 1996 Sold for $2000

981. Rookwood vase, matt glaze, figures, flowers and birds, E. Barrett, 1934, 5"h, mint 1000-1500
June 1, 1996 Sold for $2100

982. Rookwood pitcher, standard glaze, holly, E.R. Felten, 1890, #88, 5"h, hairlines 200-300
June 1, 1996 Sold for $350

983. Rookwood vase, standard glaze, floral design, E.R. Felten, 1898, #743C, 7"h, mint 500-700
June 1, 1996 Sold for $650

984. Rookwood ewer, standard glaze, fruit and leaves, C.A. Baker, 1892, #657C, 9"h, mint 600-800
June 1, 1996 Sold for $400

985. Rookwood vase, standard glaze, leaves, L. Van Briggle, 1904, #459E, 4"h, mint 350-450
June 1, 1996 Sold for $325

986. Rookwood ewer, standard glaze, floral, A.M. Bookprinter, 1891, #387B, 12"h, mint 1000-1500
June 1, 1996 Sold for $1200

987. Rookwood ewer, standard glaze, fruit, C. Schmidt, 1899, #725, 5"h, mint 550-750
June 1, 1996 Sold for $325

988. Rookwood vase, standard glaze, floral design, S.E. Coyne, 1899, #433C, 7.5"h, mint 500-700
June 1, 1996 Sold for $350

989. Rookwood vase, standard glaze, leaf design, K.C. Matchette, 1893, #607, 5"h, mint 500-700
June 1, 1996 Sold for $600

990. Rookwood vase, vellum, snow scene, F. Rothenbusch, 1909, #1121G, 10"h, repaired 800-1100
June 1, 1996 Sold for $600

991. Rookwood plaque, vellum, trees, E. Diers, 1912, 9"w x 14"h, mint 5500-7500
June 1, 1996 Sold for $4250

992. Rookwood vase, vellum, landscape, L. Asbury, 1917, #952D, 10"h, mint 1500-2000
June 1, 1996 Sold for $1500

993. Rookwood vase, standard glaze, bleeding hearts, F. Vreeland, 1901, #913, 5.5"h, mint 450-550
June 7, 1997 Sold for $425

994. Rookwood vase, standard glaze, blossoms, E.N. Lincoln, 1904, #735DD, 7.5"h, mint 450-650
June 7, 1997 Sold for $600

995. Rookwood vase, standard glaze, flowers, handles, C. Steinle, 1901, #911, 5"w x 4"h, mint 350-450
June 7, 1997 Sold for $250

996. Rookwood vase, standard glaze, rose, W. Klemm, 1901, #901C, 9"h, scratches, mint 450-650
June 7, 1997 Sold for $260

997. Rookwood vase, standard glaze, lily of valley, I. Bishop, 1901, #534D, 6"h, mint 450-650
June 7, 1997 Sold for $700

998. Rookwood creamer and sugar, standard glaze, crocus, E. Diers, #330, 4"w x 2.5"h, mint 400-500
June 7, 1997 Sold for $500

999. Rookwood vase, standard glaze, violets, K. Hickman, 1897, #765, 5.75"h, mint 350-550
June 7, 1997 Sold for $225

1000. Rookwood vase, hi-glaze, abstract design, J. Jensen, 1931, #6199D, 5"h, mint 1200-1700
June 1, 1996 Sold for $1100

1001. Rookwood vase, hi-glaze, nudes and a snake, J. Jensen, 1944, #6875, 6.5"h, mint 3500-4500
June 1, 1996 Sold for $5500

1002. Rookwood vase, matt glaze, horse, J. Jensen, 1935, 5"h, mint 1500-2500
June 1, 1996 Sold for $3250

1003. Rookwood ewer, standard glaze, floral design, J.D. Wareham, 1893, #657D, 6.5"h, line and flake 300-500
June 1, 1996 Sold for $160

1004. Rookwood vase, standard glaze, floral design, J.E. Zettel, 1900, #906C, 5.5"h, mint 400-600
June 1, 1996 Sold for $300

1005. Rookwood vase, standard glaze, tulips, L.E. Lindeman, 1905, #940D, 9"h, mint 600-800
June 1, 1996 Sold for $700

1006. Rookwood bowl, standard glaze, floral, A.M. Valentien, 1890, #228B, 10.5"w, mint 400-600
June 1, 1996 Sold for $280

1007. Rookwood vase, standard glaze, irises, S.E. Coyne, #581E, 9"h, hairlines 600-800
June 1, 1996 Sold for $475

1008. Rookwood vase, standard glaze, floral design, M. Mitchell, 1903, #901BB, 10"h, mint 700-900
June 1, 1996 Sold for $950

1009. Rookwood vase, standard glaze, tree, S.E. Coyne, 1894, #733C, 7"h, tight lines 350-450
June 1, 1996 Sold for $250

1010. Rookwood ewer, standard glaze, floral design, S. Markland, 1892, #657D, 6.5"h, mint 450-650
June 1, 1996 Sold for $350

1011. Rookwood vase, standard glaze, dandelions, J. Swing, 1903, #906E, 4"h, mint 350-550
June 7, 1997 Sold for $450

1012. Rookwood ewer, standard glaze, roses, A.M. Valentien, 1891, #387C, 11"h, crazing 500-700
June 7, 1997 Sold for $850

1013. Rookwood bowl, standard glaze, floral design, A. Pons, 1906, #1142, 3.5"w x 1.5"h, mint 250-350
June 7, 1997 Sold for $225

1014. Rookwood vase, standard glaze, roses, L.A. Fry, 1886, #269A, 15"h, mint 1500-2000
June 7, 1997 Sold for $2400

1015. Rookwood bowl, standard glaze, floral and line designs, M.L. Perkins, 8"dia. x 2.5"h, mint 600-800
June 7, 1997 Sold for $400

1016. Rookwood mug, standard glaze, mail bag and laurel, E. Noonan, 1905, 4.75"h, mint 400-600
June 7, 1997 Sold for $300

1017. Rookwood vase, standard glaze, floral design, M. Daly, 1888, #376L, 16"w, mint 1500-2000
June 1, 1996 Sold for $1000

1018. Rookwood jug, standard glaze, dogs, Cranch, not signed, 1891, #85, 6"h, mint 600-800
June 1, 1996 Sold for $400

1019. Rookwood vase, standard glaze, berries, M.A. Daly, 1889, #380A, 14.5"h, repair 900-1200
June 1, 1996 Sold for $800

1020. Rookwood vase, standard glaze, floral design, M. Nourse, 1903, #904B, 14"h, mint 3500-4500
June 1, 1996 Sold for $3250

1021. Rookwood vase, standard glaze, portrait, S. Laurence, 1896, #797, 6.5"h, mint 900-1200
June 1, 1996 Sold for $750

1022. Rookwood ewer, standard glaze, flowers, M. Daly, 1886, #101C, 8"h, mint 650-850
June 7, 1997 Sold for $400

1023. Rookwood vase, standard glaze, leaves, L. Van Briggle, #866, 1900, 6.5"h, mint 450-650
June 7, 1997 Sold for $425

1024. Rookwood chocolate pot, standard glaze, roses, L. Asbury, 1900, #772, 10"h, line to rim 350-550
June 7, 1997 Sold for $425

1025. Rookwood vase, standard glaze, blossoms, Shirayamadani, 1887, #344B, 12"w, mint 1200-1700
June 7, 1997 Sold for $900

1026. Rookwood covered jar, standard glaze, blossoms, O. Reed, 1894, #692W, 3.5"h, hairline 200-300
June 7, 1997 Sold for $150

1027. Rookwood cup, standard glaze, blossoms, S. Toohey, 1889, 4.5"w x 2"h, mint 250-350
June 7, 1997 Sold for $400

1028. Rookwood vase, standard glaze, black-eyed susan, L. Van Briggle, 1903, #735DD, 7.5"h, minor scratches 450-650
June 7, 1997 Sold for $260

1029. Rookwood basket, standard glaze, blossoms, G. Young, 1887, #45D, 7"w, mint 450-650
June 7, 1997 Sold for $325

1030. Rookwood vase, standard glaze, clover, C.A. Baker, 1894, #566DW, 7"h, mint 750-950
June 7, 1997 Sold for $425

1031. Rookwood creamer, standard glaze, blossoms, C. Steinle, 1894, #43W, 2"h, mint 150-250
June 7, 1997 Sold for $150

1032. Rookwood ewer, standard glaze, floral design, A. Valentien, 1888, #101A, 11.5"h, mint 1000-1500
June 7, 1997 Sold for $750

1033. Rookwood vase, standard glaze, floral, S.E. Coyne, 1903, #901D, 7.5"h, scratches, chip 350-450
June 7, 1997 Sold for $375

1034. Rookwood vase, standard glaze, holly, C.C. Lindeman, 1902, #584C, 5.5"h, mint 350-450
June 7, 1997 Sold for $275

1035. Rookwood vase, standard glaze, blossoms, C. Steinle, 1900, #744C, 7.5"h, mint 400-600
June 7, 1997 Sold for $250

1036. Rookwood vase, vellum, mountain scene, E. Diers, 1908, #1369D, 9"h, mint 1500-2000
June 7, 1997 Sold for $1400

1037. Rookwood vase, vellum, jonquils, I. Bishop, 1905, #30E, 8"h, mint 1000-1500
June 7, 1997 Sold for $1500

1038. Rookwood plaque, vellum, landscape, E.T. Hurley, 8.5"w x 10.5"h, mint 4000-5000
June 7, 1997 Sold for $4750

1039. Rookwood vase, vellum, grapes, S.E. Coyne, 1904, #915D, 7.5"h, mint 900-1200
June 7, 1997 Sold for $1100

1040. Rookwood vase, vellum, landscape, S.E. Coyne, 1921, #1660, 9.5"h, mint 2000-2500
June 7, 1997 Sold for $2100

1041. Rookwood vase, matt glaze, berries, K. Jones 1930, 6.5"h, mint 450-650
June 7, 1997 Sold for $425

1042. Rookwood console bowl, hi-glaze, 1922, #2573E, 8"dia., mint 300-500
June 7, 1997 Sold for $270

1043. Rookwood vase, matt glaze, blossoms, E.N. Lincoln, 1924, #1357, 9"h, mint 650-850
June 7, 1997 Sold for $750

1044. Rookwood vase, matt glaze, floral design, M.H. McDonald, 1924, #2789, 11"h, mint 800-1100
June 7, 1997 Sold for $700

1045. Rookwood vase, matt glaze, blossoms, M.H. McDonald, 1922, #955, 4.5"dia., mint 350-450
June 7, 1997 Sold for $325

1046. Rookwood vase, matt glaze, floral design, K. Jones, 1927, #551, 7"h, mint 400-600
June 7, 1997 Sold for $800

1047. Rookwood bookends, pair, matt glaze, figure of a woman, L. Abel, 7"h, mint 600-800
June 7, 1997 Sold for $2000

1048. Rookwood vase, matt glaze, butterflies, S.E. Coyne, 1925, #1369F, 6"h, mint 750-1000
June 7, 1997 Sold for $900

1049. Rookwood vase, matt glaze, floral design, S.E. Coyne, 1925, #1358F, 6"h, mint 350-550 June 7, 1997 Sold for $400

1050. Rookwood vase, matt glaze, flowers, S.E. Coyne, 1927, #951E, 7.5"h, mint 500-700 June 7, 1997 Sold for $850

1051. Sallie E. Coyne watercolor, landscape, 10"w x 15"h, in period oak frame, excellent condition 600-800 June 7, 1997 Sold for $475

1052. Rookwood vase, vellum, flowers, E.T. Hurley, 1917, #937, 10"h, mint 800-1100 June 7, 1997 Sold for $800

1053. Rookwood vase, matt glaze, flowers, Shirayamadani, 1936, #6600, 7"h, mint 1200-1500 June 7, 1997 Sold for $2200

1054. Rookwood vase, matt glaze, flowers, M.H. McDonald, 1928, #2724, 6"h, mint 500-700 June 7, 1997 Sold for $350

1055. Rookwood vase, matt glaze, berries, C. Covalenco, 1925, #2719, 6.5"h, mint 600-800 June 7, 1997 Sold for $700

1056. Rookwood vase, matt glaze, roses, M.H. McDonald, 1928, #2721, 6.5"h, mint 450-650 June 7, 1997 Sold for $700

1057. Rookwood vase, matt glaze, blossoms, E.N. Lincoln, 1927, #1918, 9"h, mint 1000-1500 June 7, 1997 Sold for $800

1058. Rookwood vase, matt glaze, stylized floral, L. Abel, 1922, #2305, 7"h, mint 550-750 June 7, 1997 Sold for $850

1059. Rookwood vase, matt glaze, blossoms, E. Barrett, 1924, #1781, 6.5"h, mint 550-750 June 7, 1997 Sold for $425

1060. Rookwood vase, matt glaze, floral design, Shirayamadani, 1935, no #, 5"h, mint 800-1100 June 7, 1997 Sold for $700

1061. Rookwood vase, iris glaze, tulips, O.G. Reed, 1910, #30E, 8"h, mint 1700-2700
June 7, 1997 Sold for $2400

1062. Rookwood vase, iris glaze, floral design, E. Diers, 1911, #1654D, 9.5"h, mint 3000-4000
June 7, 1997 Sold for $3250

1063. Rookwood vase, iris glaze, poppy, J.D. Wareham, 1897, #614E, 8"h, mint 1700-2700
June 7, 1997 Sold for $2500

1064. Rookwood vase, iris glaze, hydrangeas, H.E. Wilcox, 1895, #578, 10"h, lines 1000-1500
June 7, 1997 Sold for $1200

1065. Rookwood ewer, sea green, fish, A.R. Valentien, #T976, 13"h, repaired 1500-2500
June 7, 1997 Sold for $2900

1066. Rookwood vase, iris glaze, floral design, R. Fechheimer, 1901, #925C, 9.5"h, mint 2000-3000
June 7, 1997 Sold for $2000

1067. Rookwood vase, vellum, blossoms, M.H. McDonald, 1916, #1358F, 6"h, mint 450-650
June 7, 1997 Sold for $325

1068. Rookwood vase, vellum, butterflies, L. Epply, 1911, #1369E, 7"h, mint 1200-1700
June 7, 1997 Sold for $750

1069. Rookwood vase, vellum, blossoms, S.E. Coyne, 1905, #977, 10.5"h, mint 2000-3000
June 7, 1997 Sold for $2100

1070. Rookwood vase, vellum, blossoms, L. Epply, 1909, #1369E, 7.5"h, flakes and hairlines 500-700
June 7, 1997 Sold for $425

1071. Rookwood vase, vellum, poppies, E.F. McDermott, 1915, #943E, 7"h, mint 800-1100
June 7, 1997 Sold for $650

1072. Rookwood vase, vellum, fish, E.T. Hurley, 1910, #679, 7.5"h, mint 2500-3500
June 7, 1997 Sold for $2500

1073. Rookwood vase, vellum, geese in flight, E.T. Hurley, 1907, #943G, 10.5"h, mint 2500-3500
June 7, 1997 Sold for $2600

1074. Rookwood vase, vellum, sea horses, E.T. Hurley, 1904, #166Z, 5"h, mint 1500-2500
June 7, 1997 Sold for $2500

1075. Rookwood vase, iris glaze, floral design, L.E. Lindeman, 1906, #30F, 6.5"h, mint 800-1100
June 7, 1997 Sold for $700

1076. Rookwood vase, iris glaze, hyacinths, S. Sax, 1904, #935C, 9"h, mint 2500-3500
June 7, 1997 Sold for $4000

1077. Rookwood vase, iris glaze, lily of the valley, L. Lindeman, 1906, #952F, 5.5"h, mint 900-1200
June 7, 1997 Sold for $700

1078. Rookwood vase, vellum, carnations, F. Rothenbusch, 1905, #943D, 8"h, mint 900-1200
June 7, 1997 Sold for $900

1079. Rookwood vase, vellum, blossoms, S. Sax, 1913, #392C, 9.5"h, mint 1200-1700
June 7, 1997 Sold for $1300

1080. Rookwood vase, vellum, Queen Anne's lace, L. Asbury, 1914, #904, 11"h, mint 1500-2000
June 7, 1997 Sold for $1500

1081. Rookwood vase, vellum, blossoms, K. Jones, 1922, #955, 5"dia. x 2.5"h, line to rim 250-350
June 7, 1997 Sold for $275

1082. Rookwood vase, vellum, blossoms, E.T. Hurley, 1919, #2305, 9.5"h, repair, lines 300-400
June 7, 1997 Sold for $300

1083. Rookwood vase, vellum, lily of the valley, E.N. Lincoln, 1911, #233, 8"h, mint 600-800
June 7, 1997 Sold for $550

1084. Rookwood mug, standard glaze, Native American, S. Markland, 1897, #837, 5"h, mint 1200-1700
June 7, 1997 Sold for $2000

1085. Rookwood vase, standard glaze, "Joe Jefferson," E.R. Felten, 1902, #659C, 6"h, bruise 700-900
June 7, 1997 Sold for $1000

1086. Rookwood mug, standard glaze, Native American, S. Laurence, 1900, #837, 5.5"h, cracked 500-1000
June 7, 1997 Sold for $425

1087. Rookwood vase, vellum, flowers, M.H. McDonald, 1938, marked "S," 6"h, mint 800-1100
June 7, 1997 Sold for $1100

1088. Rookwood vase, vellum, crocus, E. Diers, 1930, #913F, 5.5"h, mint 1200-1700
June 7, 1997 Sold for $2200

1089. Rookwood vase, vellum, roses, E. Diers, 1926, #907D, 12"h, mint 3500-4500
June 7, 1997 Sold for $3250

1090. Rookwood vase, vellum, daisies, E. Diers, 1925, #356F, 5.5"h, mint 700-900
June 7, 1997 Sold for $800

1091. Rookwood vase, vellum, blossoms, E.T. Hurley, 1930, #914E, 5.5"h, mint 800-1100
June 7, 1997 Sold for $1000

1092. Rookwood vase, standard glaze, monkey, S. Laurence, 1897, #707B, 5.5"h, mint 2000-2500
June 7, 1997 Sold for $1500

1093. Rookwood vase, standard glaze, elk, R.B. Horsfall, 1895, #707A, 7.5"w x 8"h, line 1500-2500
June 7, 1997 Sold for $1900

1094. Rookwood mug, standard glaze, portrait, unsigned, G. Young, 1891, #587W, 4.5"h, mint 1000-1500
June 7, 1997 Sold for $600

1095. Rookwood vase, vellum, blossoms, E.T. Hurley, 1928, #764C, 5.5"h, mint 800-1100
June 7, 1997 Sold for $700

1096. Rookwood vase, vellum, floral design, E.F. McDermott, 1918, #295E, 7.5"h, mint 1200-1700
June 7, 1997 Sold for $1900

1097. Rookwood vase, vellum, lilies, S. Sax, 1914, #1661, 8.5"h, mint 1000-1500
June 7, 1997 Sold for $750

1098. Rookwood vase, vellum, flowers, F. Rothenbusch, 1919, #1278F, 7.5"h, mint 500-700
June 7, 1997 Sold for $400

1099. Rookwood vase, vellum, cherry blossoms, E.T. Hurley, 1910, #942D, 6"h, mint 550-750
June 7, 1997 Sold for $650

1100. Rookwood vase, vellum, landscape, E. Diers, 1919. #295E, 7.5"h, repair to base 800-1100
June 7, 1997 Sold for $550

1101. Rookwood plaque, vellum, landscape, F. Rothenbusch, 7"w x 9"h, mint 2750-3750
June 7, 1997 Sold for $2300

1102. Rookwood vase, vellum, landscape, L. Asbury, 1920, #1660D, 9.5"h, mint 1700-2700
June 7, 1997 Sold for $2400

1103. Rookwood vase, standard glaze, holly, L. Van Briggle, 1903, #583F, 5"h, scratches 350-450
June 7, 1997 Sold for $260

1104. Rookwood vase, standard glaze, blossoms, L. Asbury, 1898, #725C, 7"h, mint 500-700
June 7, 1997 Sold for $500

1105. Rookwood pitcher, standard glaze, berries, S. Sax, 1899, #564D, 9"h, mint 600-800
June 7, 1997 Sold for $750

1106. Rookwood vase, standard glaze, blossoms, H.R. Strafer, 1891, #536E W, 5.5"w x 3"h, mint 400-600
June 7, 1997 Sold for $300

1107. Rookwood vase, standard glaze, poppies, E.R. Felten, 1901, #734D, 6.5"h, mint 500-700
June 7, 1997 Sold for $550

1108. Rookwood vase, standard glaze, blossoms, M.L. Perkins, 1898, #848, 6.5"h, mint 450-650
June 7, 1997 Sold for $325

1109. Rookwood covered jar, vellum, harbor scene, C. Schmidt, 1922, #834, 6.5"h, mint 3500-4500
June 7, 1997 Sold for $2500

1110. Rookwood plaque, vellum, landscape, E. Diers, 1920, 8"w x 6"h, mint 3000-4000
June 7, 1997 Sold for $3750

1111. Rookwood vase, vellum, harbor scene, C. Schmidt, 1925, #2544, 8.5"h, mint 4000-6000
June 7, 1997 Sold for $3500

1112. Rookwood vase, standard glaze, stylized thistles, A. Pons, 1906, #924, 6"h, restored 250-350
June 7, 1997 Sold for $190

1113. Rookwood vase, standard glaze, blossoms, F. Rothenbusch, 1896, #712, 4.5"w x 5"h, mint 650-850
June 7, 1997 Sold for $400

1114. Rookwood chocolate pot, standard glaze, floral, Shirayamadani, 1891, #T589W, 10.5"h, repair 200-300
June 7, 1997 Sold for $850

1115. Rookwood ewer, standard glaze, roses, Shirayamadani, 1891, #476, 11.5"h, mint 800-1100
June 7, 1997 Sold for $800

1116. Rookwood bowl, standard glaze, poppies, J. Swing, 1903, #923, 6.5"dia. x 2.5"h, flake 300-400
June 7, 1997 Sold for $375

1117. Rookwood vase, standard glaze, irises, C. Schmidt, 1900, #639, 9"h, bruises to rim 500-700
June 7, 1997 Sold for $700

1118. Rookwood vase, standard glaze, floral design, J.E. Zettel, 1892, #654D, 3.5"h, mint 250-350
June 7, 1997 Sold for $600

1119. Rookwood vase, standard glaze, landscape, Shirayamadani, 1897, #786C, 10"h, repair 2000-3000
June 7, 1997 Sold for $1800

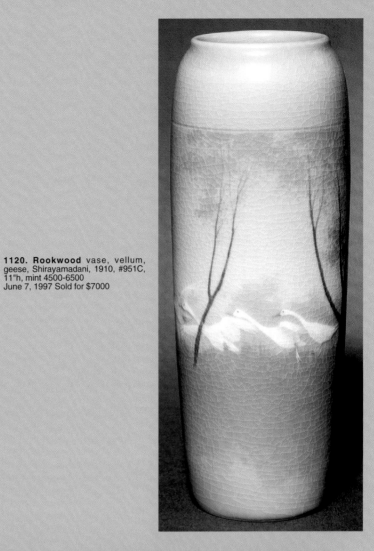

1120. Rookwood vase, vellum,
geese, Shirayamadani, 1910, #951C,
11"h, mint 4500-6500
June 7, 1997 Sold for $7000

1121. Rookwood vase, vellum, cherry blossoms, E.T.
Hurley, 1927, #272, 6.5"h, mint 600-800
June 7, 1997 Sold for $650

1122. Rookwood vase, vellum, blossoms, E. Diers,
1929, #1120, 4.5"h, mint 900-1200
June 7, 1997 Sold for $700

1123. Rookwood plaque, vellum, landscape, S.E.
Coyne, 1924, 9"w x 7"h, mint 3500-4500
June 7, 1997 Sold for $4500

1124. Rookwood vase, vellum, berries, E. Diers,
1931, #2918E, 6.5"h, flake 600-800
June 7, 1997 Sold for $800

1125. Rookwood vase, vellum, blossoms, E. Diers,
1923, #1926, 6.5"h, mint 1200-1700
June 7, 1997 Sold for $1500

1126. Rookwood vase, Black Iris glaze, dandelions, J.D. Wareham, 1899, #732A, 13"h, mint 6000-8000
June 7, 1997 Sold for $20,000

1127. Rookwood vase, Black Iris glaze, swans, Shirayaadani, 1909, #1654C, 11.5"h, scratches 15,000-25,000
June 7, 1997 Sold for $20,000

1128. Rookwood vase, vellum, blossoms, E. Diers, 1928, #2968, 7.5"h, repaired 500-700
June 7, 1997 Sold for $425

1129. Rookwood vase, vellum, roses, E. Diers, 1927, #2885, 8.5"h, mint 1200-1700
June 7, 1997 Sold for $950

1130. Rookwood plaque, vellum, landscape, C. Schmidt, 8.5"w x 5"h, mint 3000-4000
June 7, 1997 Sold for $3250

1131. Rookwood vase, vellum, blossoms, E. Diers, 1924, #2463, 8"h, mint 1500-2500
June 7, 1997 Sold for $1100

1132. Rookwood vase, vellum, blossoms, L. Asbury, 1927, #1343, 5"h, mint 900-1200
June 7, 1997 Sold for $750

1133. Rookwood vase, matt glaze, floral design, Shiraya-madani, 1904, #176CZ, 9"h, mint 5500-7500
June 7, 1997 Sold for $9000

1134. Rookwood covered vase, Limoges style, butter-fly, L. Fry, 1885, #47C, 6"h, bruise 500-700
June 7, 1997 Sold for $550

1135. Rookwood vase, Limoges style, trees, M. Daly, 1884, #49B, 10" x 2" x 11", flakes and chips 700-900
June 7, 1997 Sold for $1100

1136. Rookwood nut dish, Limoges style, flowers, bisque exterior, 1900, #279A, 6"dia., mint 200-300
June 7, 1997 Sold for $100

1137. Rookwood vase, Limoges style, mums, A.R. Valentien in 1885, #141, 11"h, mint 1000-1500
June 7, 1997 Sold for $750

1138. Rookwood vase, Limoges style, bats and blos-soms, M.L. Nichols, 1882, 11"h, tight line 1000-1500
June 7, 1997 Sold for $650

1139. Rookwood bowl, Limoges style, birds, gold highlights, 1884, #59C, 10"dia. x 4"h, mint 600-800
June 7, 1997 Sold for $450

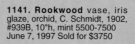

1140. Rookwood vase, matt glaze, raised stylized ferns and grasses, E. Barrett, 1927, #324, 17"h, mint 3500-4500
June 7, 1997 Sold for $2100

1141. Rookwood vase, iris glaze, orchid, C. Schmidt, 1902, #939B, 10"h, mint 5500-7500
June 7, 1997 Sold for $3750

1142. Rookwood vase, dull finish glaze, blossoms, G. Young, 1887, #355W7, 5"h, mint 500-700
June 7, 1997 Sold for $260

1143. Rookwood jug, bisque, blossoms and grass, H. Wenderoth, 1883, #19, 5"h, mint 250-350
June 7, 1997 Sold for $210

1144. Rookwood pitcher, cameo glaze, blossoms, A.M. Valentien, 1890, #487B, 7"h, crack 500-700
June 7, 1997 Sold for $210

1145. Rookwood vase, Limoges style, bird, M.A. Daly, 1886, #141Y, mint 900-1200
June 7, 1997 Sold for $650

1146. Rookwood tea set, cameo glaze, blossoms, G. Young, 1889, #473, teapot 6.5"h, chip 800-1100
June 7, 1997 Sold for $750

1147. Rookwood water jug, Limoges style, birds, A.R. Valentien, 1886, #41, 9.5"h, mint 1500-2000
June 7, 1997 Sold for $1100

1148. Rookwood vase, vellum, landscape, E. Diers, #940D, 1917, 10.5"h, tiny chip and lines 1000-1500
June 7, 1997 Sold for $900

1149. Rookwood vase, vellum, winter landscape, F. Rothenbusch, 1914, #922E, 11"h, mint 1700-2500
June 7, 1997 Sold for $1500

1150. Rookwood vase, vellum, Oriental boats, S.E. Coyne, 1914, #1343, 5"h, mint 1200-1700
June 7, 1997 Sold for $800

1151. Rookwood vase, vellum, underwater scene, E.T. Hurley, 1907, #927D, 9"h, mint 1500-2500
June 7, 1997 Sold for $3250

1152. Rookwood vase, hi-glaze, floral design, L. Epply, 1922, #2191, 5"h, mint 800-1100
June 7, 1997 Sold for $1300

1153. Rookwood bowl, Black Opal glaze, butterflies, S. Sax, 1926, #2813C, 13"dia., scratches 2000-3000
June 7, 1997 Sold for $2600

1154. Rookwood vase, vellum , blossoms, L. Epply, 1922, #2308, 7"h, mint 800-1100
June 7, 1997 Sold for $750

1155. Kenton Hills vase, vellum, floral design, initialed, impressed mark, 6"h, mint 400-600
June 7, 1997 Sold for $350

1156. Rookwood vase, vellum, floral design, L. Epply, 1921, #913F, 5.5"h, mint 750-1000
June 7, 1997 Sold for $475

1157. Rookwood vase, vellum, snowy landscape, Shirayamadani, #534C, 1912, 7.5"h, flake 900-1200
June 7, 1997 Sold for $850

1158. Rookwood plaque, vellum, landscape, L. Asbury, 1923, 9"w x 7"h, hairlines 1200-1700
June 7, 1997 Sold for $1600

1160. Rookwood vase, vellum, landscape, E. Diers, #328B, 1916, 6.5"h, mint 1200-1700
June 7, 1997 Sold for $2000

1159. Rookwood tray, matt glaze, rook design, 1914, #2024, 11"w x 5"d x 3"h, mint 500-700
June 7, 1997 Sold for $500

1161. Rookwood vase, matt glaze, violets, S.E. Coyne, 1905, #1124E, 7"h, mint 1000-1500
June 7, 1997 Sold for $1000

1162. Rookwood vase, matt glaze, mushrooms, J.D. Wareham, 1901, #909, 9"h, mint 1200-1700
June 7, 1997 Sold for $1500

1163. Rookwood vase, matt glaze, holly, S. Toohey, 1905, #214, 6.5"dia., mint 1500-2000
June 7, 1997 Sold for $1000

1164. Rookwood plaque, matt glaze, landscape, S. Toohey, 7"w x 9"h, mint 4000-6000
June 7, 1997 Sold for $4750

1165. Rookwood vase, matt glaze, stripes and circles, C.S. Todd, 1916, #214C, 5.5"dia., line 300-400
June 7, 1997 Sold for $240

1166. Rookwood vase, matt glaze, Arts & Crafts design, C.S. Todd, 1912, #535C, 11"h, mint 800-1100
June 7, 1997 Sold for $2100

1167. Rookwood vase, matt glaze, swirled design, C.A. Duell, 1908, #1124E, 6.5"h, lines 350-550
June 7, 1997 Sold for $425

1168. Rookwood vase, vellum, landscape, F. Rothenbusch, 1923, #1779, 7.5"h, mint 2000-2500
June 7, 1997 Sold for $1500

1169. Rookwood plaque, vellum, landscape, L. Asbury, 8"w x 4"h, mint 1500-2000
June 7, 1997 Sold for $1300

1170. Rookwood vase, vellum, birds, L. Asbury, 1908, #938D, 7"h, mint 1200-1700
June 7, 1997 Sold for $1000

1171. Rookwood vase, vellum, cherry blossoms, E.T. Hurley, 1919, #2038, 5.5"dia. x 4"h, mint 450-650
June 7, 1997 Sold for $500

1172. Rookwood vase, vellum, berries, L. Asbury, 1922, #604F, 6.5"h, minor bruise to rim 500-700
June 7, 1997 Sold for $500

1173. Rookwood bowl, vellum, blossoms, M.H. McDonald, 1919, #2119, 5"dia., mint 400-500
June 7, 1997 Sold for $180

1174. Rookwood vase, vellum, blossoms, P. Conant, 1916, #939D, 8"h, mint 800-1100
June 7, 1997 Sold for $550

1175. Rookwood vase, vellum, floral, unknown signature, 1920, #892B, 11.5"h, glaze miss 1200-1700
June 7, 1997 Sold for $1100

1176. Rookwood vase, vellum, stylized design, C.S. Todd, 1921, #2105, 5"h, mint 500-700
June 7, 1997 Sold for $375

1177. Rookwood vase, matt glaze, floral design, M.H. McDonald, #2102, 1921, 7.5"h, mint 800-1100
June 7, 1997 Sold for $500

1178. Rookwood vase, vellum, berries, unknown signature, 1919, #1356F, 6"h, mint 500-700
June 7, 1997 Sold for $400

1179. Rookwood vase, vellum, stylized flowers, C.S. Todd, 1916, #1929, 4.5"h, mint 800-1100
June 7, 1997 Sold for $500

1180. Rookwood vase, vellum, wreathes, H.E. Wilcox, 1925, #2301E, 8"h, line to base 350-550
June 7, 1997 Sold for $475

1181. Rookwood plaque, vellum, landscape, F. Rothenbusch, 8.5"w x 11"h, mint 3500-4500
June 7, 1997 Sold for $4000

1182. Rookwood vase, matt glaze, interlocking design, S. Sax, 1909, #852, 6"h, hard to find line 300-400
June 7, 1997 Sold for $500

1183. Rookwood vase, matt glaze, stylized vine, C.S. Todd, 1920, #654C, 5.5"h, hairline 300-400
June 7, 1997 Sold for $220

1184. Rookwood vase, vellum, floral, K. Van Horne, 1926, #1779, 7.5"h, mint 500-700
June 7, 1997 Sold for $750

1185. Rookwood vase, vellum, blossoms, H.E. Wilcox, 1923, #614E, 8.5"h, mint 1200-1700
June 7, 1997 Sold for $1100

1186. Rookwood vase, vellum, blossoms, F. Rothenbusch, 1924, 9.5"h, mint 1700-2700
June 7, 1997 Sold for $1500

1187. Rookwood vase, matt glaze, blossoms, J. Jensen, 1931, #927E, 7.5"h, mint 1200-1700
June 7, 1997 Sold for $1100

1188. Rookwood vase, vellum, blossoms, L. Asbury, 1923, #2547, 9.5"h, mint 1700-2700
June 7, 1997 Sold for $1400

1189. Rookwood vase, vellum, crocus, M.H. McDonald, 1938, 7"h, mint 1000-1500
June 7, 1997 Sold for $700

1190. Rookwood vase, standard glaze, flowers, silver overlay, I. Bishop, 1903, #903C, 8"h, mint 2500-3500
June 7, 1997 Sold for $2700

1191. Rookwood jug, standard glaze, clover, wire mesh, M. Daly, 1893, #512W, 9.5"h, mint 2000-3000
June 7, 1997 Sold for $2100

1192. Rookwood vase, standard, silver overlay, dogwood, E. Foertmeyer, 1903, #900C, 8"h, mint 2500-3500
June 7, 1997 Sold for $2700

1193. Rookwood vase, matt glaze, blossom and leaf, W.E. Hentschel, 1914, #2100, 5"h, mint 750-1000
June 7, 1997 Sold for $700

1194. Rookwood vase, matt glaze, leaf and berry design, E. Barrett, 1927, #1348, 5"h, mint 900-1200
June 7, 1997 Sold for $1800

1195. Rookwood dish, matt glaze, lizard, Shiraya-madani, 1907, #1080E, 3.5"dia., mint 400-600
June 7, 1997 Sold for $500

1196. Rookwood vase, matt glaze, stylized leaves, W.E. Hentschel, 1926, #2903, 10"h, mint 1500-2000
June 7, 1997 Sold for $1100

1197. Rookwood vase, matt glaze, stylized leaves, W.E. Hentschel, 1926, #1929, 6.5"dia., mint 1000-1500
June 7, 1997 Sold for $800

1198. Rookwood vase, matt glaze, stylized leaves, W.E. Hentschel, 1927, #915D, 7.5"h, mint 1000-1500
June 7, 1997 Sold for $1800

1199. Rookwood vase, standard glaze, Native American, S. Laurence, 1898, #829, 9.25"h, mint 3500-5500
June 7, 1997 Sold for $4000

1200. Rookwood mug, standard glaze, gnome in cemetery, G. Young, 1897, #587C, 5"h, mint 1200-1700
June 7, 1997 Sold for $1200

1201. Rookwood stein, standard glaze, portrait, M. Daly, 1896, #775, ornate handle, 8.5"h, mint 3500-5500
June 7, 1997 Sold for $2400

1202. Rookwood vase, hi-glaze, flowers, Shirayamadani, 1939, #6735, 6.5"h, mint 1500-2000
June 7, 1997 Sold for $950

1203. Rookwood vase, Black Opal glaze, floral design, 1927, S. Sax, #2996, 9"h, mint 1500-2500
June 7, 1997 Sold for $1200

1204. Rookwood vase, hi-glaze, daisies, K. Ley, 1945, #2917E, 6"h, mint 800-1100
June 7, 1997 Sold for $1300

1205. Kenton Hills vase, butterfat glaze, chickens, W. Hentschel, 9"h, mint 700-900
June 7, 1997 Sold for $550

1206. Rookwood vase, hi-glaze, floral design, F. Rothenbusch, 1922, #77C, 5.5"h, chip 350-450
June 7, 1997 Sold for $160

1207. Rookwood vase, hi-glaze, bird, J. Jensen, 1946, #6204C, 8792, 7"h, mint 1500-2000
June 7, 1997 Sold for $1200

1208. Rookwood vase, Chinese Plum glaze, floral, Shirayamadani, 1925, #130, 6.5"h, mint 1500-2000
June 7, 1997 Sold for $2200

1209. Rookwood vase, standard glaze, birds, A.R. Valentien, about 1897, 7.5"h, mint 1500-2500
June 7, 1997 Sold for $2100

1210. Rookwood vase, green standard, dragons, Shirayamadani, 1887, #346B S, 6.5"h, mint 2500-3500
June 7, 1997 Sold for $1600

1211. Rookwood vase, yellow standard, dragon, A.R. Valentien, 1885, #218, 11"h, mint 2500-3500
June 7, 1997 Sold for $1600

1212. Rookwood vase, hi-glaze drip, 1949, #6644E, 7"h, mint 200-300
June 7, 1997 Sold for $450

1213. Rookwood vase, hi-glaze, tulips, M.H. McDonald, 1946, #6659, 7.5"h, bruise 350-550
June 7, 1997 Sold for $400

1214. Rookwood vase, hi-glaze, 1920, #356R, 5.5"h, mint 250-350
June 7, 1997 Sold for $550

1215. Rookwood vase, hi-glaze, blue jays, O. King, 1949, #6933, 11.5"h, drilled hole, mint 1500-2000
June 7, 1997 Sold for $850

1216. Rookwood vase, hi-glaze, snails, J.D. Wareham, 1952, 6.5"h, mint 1000-1500
June 7, 1997 Sold for $1200

1217. Rookwood vase, hi-glaze, irises, L. Holtkamp, 1951, #6933, 11.5"h, drilled, mint 1000-1500
June 7, 1997 Sold for $700

1218. Rookwood vase, hi-glaze, floral design, J. Jensen, 1945, #6873, #8149, 7"h, mint 800-1100
June 7, 1997 Sold for $1400

1219. Rookwood vase, hi-glaze, blossoms, K. Ley, 1946, #778, 4443, 10"h, minor glaze chip 450-650
June 7, 1997 Sold for $375

1220. Rookwood vase, hi-glaze, design of woman and stars, handles, 1935, #6539, 9"h, mint 300-400
June 7, 1997 Sold for $200

1221. Rookwood vase, hi-glaze, pansies, S. Markland, 1892, #533E, 6.5"h, minute flake 300-400
June 3, 2000 Sold for $450

1222. Rookwood vase, hi-glaze, maple leaves, Shirayamadani, 1890, #S911, 13"h, mint 2000-2500
June 3, 2000 Sold for $2900

1223. Rookwood covered vessel, hi-glaze, weasels, B.R. Horsfall, 1894, #234, 5.5"h, mint 1500-2500
June 3, 2000 Sold for $2500

1224. Rookwood vase, hi-glaze, R.E. Menzel, 1949, 7"h, mint 350-450
June 7, 1997 Sold for $260

1225. Rookwood vase, hi-glaze, stylized blossoms, artist signed, 1945, #2110, 5"h, mint 250-350
June 7, 1997 Sold for $150

1226. Rookwood vase, hi-glaze, houses, L. Holtkamp, 1951, 7.5"h, mint 700-900
June 7, 1997 Sold for $375

1227. Rookwood vase, matt glaze, rooks, five-sided, 1922, #1795, 5"h, mint 200-300
June 7, 1997 Sold for $350

1228. Rookwood tile, matt glaze, rook and geometric design, 1924, #1794, 5.5"sq., mint 300-400
June 7, 1997 Sold for $450

1229. Rookwood vase, hi-glaze, 1951, #2551, 14"h, mint 500-700
June 7, 1997 Sold for $300

1230. Rookwood vase, matt glaze, rooks, five-sided, 1911, #1795, 5"h, mint 250-350
June 7, 1997 Sold for $325

1231. Rookwood vase, hi-glaze, houses, L. Holtkamp, 1951, 7.5"h, line to rim 400-600
June 7, 1997 Sold for $425

1232. Rookwood vase, hi-glaze, floral design, 1943, #6194P, 5"h, mint 250-350
June 7, 1997 Sold for $190

1233. Rookwood vase, porcelain drip glaze, flowers, W.E. Hentschel, 1922, #1348, 6"w, mint 500-700
June 6, 1998 Sold for $400

1234. Rookwood vase, matt glaze, floral design, E.T. Hurley, 1937, #6666, 6"h, mint 1000-1500
June 6, 1998 Sold for $1100

1235. Rookwood vase, matt glaze, flowers, Shirayamadani, 1932, 6"h, mint 2000-3000
June 6, 1998 Sold for $1800

1236. Rookwood tray, hi-glaze, young lady and horse, 1940s, 15.5"l x 11"w, mint 800-1100
June 6, 1998 Sold for $700

1237. Rookwood vase, matt glaze, daffodils, Shirayamadani, 1942, 6.5"h, mint 1500-2000
June 6, 1998 Sold for $1200

1238. Rookwood vase, matt glaze, grapes, M.H. McDonald, 1929, #6114C, 11"h, mint 1000-1500
June 6, 1998 Sold for $1000

1239. Rookwood vase, iris glaze, floral design, C.A. Baker, 1902, #922E, 5.5"h, mint 800-1100
June 7, 1997 Sold for $550

1240. Rookwood vase, iris glaze, heron, C. Schmidt, 1905, #941C, 9.5"h, minor flaw 2000-3000
June 7, 1997 Sold for $1200

1241. Rookwood vase, iris glaze, tropical leaves, E. Diers, 1907, #1126C, 9"h, glaze misses 1200-1700
June 7, 1997 Sold for $650

1242. Rookwood vase, sea green, ocean scene, Shirayamadani, 1897, 6"h, repair to rim 1000-1500
June 7, 1997 Sold for $1100

1243. Rookwood vase, iris glaze, blossoms, L. Asbury, 1904, #909C, 8.5"h, mint 1500-2000
June 7, 1997 Sold for $1500

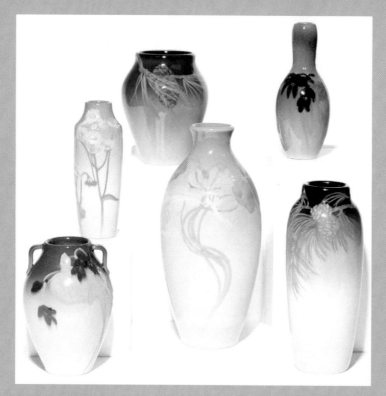

1244. Rookwood vase, iris glaze, flowers, V. Demarest, 1901, #604E, 6"h, mint 700-900 June 6, 1998 Sold for $950

1245. Rookwood vase, flowers, I. Bishop, 1905, #941E, 6.5"h, mint 900-1200 June 6, 1998 Sold for $1100

1246. Rookwood vase, iris glaze, pinecones, K. Van Horne, 1907, #915E, 5.5"h, mint 650-850 June 6, 1998 Sold for $850

1247. Rookwood vase, iris glaze, flowers, E. Diers, 1904, #732B, 10.5"h, mint 1700-2700 June 6, 1998 Sold for $1600

1248. Rookwood vase, iris glaze, pinecones, L. Asbury, 1906, #907E, 8.5"h, mint 1700-2700 June 6, 1998 Sold for $2400

1249. Rookwood vase, sea green, flowers, M. Mitchell, 1901, #921, 6"h, mint 1200-1700 June 6, 1998 Sold for $850

1250. Rookwood vase, matt glaze, flowers, L. Abel, 1927, #2905, 9.5"h, mint 550-750 June 7, 1997 Sold for $375

1251. Rookwood vase, matt glaze, blossoms, M.H. McDonald, 1937, #6629, 6"h, mint 800-1100 June 7, 1997 Sold for $325

1252. Rookwood vase, matt glaze, floral, E.N. Lincoln, 1925, #2040C, 12"h, mint 600-800 June 7, 1997 Sold for $850

1253. Rookwood bowl, matt glaze, foliage, V. Tischler, 1922, #214E, 5"dia. x 2"h, mint 250-350 June 7, 1997 Sold for $275

1254. Rookwood vase, matt glaze, flowers, M.H. McDonald, 1929, #9150, 7.5"h, mint 400-600 June 7, 1997 Sold for $375

1255. Rookwood vase, matt glaze, crocus, Shirayamadani, 1934, 5.5"h, mint 900-1200 June 7, 1997 Sold for $1000

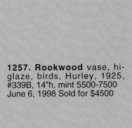

1256. Rookwood vase, French Red, S. Sax, 1922, #1667, 11"h, mint 3000-4000
June 6, 1998 Sold for $9500

1257. Rookwood vase, hi-glaze, birds, Hurley, 1925, #339B, 14"h, mint 5500-7500
June 6, 1998 Sold for $4500

1258. Rookwood vase, standard glaze, floral design, I. Bishop, 1900, #731, 3.5"h, missing top 250-350
June 6, 1998 Sold for $400

1259. Rookwood vase, standard glaze, floral design, L. Asbury, 1899, #753, 6.5"h, mint 400-600
June 6, 1998 Sold for $575

1260. Rookwood vase, matt glaze, molded rooks, 1919, #1815, 6"h, minor roughness to top 250-350
June 6, 1998 Sold for $270

1261. Rookwood pitcher, Limoges style, butterfly and spider, 1882, #65, 9.5"h, mint 800-1100
June 6, 1998 Sold for $650

1262. Rookwood vase, standard glaze, hyacinth, S.E. Coyne, 1903, #901, 9.5"h, drilled 350-550
June 6, 1998 Sold for $600

1263. Rookwood box, standard glaze, flowers, C.J. Dibowski, 1893, #601C, 5.5"dia. x 2"h, mint 400-600
June 6, 1998 Sold for $425

1264. Rookwood covered urn, hi-glaze, hand thrown form, 1920, #2300, 11.5"h, mint 400-600
June 6, 1998 Sold for $750

1265. Rookwood vase, vellum, mallards, Shiryamadani, 1907, #950C, 10.5"h, mint 4500-6500
June 6, 1998 Sold for $4000

1266. Rookwood vase, hi-glaze, parrots, Shiryamadani, #S1772, 10.5"h, mint 9000-1200
June 6, 1998 Sold for $14,000

1267. Rookwood vase, aventurine glaze, 1920, #1656D, 9.5"h, mint 700-1000
June 6, 1998 Sold for $425

1268. Rookwood vase, standard glaze, mums, H. Altman, 1903, #534C, 7.5"h, mint 550-750
June 6, 1998 Sold for $325

1269. Rookwood vase, matt glaze, molded vertical leaves, 1923, #2403, 7"h, mint 250-350
June 6, 1990 Sold for $400

1270. Rookwood vase, standard glaze, roses, A. Van Briggle, 1888, #464, 8"h, mint 900-1200
June 6, 1998 Sold for $1200

1271. Rookwood vase, standard glaze, flowers, A.R. Valentien, 1897, #815, 7.5"w x 7"h, mint 800-1100
June 6, 1998 Sold for $700

1272. Rookwood vase, matt glaze, six-sided form, stylized flowers, 1922, #2584, 10"h, mint 350-450
June 6, 1998 Sold for $375

1273. Rookwood vase, standard glaze, iris, L. Asbury, 1900, #762C, 7"w x 6"h, mint 800-1100
June 6, 1998 Sold for $850

1274. Rookwood vase, matt glaze, molded stylized design, 1929, #2318, 9.5"h, mint 300-400
June 6, 1998 Sold for $400

1275. Rookwood vase, standard glaze, water lilies and poppies, Shirayamadani, 1890, 17"h, mint 4500-6500
June 6, 1998 Sold for $6000

1276. Rookwood vase, iris glaze, geese, A.R. Valentien, 1898, #S1410B, 12.5"h, repaired drill hole in base 5500-7500
June 6, 1998 Sold for $7000

1277. Rookwood vase, vellum, landscape, F. Rothenbusch, 1916, #1358D, 9"h, mint 1750-2250
June 6, 1998 Sold for $1300

1278. Rookwood vase, vellum, landscape, E. Diers, 1910, #907F, 7.5"h, mint 1700-2700
June 6, 1998 Sold for $1500

1279. Rookwood plaque, vellum, landscape, F. Rothenbusch, 1917, 10"h x 13"w, mint 4000-5000
June 6, 1998 Sold for $4000

1280. Rookwood vase, vellum, landscape, S.E. Coyne, 1911, #940D, 10"h, mint 1700-2700
June 6, 1998 Sold for $1600

1281. Rookwood vase, vellum, landscape, E. Diers, 1915, #959E, 7.5"h, mint 600-800
June 6, 1998 Sold for $750

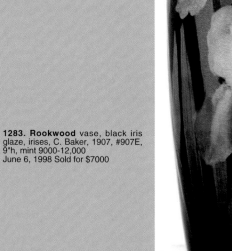

1282. Rookwood vase, sea green, silver overlay, irises, M. Daly, 1900, #S1574, 12.5"h, mint 15,000-25,000
June 6, 1998 Sold for $12,000

1283. Rookwood vase, black iris glaze, irises, C. Baker, 1907, #907E, 9"h, mint 9000-12,000
June 6, 1998 Sold for $7000

1284. Rookwood vase, vellum, flowers, F. Rothenbusch, 1924, #1356E, 7.5"h, mint 1200-1500
June 6, 1998 Sold for $1400

1285. Rookwood vase, vellum, flowers, L. Asbury, 1924, #922D, 7.5"h, mint 1200-1700
June 6, 1998 Sold for $2100

1286. Rookwood plaque, vellum, seascape, E.T. Hurley, 1915, 8.5" x 11"w, mint 1500-2500
June 6, 1998 Sold for $1800

1287. Rookwood vase, vellum, mushrooms, 1916, unknown signature, #2066, 7.5"h, mint 1200-1700
June 6, 1998 Sold for $1100

1288. Rookwood vase, vellum, irises, S.E. Coyne, 1910, #904CC, 10.5"h, mint 1700-2700
June 6, 1998 Sold for $3250

1289. Rookwood plaque, vellum, landscape, E.T. Hurley, 1920, 11"h x 14"w, mint 5500-7500
June 6, 1998 Sold for $6500

1290. Rookwood vase, vellum, flowers, E. Diers, 1906, #950D, 9"h, mint 1000-1500
June 6, 1998 Sold for $1100

1291. Rookwood vase, vellum, cherry blossoms, L. Asbury, 1921, #943E, 7"h, mint 700-900
June 6, 1998 Sold for $850

1292. Rookwood plaque, nocturnal scene, K. Van Horne, 1914, 9.25"w x 5.25"h, mint 1200-1700
June 6, 1998 Sold for $2400

1293. Rookwood vase, vellum, water lily, Ed Diers, 1907, #900C, 8.5"h, mint 1200-1700
June 6, 1998 Sold for $900

1294. Rookwood vase, vellum, flowers, C. Steinle, 1916, #995E, 6.5"w x 5.5"h, mint 1000-1500
June 6, 1998 Sold for $600

1295. Rookwood vase, vellum, flowers, M.H. McDonald, 1918, #1660E, 7.5"h, bruise 300-500
June 6, 1998 Sold for $400

1296. Rookwood bowl, vellum, flowers, E.F. McDermott, 1915, #214E, 4.5"dia., mint 300-500
June 6, 1998 Sold for $325

1297. Rookwood plaque, vellum, birches and mountains, E.T. Hurley, 1946, 12" x 14", mint 12,000-17,000
June 6, 1998 Sold for $16,000

1298. Rookwood vase, matt glaze, flowers, M.H. McDonald, 1938, 5.5"h, glaze loss 550-750
June 6, 1998 Sold for $700

1299. Rookwood vase, vellum, roses, Ed Diers, 1907, #939C, 9"h, mint 1200-1500
June 6, 1998 Sold for $1300

1300. Rookwood plaque, vellum, landscape, E.T. Hurley, 1915, 9.5" x 5.5", mint 2750-3750
June 6, 1998 Sold for $2600

1301. Rookwood vase, vellum, stylized flowers, K. Van Horne, 1910, #1659E, 7.5"h, mint 800-1100
June 6, 1998 Sold for $475

1302. Rookwood vase, vellum, boats, L. Asbury, 1912, #1658F, 6.5"h, mint 900-1200
June 6, 1998 Sold for $1200

1303. Rookwood vase, vellum, stylized tulips, S. Sax, 1907, #932E, 8"h, mint 900-1200
June 6, 1998 Sold for $600

1304. Rookwood vase, iris glaze, irises, 1903, C. Schmidt, #S1707A, 10"h, mint 6500-8500
June 6, 1998 Sold for $10,000

1305. Rookwood vase, vellum, Venetian scene, C. Schmidt, 1920, #907C, 15"h, mint 7500-8500
June 6, 1998 Sold for $10,000

1306. Rookwood vase, vellum, wisteria, E. Diers, 1925, #2720, 6.5"h, mint 1000-1500
June 6, 1998 Sold for $1600

1307. Rookwood vase, vellum, holly, M.H. McDonald, 1913, #2041E, 7"h, bruise 300-400
June 6, 1998 Sold for $400

1308. Rookwood plaque, vellum, sailboat, S. Sax, 1920, 5"h x 8"w, mint 2000-3000
June 6, 1998 Sold for $3250

1309. Rookwood vase, vellum, berries, L. Asbury, 1927, #1779, 8"h, mint 1500-2000
June 6, 1998 Sold for $1200

1310. Rookwood vase, vellum, flowers, E. Diers, 1928, #614F, 7"h, mint 700-900
June 6, 1998 Sold for $600

1311. Rookwood vase, vellum, stylized floral, F. Rothenbusch, 1923, #1358F, 6"h, mint 900-1200
June 6, 1998 Sold for $1000

1312. Rookwood vase, vellum, cherry blossoms, E. Noonan, 1907, #941D, 8.5"h, mint 700-900
June 6, 1998 Sold for $900

1313. Rookwood vase, vellum, snow scene, L. Asbury, 1916, #907D, 12"h, mint 3500-5500 June 6, 1998 Sold for $6000

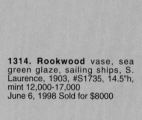

1314. Rookwood vase, sea green glaze, sailing ships, S. Laurence, 1903, #S1735, 14.5"h, mint 12,000-17,000 June 6, 1998 Sold for $8000

1315. Rookwood vase, vellum, cherry blossoms, E. Diers, 1910, #1356D, 8.5"h, mint 900-1200 June 6, 1998 Sold for $1000

1316. Rookwood vase, matt glaze, flowers, M. H. McDonald, 1924, #2723, 6"h, mint 550-750 June 6, 1998 Sold for $450

1317. Rookwood plaque, vellum, landscape, F. Rothenbusch, 1914, 8" x 6", mint 2000-2500 June 6, 1998 Sold for $1700

1318. Rookwood vase, vellum, dogwood, S. Sax, 1904, #915D, 7.5"h, mint 1000-1500 June 6, 1998 Sold for $1100

1319. Rookwood vase, vellum, carnations, L. Epply, 1907, #614F, 6"h, bruise 350-450 June 6, 1998 Sold for $500

1320. Rookwood vase, vellum, cherry blossom, 1907, L. Epply, #907F, 7.5"h, mint 650-850 June 6, 1998 Sold for $500

1321. Rookwood vase, vellum, dogwood, E.N. Lincoln, 1906, #942D, 6"h, mint 500-700 June 6, 1998 Sold for $525

1322. Rookwood vase, vellum, landscape, L. Epply, 1917, #925C, 10.5"h, mint 2500-3500
June 6, 1998 Sold for $1800

1323. Rookwood vase, vellum, landscape, Shirayamadani, 1912, #1278E, 9"h, mint 1000-1500
June 6, 1998 Sold for $900

1324. Rookwood plaque, vellum, landscape, F. Rothenbusch, 9"h x 7"w, mint 1700-2700
June 6, 1998 Sold for $2200

1325. Rookwood vase, vellum, landscape, F. Rothenbusch, 1923, #839B, 9.5"h, mint 2500-3500
June 6, 1998 Sold for $2600

1326. Rookwood vase, vellum, landscape, F. Rothenbusch, 1923, #1358E, 7.5"h, mint 2000-3000
June 6, 1998 Sold for $2400

1327. Rookwood vase, vellum, landscape, E. Diers, 1922, #904D, 9"h, restoration 2000-3000
June 6, 1998 Sold for $1200

1328. Rookwood vase, matt glaze, flowers, J. Jensen, 1920, #2720, 6"h, mint 500-700
June 6, 1998 Sold for $750

1329. Rookwood vase, matt glaze, flowers, M.H. McDonald, 1937, #6629, 6"h, mint 550-750
June 6, 1998 Sold for $750

1330. Rookwood plaque, vellum, landscape, L. Epply, 1916, 9" x 11", mint 4000-5000
June 6, 1998 Sold for $3500

1331. Rookwood vase, matt glaze, floral design, W.E. Hentschel, 1921, #1844, 5.5"w, mint 550-750
June 6, 1998 Sold for $700

1332. Rookwood vase, matt glaze, flowers, J. Jensen, 1929, #2831, 5.5"h, mint 350-550
June 6, 1998 Sold for $750

1333. Rookwood vase, matt glaze, flowers, L. Abel, 1922, #950D, 9.5"h, mint 900-1200
June 6, 1998 Sold for $800

1334. Rookwood vase, vellum, landscape, E. Diers, 1925, #925A, 15.5"h, filled drill hole 2500-3500
June 6, 1998 Sold for $3250

1335. Rookwood plaque, vellum, landscape, S. Sax, 8" x 6", mint 1700-2700
June 6, 1998 Sold for $1500

1336. Rookwood vase, vellum, landscape, E. Diers, 1918, #30E, 9"h, mint 1750-2750
June 6, 1998 Sold for $2100

1337. Rookwood vase, vellum, landscape, E.F. McDermott, 1920, #808, 8"h, mint 2000-2500
June 6, 1998 Sold for $2200

1338. Rookwood vase, crystalline glaze, 1919, #2247C, 13.5"h, mint 1500-2500
June 6, 1998 Sold for $1500

1339. Rookwood vase, matt glaze, flowers, M.H. McDonald, 1931, #6206F, 5"h, mint 450-650
June 6, 1998 Sold for $400

1340. Rookwood vase, matt glaze, dogwood, Shiryamadani, 1938, 7"h, mint 1200-1700
June 6, 1998 Sold for $1200

1341. Rookwood plaque, vellum, landscape, E.T. Hurley, 9"h x 11"w, mint 3750-4750
June 6, 1998 Sold for $3000

1342. Rookwood vase, matt glaze, leaves, J. Jensen, 1930, #2078, 5"h, mint 450-650
June 6, 1998 Sold for $600

1343. Rookwood vase, matt glaze, flowers, S.E. Coyne, 1925, #2070, 7.5"h, mint 550-750
June 6, 1998 Sold for $600

1344. Rookwood vase, standard glaze, holly, J. Zettel, 1892, #636W, 6"w, two tight lines 250-350
June 6, 1998 Sold for $400

1345. Rookwood vase, standard glaze, roses, 1890, #415C, 6"h, mint 500-700
June 6, 1998 Sold for $450

1346. Rookwood vase, matt glaze, bamboo, 1935, #2480, 10"h, mint 350-550
June 6, 1998 Sold for $650

1347. Rookwood vase, standard glaze, flowers, A.B. Sprague, 1899, #537C, 16"h, mint 2000-3000
June 6, 1998 Sold for $1700

1348. Rookwood teapot, standard glaze, carnations, E.N. Lincoln, 1894, #552, 7.5"h, mint 700-900
June 6, 1998 Sold for $700

1349. Rookwood vase, matt glaze, molded stylized floral design, 1929, #2401, 7"h, mint 250-350
June 6, 1998 Sold for $350

1350. Rookwood vase, standard glaze, floral design, 1904, C. Steinle, #941, 9.5"h, mint 700-900
June 6, 1998 Sold for $900

1351. Rookwood jug, standard glaze, corn, C. Steinle, 1900, #512C, 5.5"h, minor scratches 300-400
June 6, 1998 Sold for $300

1352. Rookwood vase, matt glaze, rooks, 1921, #2326, 6"h, mint 300-400
June 6, 1998 Sold for $375

1353. Rookwood vessel, dull finish glaze, flowers, Shirayamadani, 1887, #344B, 12"l, mint 1200-1700
June 6, 1998 Sold for $1400

1354. Rookwood vase, standard glaze, floral design, S. Sax, 1899, #611D, 8"h, mint 500-750
June 6, 1998 Sold for $650

1355. Rookwood ewer, standard glaze, berries, A.M. Valentien, 1894, #611B, 10"h, restoration 400-600
June 6, 1998 Sold for $500

1356. Rookwood vase, matt glaze, 1930, #2587F, 4"h, mint 300-400
June 6, 1998 Sold for $300

1357. Rookwood vase, standard glaze, clover, C. Steinle, 1897, #731, 3.5"h, missing top, mint 200-300
June 6, 1998 Sold for $280

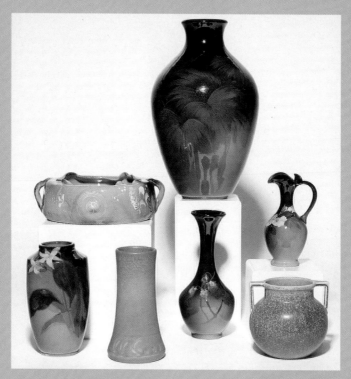

1358. Rookwood vase, standard glaze, lilies, C. Steinle, 1900, #735D, 7.5"h, mint 400-600
June 6, 1998 Sold for $425

1359. Rookwood bowl, hi-glaze, flowers and circles, L. Perkins, 9.5"dia. x 3"h, mint 500-700
June 6, 1998 Sold for $350

1360. Rookwood vase, matt glaze, incised stylized design, 1908, #1358E, 7"h, mint 250-350
June 6, 1998 Sold for $350

1361. Rookwood vase, standard glaze, palm, M. Daly, 1898, #S1411C, 13.5"h, abrasions 1200-1700
June 6, 1998 Sold for $1100

1362. Rookwood vase, standard glaze, berries, R. Fechheimer, 1898, #557, 7"h, mint 550-750
June 6, 1998 Sold for $550

1363. Rookwood vase, crystalline glaze, handled, 922, #2078, 5"h, mint 250-350
June 6, 1998 Sold for $375

1364. Rookwood ewer, standard glaze, roses, C. Schmidt, 1897, #639D, 6.5"h, mint 450-650
June 6, 1998 Sold for $550

1365. Rookwood vase, matt glaze, molded stylized flowers, 1930, #2852, 7"h, mint 300-400
June 6, 1998 Sold for $450

1366. Rookwood vase, mahogany glaze, floral design, M. Daly, 1888, #419, 7.5"h, mint 1200-1700
June 6, 1998 Sold for $1200

1367. Rookwood pilgrim flask, Limoges style, geese, A.R. Valentien, 1882, 7"h, mint 800-1100
June 6, 1998 Sold for $800

1368. Rookwood vase, standard glaze, tulips, J. Swing, 1903, #915C, 7.5"h, mint 700-900
June 6, 1998 Sold for $800

1369. Rookwood vase, standard glaze, palm, M. Daly, 1896, #825, 11.5"h, minor abrasions 900-1200
June 6, 1998 Sold for $1100

1370. Rookwood bowl, Limoges style, butterflies, 1883, N.J. Hirschfeld, #166, 7"dia., mint 650-850
June 6, 1998 Sold for $375

1371. Rookwood vase, matt glaze, rooks, 1922, #2326, 6"h, mint 300-400
June 6, 1998 Sold for $400

1372. Rookwood vase, standard glaze, clover, silver overlay, C. Steinle, 1892, #459E, 4"h, mint 3500-4500
June 6, 1998 Sold for $4500

1373. Rookwood ewer, standard glaze, floral, silver overlay, Strafer, 1892, #510, 7"h, fracture 2000-3000
June 6, 1998 Sold for $3500

1374. Rookwood vessel, standard glaze, men, silver overlay, Wilcox, 1891, #259B, 8"h, hairlines 2000-3000
June 6, 1998 Sold for $4750

1375. Rookwood inkwell, standard glaze, clover, silver overlay, Baker, 1899, #586C, 10"l, mint 2000-3000
June 6, 1998 Sold for $1600

1376. Rookwood vase, standard glaze, roses, silver overlay, Lindeman, 1902, #568C, 7.5"h,
mint 3500-4500
June 6, 1998 Sold for $4000

1377. Rookwood vase, vellum, flowers, E. Diers, 1925, #2831, 5.5"h, glaze flaking 600-800
June 6, 1998 Sold for $500

1378. Rookwood vase, vellum, wisteria, E. Diers, 1926, #356D, 8.5"h, mint 1500-2000
June 6, 1998 Sold for $1700

1379. Rookwood plaque, vellum, landscape, L. Asbury, 1919, 11"w x 9"h, mint 4000-5000
June 6, 1998 Sold for $5500

1380. Rookwood vase, vellum, cherry blossoms, S. Sax, 1908, #1929, 7"w, mint 800-1100
June 6, 1998 Sold for $700

1381. Rookwood vase, vellum, roses, E. Diers, 1928, #900D, 7"h, mint 1200-1700
June 6, 1998 Sold for $1300

1382. Rookwood vase, standard glaze, cherries, silver overlay, Perkins, 1894, #T871, 4"h, mint 3500-4500
June 6, 1998 Sold for $5400

1383. Rookwood vase, standard glaze, floral, silver overlay, Markland, 1898, #842C, 7"h, mint 3750-4750
June 6, 1998 Sold for $5350

1384. Rookwood vase, standard glaze, corn, silver overlay, Valentien, 1895, #659, 8"h, cracked 2000-3000
June 6, 1998 Sold for $3750

1385. Rookwood vase, standard glaze, pansies, silver overlay, 1891, #628, restoration 1500-2000
June 6, 1998 Sold for $1200

1386. Rookwood vase, standard glaze, holly, silver overlay, Dibowski, 1894, #623, 5.5"h, mint 3750-4750
June 6, 1998 Sold for $4750

1387. Rookwood vase, vellum, snow scene, S.E. Coyne, 1920, #943E, 7"h, mint 1200-1700
June 6, 1998 Sold for $1200

1388. Rookwood vase, vellum, landscape, E.T. Hurley, 1938, #907F, 7.5"h, mint 2000-2500
June 6, 1998 Sold for $1500

1389. Rookwood plaque, vellum, landscape, F. Rothenbusch, 1935, 9"h x 12"w, mint 4000-5000
June 6, 1998 Sold for $4250

1390. Rookwood vase, vellum, landscape, F. Rothenbusch, 1924, #614C, 10.5"h, mint 2700-3700
June 6, 1998 Sold for $2300

1391. Rookwood vase, vellum, landscape, F. Rothenbusch, 1909, #1369D, 9"h, mint 1700-2700
June 6, 1998 Sold for $1500

1392. Rookwood vase, vellum, landscape, no signature, 1912, #2041C, 11"h, mint 1200-1700
June 6, 1998 Sold for $1200

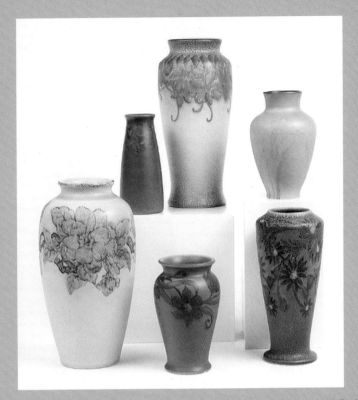

1393. Rookwood vase, matt glaze, flowers, C. Covalenco, 1925, #614D, 11"h, mint 900-1200
June 6, 1998 Sold for $1500

1394. Rookwood vase, matt glaze, flowers, S.E. Coyne, 1927, #1660F, 6"h, mint 400-600
June 6, 1998 Sold for $600

1395. Rookwood vase, matt glaze, flowers, L. Abel, 1925, #2720, 6.5"h, uncrazed, mint 450-650
June 6, 1998 Sold for $650

1396. Rookwood vase, matt glaze, floral, M.H. McDonald, 1925, #1664D, 10.5"h, mint 1000-1500
June 6, 1998 Sold for $1200

1397. Rookwood vase, matt glaze, floral design, Shirayamadani, 1935, 6.5"h, mint 1200-1700
June 6, 1998 Sold for $1100

1398. Rookwood vase, matt glaze, flowers, L. Abel, 1922, #1356D, 9"h, mint 1000-1500
June 6, 1998 Sold for $1100

1399. Rookwood mug, vellum, clover, S. Sax, 1905, 5.5"h, mint 900-1200
June 6, 1998 Sold for $700

1400. Rookwood vase, vellum, berries and leaves, S. Sax, 1907, #S1306, 8.5"h, mint 1200-1700
June 6, 1998 Sold for $2200

1401. Rookwood plaque, vellum, landscape, L. Asbury, 8"w x 5"h, mint 2200-2700
June 6, 1998 Sold for $2600

1402. Rookwood vase, vellum, flowers, M.H. McDonald, 1914, #551, 7"h, glaze flaw 300-400
June 6, 1998 Sold for $300

1403. Rookwood vase, vellum, cherry blossoms, E. Noonan, 1907, #932F, 6.5"h, mint 500-700
June 6, 1998 Sold for $550

1404. Rookwood vase, vellum, cherry blossoms, S.E. Coyne, 1909, #1665, 11.5"h, mint 1200-1700
June 6, 1998 Sold for $1200

1405. Rookwood vases, pair, aventurine glaze, 1930, #5675, 4"h, both mint 500-750
June 6, 1998 Sold for $850

1406. Rookwood vase, aventurine glaze, 1935, 5.5"h, mint 300-400
June 6, 1998 Sold for $600

1407. Rookwood vase, crystalline glaze, hand thrown form, 1933, #6364, 5.5"h, mint 350-450
June 6, 1998 Sold for $325

1408. Rookwood vase, crystalline hi-glaze, 1950, #778, 10"h, mint 700-1200
June 6, 1998 Sold for $600

1409. Rookwood vase, aventurine glaze, 1939, #6311, 7.5"h, hole in base for lamp 350-550
June 6, 1998 Sold for $750

1410. Rookwood vase, miniature form, aventurine glaze, 1932, impressed mark, 4"h, mint 350-550
June 6, 1998 Sold for $550

1411. Rookwood vase, aventurine glaze, 1943, #6823, 8"h, mint 250-350
June 6, 1998 Sold for $250

1412. Rookwood vase, aventurine glaze, molded ducks, 1939, #6550, 6"h, mint 400-600
June 6, 1998 Sold for $400

1413. Rookwood vase, vellum, landscape, F. Rothenbusch, 1930, #614D, 10.5"h, mint 3000-4000
June 6, 1998 Sold for $2800

1414. Rookwood vase, vellum, landscape, S.E. Coyne, 1924, #2032E, 8"h, mint 2200-2700
June 6, 1998 Sold for $3000

1415. Rookwood plaque, vellum, six ships, C. Schmidt, 1920s, 9" x 11.5", mint 4500-6500
June 6, 1998 Sold for $4500

1416. Rookwood vase, vellum, landscape, F. Rothenbusch, 1921, #233, 8.5"h, mint 2000-2500
June 6, 1998 Sold for $2500

1417. Rookwood vase, vellum, landscape, F. Rothenbusch, 1929, #925C, 11"h, mint 2750-3750
June 6, 1998 Sold for $6000

1418. Rookwood vase, vellum, geese, Shirayamadani, 1910, #1667, 11"h, mint 5500-7500
June 6, 1998 Sold for $4000

1419. Rookwood vase, Limoges style, bats, egret and frogs, M.L. Nichols, 1882, #102, 9.5"h, mint 4000-6000
June 6, 1998 Sold for $3750

1420. Rookwood stein, standard glaze, portrait, M. Daly, 1896, #775, 9.5"h, restoration 2000-3000
June 6, 1998 Sold for $1600

1421. Rookwood vase, standard glaze, Native American, G. Young, 1899, #895B, metalwork by Shiryamadani, 8"h, restored 7000-9000
June 6, 1998 Sold for $9500

1422. Rookwood vessel, standard glaze, Native American, Markland, 1898, #837, 5"h, mint 2500-3500
June 6, 1998 Sold for $1700

1423. Rookwood vase, standard glaze, Native American, Laurence, 1899, #614E, 8"h, mint 5000-7000
June 6, 1998 Sold for $4500

1424. Rookwood vase, black iris glaze, swans, C. Schmidt, 1904, 9"h, mint 9000-12,000
June 6, 1998 Sold for $14,000

1425. Rookwood vase, iris glaze, irises, C. Schmidt, 1910, #907C, 14"h, mint 15,000-20,000
June 6, 1998 Sold for $13,000

1426. Rookwood vase, vellum, geese, E. Noonan, 1907, #938D, 6.5"h, mint 1200-1700
June 6, 1998 Sold for $2200

1427. Rookwood vase, vellum, five fish, E. Noonan, 1909, 1120, 5"h, mint 1000-1500
June 6, 1998 Sold for $1500

1428. Rookwood vase, vellum, nocturnal landscape, L. Asbury, 1910, #1652D, 9.5"h, mint 2500-3500
June 6, 1998 Sold for $3000

1429. Rookwood vase, vellum, a rook, S.E. Coyne, 1908, #951D, 9"h, mint 2750-3750
June 6, 1998 Sold for $4000

1430. Rookwood vase, vellum, two fish, E.T. Hurley, 1907, 942C, 7"h, hairlines 800-1100
June 6, 1998 Sold for $900

1431. Rookwood vase, vellum, four fish, E. Noonan, 1908, #1358E, 7"h, tight hairline 700-900
June 6, 1998 Sold for $700

1432. Rookwood handled vessel, standard glaze, boy, A. Van Briggle, 1891, #587, 5"h, mint 900-1200
June 6, 1998 Sold for $650

1433. Rookwood vase, matt glaze, butterflies, 1926, #2072, 6"h, mint 200-300
June 6, 1998 Sold for $300

1434. Rookwood handled vessel, standard glaze, dog, H. Wilcox, 1891, #587, 5"h, minor flaws 600-800
June 6, 1998 Sold for $400

1435. Rookwood plate, Limoges style, water bird, N.J. Hirschfeld, 1882, #87, 6.5"dia., minor flakes 150-250
June 6, 1998 Sold for $180

1436. Rookwood vessel, standard glaze, bee and tadpoles, Valentien, 1889, #328, 6"h, mint 900-1200
June 6, 1998 Sold for $1000

1437. Rookwood vase, matt glaze, molded peacock feather design, 1919, #1905, 8"h, mint 200-300
June 6, 1998 Sold for $350

1438. Rookwood vase, matt glaze, floral design, W.E. Hentschel, 1914, #692, 9.5"h, mint 1200-1700
June 6, 1998 Sold for $1800

1439. Rookwood vase, matt glaze, geometric design, W.E. Hentschel, 1910, #967, 5"w, repair 300-400
June 6, 1998 Sold for $250

1440. Rookwood vase, matt glaze, flowers, W.E. Hentschel, 1913, #1343, 5"h, mint 650-850
June 6, 1998 Sold for $1100

1441. Rookwood tile, matt glaze, landscape, 12"sq., excellent condition 2500-3500
June 6, 1998 Sold for $3000

1442. Rookwood inkwell, matt glaze, peacock feathers, 1905, #1073A, 6"w, repaired 350-550
June 6, 1998 Sold for $425

1443. Rookwood vase, matt glaze, stylized floral design, E. Barrett, 1929, #6115, 10"h, mint 800-1100
June 6, 1998 Sold for $650

1444. Rookwood vase, matt glaze, stylized flowers, C. Duell, 1907, #830E, 4.5"h, mint 400-600
June 6, 1998 Sold for $650

1445. Rookwood vase, Limoges style, poppy and daisies, 1882, M.L. Nichols, 10.5"h, mint 1000-1500
June 6, 1998 Sold for $1500

1446. Rookwood handled vessel, Limoges style, satyr, E.P. Cranch, 1884, 6.5"h, mint 1500-2500
June 6, 1998 Sold for $1600

1447. Rookwood Turkish pot, Limoges style, ducks, M.L. Nichols, 1882, 11.5"h, mint 2500-3500
June 6, 1998 Sold for $2000

1448. Mary Louise McLaughlin vase, Limoges style, floral design, 1887, 11.5"h, minor damage 800-1100
June 6, 1998 Sold for $750

1449. Rookwood vase, matt glaze, flowers and leaves, E. Lincoln, 1927, #1929, 7"w, mint 600-800
June 6, 1998 Sold for $750

1450. Rookwood bowl, matt glaze, flowers, V. Tischler, 1922, #2239, 6.5"w, mint 450-650
June 6, 1998 Sold for $300

1451. Rookwood plaque, matt glaze, landscape, 1904, #1226, 12"sq., mint 2500-3500
June 6, 1998 Sold for $1800

1452. Rookwood tray, matt glaze, feathers, 1921, #1668, 6.5"l, mint 150-250
June 6, 1998 Sold for $150

1453. Rookwood vase, matt glaze, geometric design, 1901, #95Z, 4"w, mint 300-400
June 6, 1998 Sold for $500

1454. Rookwood bowl, matt glaze, mushrooms, W. Hentschel, 1913, #956, 5.5"dia., mint 500-700
June 6, 1998 Sold for $700

1455. Rookwood vase, matt glaze, flowers, C.S. Todd, 1919, #2103, 5.5"h, mint 550-750
June 6, 1998 Sold for $700

1456. Rookwood plaque, matt glaze, rook, S. Toohey, 1904, 5"h x 9"w, mint 3500-5500
June 6, 1998 Sold for $7000

1457. Rookwood vase, iris glaze, irises, C. Schmidt, 1902, #907C, 14"h, line 5000-7500
June 6, 1998 Sold for $7500

1458. Rookwood vase, i-glaze, geometric design, L. Epply, 1930, #2917E, 6"h, mint 400-600
June 6, 1998 Sold for $600

1459. Rookwood vase, hi-glaze, flowers, J. Harris, 1930, #2587D, 5.5"h, mint 450-650
June 6, 1998 Sold for $600

1460. Rookwood covered jar, Black Opal glaze, floral design, S. Sax, 1923, #2249, 4.5"h, mint 1000-1500
June 6, 1998 Sold for $2000

1461. Rookwood bowl, i-glaze, roses and star, W.E. Hentschel, 1920, 2239, 6.5"w, mint 400-600
June 6, 1998 Sold for $450

1462. Rookwood vase, Black Opal glaze, floral, L. Epply, 1926, #2933, 12"h, mint 3500-4500
June 6, 1998 Sold for $2300

1463. Rookwood vase, hi-glaze, flowers, 1946, #6133F, painted #360A, 4.5"h, mint 400-600
June 6, 1998 Sold for $250

1464. Rookwood vase, hi-glaze, flowers, M.H. McDonald, 1942, 7.5"h, mint 500-700
June 6, 1998 Sold for $500

1465. Rookwood plaque, vellum, snow scene, S. Sax, 1919, 9" x 11", mint 5000-7000
June 6, 1998 Sold for $5500

1466. Rookwood vase, cameo glaze, three girls, H.E. Wilcox, 1891, #484D, 9"dia. x 7"h, mint 5500-7500
June 6, 1998 Sold for $2100

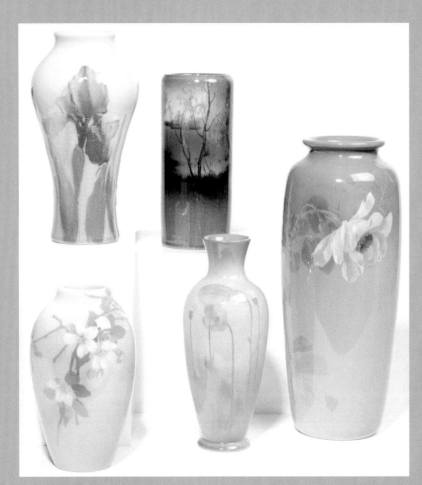

1467. Rookwood vase, iris glaze, carved irises, M. Daly, 1900, #909C, 9.5"h, mint 2000-3000
June 6, 1998 Sold for $1900

1468. Rookwood vase, iris glaze, flowers, L. Asbury, 1907, #900C, 8"h, insignificant line 700-900
June 6, 1998 Sold for $750

1469. Rookwood vase, iris glaze, landscape, Shirayamadani, 1906, #952D, 8.5"h, mint 2000-3000
June 6, 1998 Sold for $1600

1470. Rookwood vase, iris glaze, poppies, Shirayamadani, 1896, #562, 9.5"h, restoration 1000-1500
June 6, 1998 Sold for $750

1471. Rookwood vase, iris glaze, a rose, A.R. Valentien, 1902, #904B, 13.5"h, mint 2750-3750
June 6, 1998 Sold for $1600

1472. Rookwood pitcher, cameo glaze, wild roses, A.M. Valentien, 1889, #13, 6"h, mint 700-900
June 6, 1998 Sold for $450

1473. Rookwood jug, Limoges style, birds, 1882, unknown artist signature, 5"h, mint 300-400
June 6, 1998 Sold for $270

1474. Rookwood handled vessel, dull finish glaze, birds, 1885, M. Daly, #101A, 11"h, mint 900-1200
June 6, 1998 Sold for $750

1475. Rookwood chalice, early standard glaze, gargoyles, 1888, #350, 8"h, restoration 700-900
June 6, 1998 Sold for $550

1476. Rookwood vase, attribution, Limoges style, butterfly, M. Daly, 8"h, mint 1000-1500
June 6, 1998 Sold for $650

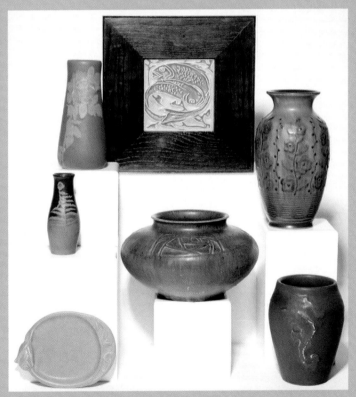

1477. Rookwood tray, matt glaze, rose, Shirayamadani, 1912, #1640, 6.5"l, mint 250-350
June 6, 1998 Sold for $350

1478. Rookwood vase, matt glaze, fern fronds, H. Wilcox, 1904, #37FZ, 5"h, mint 800-1100
June 6, 1998 Sold for $1200

1479. Rookwood vase, matt glaze, rose, O.G. Reed, 1907, #950E, 7"h, mint 1500-2000
June 6, 1998 Sold for $1900

1480. Rookwood tile, matt glaze, molded fish, 1919, #1946, 5"sq., mint 400-600
June 6, 1998 Sold for $700

1481. Rookwood vase, matt glaze, floral design, W.E. Hentschel, 1913, #494A, 9"dia., mint 1000-1500
June 6, 1998 Sold for $1300

1482. Rookwood vase, matt glaze, flowers, W.E. Hentschel, 1926, #704, 9"h, mint 900-1200
June 6, 1998 Sold for $800

1483. Rookwood vase, matt glaze, carved sea horses, S. Toohey, 1905, #942C, 6.5"h, mint 800-1100
June 6, 1998 Sold for $900

1484. Rookwood vase, standard glaze, portrait, S. Laurence, 1897, #732B, 10.5"h, mint 1200-1700
June 6, 1998 Sold for $850

1485. Rookwood handled vessel, standard glaze, portrait, G. Young, 1899, #656, 9"h, mint 3000-4000
June 6, 1998 Sold for $2300

1486. Rookwood vase, standard glaze, portrait, silver rim, M. Daly, 1896, #656C, 6"h, restored 600-800
June 6, 1998 Sold for $550

1487. Rookwood vase, standard glaze, portrait, S. Laurence, 1899, #568C, 7.5"h, mint 800-1100
June 6, 1998 Sold for $800

1488. Rookwood jug, standard glaze, portrait, H. Wilcox, 1896, #747C, 6"h, mint 600-800
June 6, 1998 Sold for $500

1489. Rookwood vase, matt glaze, stylized flowers, W. Rehm, 1928, #764C, 5"h, mint 800-1100
June 6, 1998 Sold for $1200

1490. Rookwood vase, crystalline matt glaze, deer and flowers, 1937, #6053, 7.5"h, mint 300-400
June 6, 1998 Sold for $400

1491. Rookwood tile, matt glaze, Griffin, 1913, #1203, 6"sq., mint 300-400
June 6, 1998 Sold for $550

1492. Rookwood vase, crystalline matt glaze, molded fish, 1931, #6215, 7"h, mint 250-350
June 6, 1998 Sold for $450

1493. Rookwood vase, matt glaze, geometric design, W. Rehm, 1930, #6195E, 5.5"h, mint 450-650
June 6, 1998 Sold for $600

1494. Rookwood vase, matt glaze, hollyhocks, Shiraya-madani, 1940, 12"h, mint 3000-4000
June 6, 1998 Sold for $3000

1495. Rookwood vase, matt glaze, floral decoration, W.E. Hentschel, 1921, #2038, 5.5"w x 4"h, mint 600-800
June 6, 1998 Sold for $600

148

1496. Rookwood vase, vellum, landscape, S.E. Coyne, 1914, #2067, 8"h, mint 1200-1700
June 5, 1999 Sold for $1500

1497. Rookwood plaque, vellum, landscape, E. Diers, 1921, 8"w x 6"h, mint 3000-4000
June 5, 1999 Sold for $3750

1498. Rookwood vase, vellum glaze, landscape, E.F. McDermott, 1916, #1358E, 7.5"h, mint 1200-1700
June 5, 1999 Sold for $1000

1499. Rookwood vase, standard glaze, floral decoration, A.R. Valentien, 1885, #219, 10.5"h, mint 1000-1500
June 6, 1998 Sold for $1400

1500. Rookwood vase, standard glaze, wild roses, K. Shiraya-madani, 1888, #420, 9"h, mint 1700-2700
June 6, 1998 Sold for $1800

1501. Rookwood vase, aventurine glaze, molded rooks, 1924, #2705, 7"h, mint 700-900
June 6, 1998 Sold for $700

1502. Rookwood vase, vellum, harbor scene, C. Schmidt, 1924, #1664D, 11"h, mint 5000-7000
June 6, 1998 Sold for $6000

1503. Rookwood vase, vellum, harbor scene, C. Schmidt, 1921, #900C, 8.5"h, mint 2500-3500
June 6, 1998 Sold for $1300

1504. Rookwood vase, vellum, Venetian scene, C. Schmidt, 1922, #834, 6.5"h, mint 2500-3500
June 6, 1998 Sold for $3500

1505. Rookwood vase, vellum, landscape, E. Diers, 1922, #1873, 6"h, mint 1000-1500
June 5, 1999 Sold for $1600

1506. Rookwood plaque, vellum, landscape, E.F. McDermott, 1918, 9.5" x 5.5"h, mint 3000-4000
June 5, 1999 Sold for $3500

1507. Rookwood vase, vellum, landscape, L. Asbury, 1912, #1871, 6.5"h, mint 800-1100
June 5, 1999 Sold for $1200

1508. Rookwood vase, French Red glaze, grapes, H. Wilcox, 1924, #1918, 9"h, mint 3500-5500
June 6, 1998 Sold for $3750

1509. Rookwood vase, French Red glaze, grapes, H. Wilcox, 1924, #2721, 6"h, mint 1200-1700
June 6, 1998 Sold for $2100

1510. Rookwood vase, hi-glaze, stylized flowers, S. Sax, 1923, #1110, 5.5"w, mint 1000-1500
June 6, 1998 Sold for $1000

1511. Rookwood vase, sea green glaze, thistles, R. Fechheimer, 1901, #589F, 7.5"h, mint 3500-5500
June 6, 1998 Sold for $3000

1512. Rookwood vase, sea green glaze, serpent, M. Daly, 1895, #184 and #765, 5.5"h, mint 1500-2500
June 6, 1998 Sold for $3250

1513. Rookwood vase, sea green glaze, frogs, A.R. Valentien, 1896, #786D, 8"h, lines 2500-3500
June 6, 1998 Sold for $1600

1514. Rookwood bowl, matt glaze, floral design, C.S. Todd, 1919, #957C, 8"dia., mint 550-750
June 6, 1998 Sold for $550

1515. Rookwood vase, matt glaze, floral design, L. Abel, 1920, #419, 8.5"h, mint 600-800
June 6, 1998 Sold for $450

1516. Rookwood vase, matt glaze, floral design, E.N. Lincoln, 1919, #800A, 14.5"h, mint 1700-2700
June 6, 1998 Sold for $2000

1517. Rookwood plaque, matt glaze, gentleman in overcoat, 6"sq., mint 700-900
June 6, 1998 Sold for $850

1518. Rookwood vase, matt glaze, grapes, S.E. Coyne, 1929, #900C, 8.5"h, mint 800-1100
June 6, 1998 Sold for $1100

1519. Rookwood vase, matt glaze, flowers, S. Coyne, 1928, #954, 5"h, mint 350-550
June 6, 1998 Sold for $500

1520. Rookwood vase, standard glaze, flowers, M. Nourse, 1902, #905C, 10"h, mint 700-900
June 6, 1998 Sold for $900

1521. Rookwood vase, matt glaze, feather, 1927, #1902, 5.5"h, mint 200-300
June 6, 1998 Sold for $210

1522. Rookwood vase, unusual hi-glaze, 1930, #5204F, 4.5"h, minor scratches, mint 150-250
June 6, 1998 Sold for $140

1523. Rookwood vase, matt glaze, feather, 1916, #1904, 6"h, mint 200-300
June 6, 1998 Sold for $150

1524. Rookwood vase, standard glaze, leaves, S. Laurence, 1902, #925B, 12.5"h, drilled hole 450-650
June 6, 1998 Sold for $550

1525. Rookwood vase, hi-glaze, 1921, #2545C, 11"h, mint 300-400
June 6, 1998 Sold for $550

1526. Rookwood Turkish water jug, Limoges style, butterflies, M. Daly, 1886, #41, 9.5"h, mint 1200-1700
June 6, 1998 Sold for $1100

1527. Rookwood vase, standard glaze, wild rose, E. Diers, 1901, #883F, 4.5"h, mint 350-550
June 6, 1998 Sold for $425

1528. Rookwood vase, matt glaze, flowers, 1910, W.E. Hentschel, #1348, 6"w, mint 450-650
June 6, 1998 Sold for $550

1529. Rookwood vase, matt glaze, butterflies, L. Abel, 1920, #1097C, 10"h, mint 1200-1700
June 6, 1998 Sold for $800

1530. Rookwood plaque, matt glaze, Dutch woman, 6"sq., mint 700-900
June 6, 1998 Sold for $850

1531. Rookwood vase, matt glaze, floral design, W. Rehm, 1928, #2963, 7.5"h, mint 350-550
June 6, 1998 Sold for $325

1532. Rookwood vase, matt glaze, leaf and flower, K. Shirayamadani, 1927, #2997, 13.5"h, mint 800-1100
June 6, 1998 Sold for $950

1533. Rookwood vase, matt glaze, flowers, 1927, K. Jones, #2745, 9.5"h, mint 800-1100
June 6, 1998 Sold for $800

1534. Rookwood vase, matt glaze, flowers, E.N. Lincoln, 1923, #1865, 7.5"h, mint 800-1100
June 6, 1998 Sold for $900

1535. Rookwood covered box, matt glaze, five-sided form, 1920, #2009, 5"dia., mint 200-300
June 6, 1998 Sold for $300

1536. Rookwood vase, standard glaze, cherries, E.T. Hurley, 1900, #830F, 4.5"h, mint 400-600
June 6, 1998 Sold for $375

1537. Rookwood handled vessel, dull finish, flowers and leaves, H. Wenderoth, 1882, 12.5"h, mint 600-800
June 6, 1998 Sold for $500

1538. Rookwood pilgrim flask, Limoges style, butterfly, 1882, 6.5"h, minor glaze loss 450-650
June 6, 1998 Sold for $375

1539. Rookwood vase, standard glaze, violets, I. Bishop, 1905, #241C, 5.5"h, mint 350-550
June 6, 1998 Sold for $375

1540. Rookwood jug, standard glaze, corn, S.E. Coyne, 1899, #674, 7"h, slip crawling and heavy craze line 250-350
June 6, 1998 Sold for $200

1541. Rookwood vase, hi-glaze, hand thrown form, R. Menzel, 1959, 6.5"h, mint 250-350
June 6, 1998 Sold for $350

1542. Rookwood covered box, standard glaze, flowers, A.M. Bookprinter, #44A, 6.5"l, minor chips 400-600
June 6, 1998 Sold for $210

1543. Rookwood tray, matt glaze, molded bat, 1922, #994, 5.5"w, mint 250-350
June 6, 1998 Sold for $425

1544. Rookwood vase, standard glaze, flowers, L. Fry, 1886, #30B, 11.5"h, mint 1200-1700
June 6, 1998 Sold for $1900

1545. Rookwood cup/saucer, cherry blossom, 1886, A. Bookprinter, #208, 5"dia. and 3"h, mint 250-350
June 6, 1998 Sold for $240

1546. Rookwood cup/saucer, cherry blossoms, A. Bookprinter, 1886 #208, 5"dia. and 3"h, mint 250-350
June 6, 1998 Sold for $250

1547. Rookwood vase, matt glaze, dragonflies, 1924, #2704, 7"h, mint 300-400
June 6, 1998 Sold for $400

1548. Rookwood pitcher, standard glaze, chestnuts, A. Van Briggle, 1888, #251, 7"h, mint 500-750
June 6, 1998 Sold for $800

1549. Rookwood vase, standard glaze, roses, K. Matchette, 1891, #584C, 5.5"h, mint 400-600
June 6, 1998 Sold for $400

1550. Rookwood covered urn, matt glaze, vines, W.E. Hentschel, 1915, #1708, 7"h, mint 1200-1700
June 6, 1998 Sold for $2200

1551. Rookwood vase, matt glaze, vertical leaves, W.E. Hentschel, 1910, #1652D, 9.5"h, mint 1000-1500
June 6, 1998 Sold for $1100

1552. Rookwood plaque, matt glaze, landscape, 1904, #1226, 12"sq., heavy craze line 1500-2500
June 6, 1998 Sold for $2000

1553. Rookwood vase, matt glaze, lizard, 1908, #952F, 6"h, mint 700-900
June 6, 1998 Sold for $1200

1554. Rookwood vase, matt glaze, Arts & Crafts design, 1906, #907F, 7"h, mint 450-650
June 6, 1998 Sold for $900

1555. Rookwood vase, matt glaze, organic form, W.E. Hentschel, 1915, #339B, 14.5"h, mint 1700-2700
June 6, 1998 Sold for $1800

1556. Rookwood vase, matt glaze, flowers and swags, C.S. Todd, 1918, #534D, 7"h, mint 500-750
June 6, 1998 Sold for $700

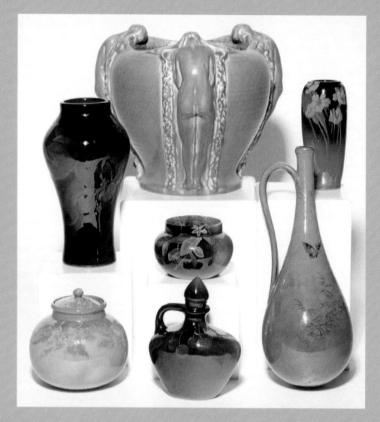

1557. Rookwood covered vessel, standard glaze, roses, A.M. Valentien, 1889, #282D, 5"h, mint 700-900
June 6, 1998 Sold for $800

1558. Rookwood vase, standard glaze, tulips, E.T. Hurley, 1902, #909C, 9"h, minor flake 400-600
June 6, 1998 Sold for $400

1559. Rookwood jardiniere, matt glaze, nudes, 1920, E.B. Haswell, #2280, 11"w, minor chips 1000-1500
June 6, 1998 Sold for $1900

1560. Rookwood covered jar, standard glaze, flowers, C.J. Dibowski, 1892, #622C, 4"dia., mint 500-700
June 6, 1998 Sold for $600

1561. Rookwood jug, original stopper, standard glaze, cherries, I. Bishop, 1901, #706, 6"h, mint 500-750
June 6, 1998 Sold for $475

1562. Rookwood gourd, limoges style, butterfly, A.R. Valentien, 1884, #52, 12"l, mint 900-1200
June 6, 1998 Sold for $700

1563. Rookwood vase, standard glaze, flowers, E. Noonan, 1905, #951F, 6"h, minor flakes 250-350
June 6, 1998 Sold for $260

1564. Rookwood vase, iris glaze, geese, L. Asbury, 1909, #604D, 7"h, harmless line to top 900-1200
June 6, 1998 Sold for $850

1565. Rookwood vase, iris glaze, irises, S. Sax, 1902, #932D, 9"h, mint 2200-3200
June 6, 1998 Sold for $1600

1566. Rookwood plaque, matt glaze, Seagull, 1905, in an Arts & Crafts oak frame, 6" x 8", mint 700-900
June 6, 1998 Sold for $1600

1567. Rookwood vase, vellum, flowers, E. Diers, 1927, #927E, 7.5"h, mint 2200-3200
June 6, 1998 Sold for $1100

1568. Rookwood vase, vellum, narcissus, E.T. Hurley, 1928, #913D, 8"h, mint 2200-3200
June 6, 1998 Sold for $1400

1569. Rookwood vase, hi-glaze, impressionistic design, E.T. Hurley, 1924, #2548, 8.5"h, mint 700-900
June 6, 1998 Sold for $800

1570. Rookwood vase, hi-glaze, birds, L. Epply, 1919, 9.5"h, restored 1000-1500
June 6, 1998 Sold for $1100

1571. Rookwood bowl and flower frog, hi-glaze, floral, L. Epply, 1927, #2268B, 13"dia., mint 800-1100
June 6, 1998 Sold for $900

1572. Rookwood vase, hi-glaze, pansies, E.T. Hurley, 1946, #6199F, 4"h, mint 400-600
June 6, 1998 Sold for $500

1573. Rookwood vase, hi-glaze, flowers, W. Hentschel, 1924, #2785, 13"h, mint 1200-1700
June 6, 1998 Sold for $1700

1574. Rookwood vase, hi-glaze, cherry blossoms, 1919, C.J. McLaughlin, #2190, 6"h, mint 550-750
June 6, 1998 Sold for $700

1575. Kenton Hills vase, hi-glaze, striped design, W.E. Hentschel, #105, 4"h, mint 250-350
June 6, 1998 Sold for $375

1576. Rookwood vase, hi-glaze, leaves, R. Menzel, 1942, #6737, 5"h, mint 550-750
June 6, 1998 Sold for $550

1577. Rookwood vase, matt and semigloss glazes, leaves, W.E. Hentschel, 1931, #6206F, 5"h, mint 700-900
June 6, 1998 Sold for $950

1578. Kenton Hills ashtray, hi-glaze, horse, #182, D. Seyler, 6"l, mint 150-250
June 6, 1998 Sold for $110

1579. Rookwood vase, hi-glaze, nude in panel, W. Rehm, 1940s, #6292C, 7.5"h, mint 550-750
June 6, 1998 Sold for $300

1580. Rookwood vase, hi-glaze, fish and birds, J. Jensen, 1944, #6204C, 7.5"h, mint 1200-1700
June 6, 1998 Sold for $2200

1581. Rookwood vase, hi-glaze, geometric design, L. Holtkamp, 1952, #6660F, 5"dia., mint 450-650
June 6, 1998 Sold for $450

1582. Kenton Hills vase, hi-glaze, gazelles, W.E. Hentschel, #134, 6.5"h, mint 300-400
June 6, 1998 Sold for $400

1583. Rookwood vase, hi-glaze, flowers, L. Furukawa, 1946, #6199F, 4"h, mint 450-650
June 6, 1998 Sold for $400

1584. Rookwood vase, hi-glaze, berries, S. Sax, 1921, #808, 8"h, mint 800-1100
June 6, 1998 Sold for $750

1585. Rookwood vase, hi-glaze, tulips, J. Jensen, 1951, #S2136, 13.5"h, original hole, mint 800-1100
June 6, 1998 Sold for $550

1586. Rookwood bowl, hi-glaze, bouquets, L. Epply, 1925, #2725, 8"w x 3"h, mint 400-600
June 6, 1998 Sold for $550

1587. Rookwood vase, hi-glaze, pansies, Hurley, 1946, #6199F, 4"h, mint 400-600
June 6, 1998 Sold for $475

1588. Rookwood vase, hi-glaze, lettuce leaves, 1946, artist unknown, #6818, 6.5"h, mint 250-350
June 6, 1998 Sold for $150

1589. Rookwood vase, hi-glaze, flowers, W.E. Hentschel, 1922, #2078, 5"h, mint 400-600
June 6, 1998 Sold for $375

1590. Rookwood vase, hi-glaze, landscape, M.H. McDonald, 1935, #892C, 9"h, mint 1500-2500
June 6, 1998 Sold for $950

1591. Rookwood vase, hi-glaze, wild roses, H. Wilcox, 1921, #230S, 9.5"h, mint 2000-2500
June 6, 1998 Sold for $1900

1592. Rookwood vase, hi-glaze, berries, Shirayamadani, 1926, #654D, 4.5"h, mint 1200-1700
June 6, 1998 Sold for $1400

1593. Rookwood tea set, three pieces, hi-glaze, flowers, S. Sax, 1910, #S1844, teapot 8"h, mint 1200-1700
June 6, 1998 Sold for $1000

1594. Rookwood vase, hi-glaze, flowers, W. Hentschel, 1922, #935C, 9.5"h, mint 1500-2000
June 6, 1998 Sold for $1200

1595. Rookwood urn, hi-glaze, floral design, A. Conant, 1921, #2448, 14.5"h, line 2000-3000
June 6, 1998 Sold for $6000

1596. Rookwood vase, iris glaze, clover, C. Lindeman, 1907, #917E, 5.5"h, hairline 400-600 June 5, 1999 Sold for $350

1597. Rookwood vase, iris glaze, grape design, L. Asbury, 1916, 10"h, restored 1200-1700 June 5, 1999 Sold for $2500

1598. Rookwood vase, iris glaze, dogwood, L. Asbury, 1905, #905D, 8"h, mint 1200-1700 June 5, 1999 Sold for $1600

1599. Rookwood vase, drip hi-glaze, 1932, #6316, 3.75"h, mint 350-450 June 5, 1999 Sold for $375

1600. Rookwood vase, crystalline glaze, women and stars, J.D. Wareham, 1951, #6539, 9"h, mint 450-650 June 5, 1999 Sold for $260

1601. Rookwood vase, drip hi-glaze, 1933, #6369, 5"h, mint 350-450 June 5, 1999 Sold for $170

1602. Rookwood vase, drip hi-glaze, 1950, #6644E, 6.75"h, mint 350-450 June 5, 1999 Sold for $325

1603. Rookwood vase, goldstone glaze, geese, Shiraya-madani, 1939, #6550, 6.5"h, mint 550-750 June 5, 1999 Sold for $650

1604. Rookwood vase, coromandel glaze, 1932, #6308C, 7"h, mint 550-750 June 5, 1999 Sold for $375

1605. Rookwood vase, drip hi-glaze, probably 1932, 3"h, mint 200-300 June 5, 1999 Sold for $250

1606. Rookwood vase, drip hi-glaze, 1932, #6320, 8.5"h, mint 650-750 June 5, 1999 Sold for $250

1607. Rookwood vase, drip glaze, 1932, #6503, #H2052, 4.25"h, mint 200-300 June 5, 1999 Sold for $150

1608. Rookwood vase, iris glaze, violets, F. Rothenbusch, 1902, #917D, 7"h, mint 900-1200
June 5, 1999 Sold for $1500

1609. Rookwood vase, iris glaze, irises, C. Schmidt, 1903, #939A, 13"h, restoration 2000-3000
June 5, 1999 Sold for $1500

1610. Rookwood vase, iris glaze, grapes, L. Asbury, 1907, #917C, 7.5"h, mint 1200-1700
June 5, 1999 Sold for $1600

1611. Rookwood vase, coromandel glaze, 1932, #6308C, 7"h, minute flakes to base 450-650
June 5, 1999 Sold for $300

1612. Rookwood bowl, hi-glaze drip, 1932, #6313, 8"dia., mint 300-400
June 5, 1999 Sold for $150

1613. Rookwood vase, hi-glaze drip, 1932, #6303, 4"h, mint 300-400
June 5, 1999 Sold for $300

1614. Rookwood vases, pair, coromandel glaze, tulips, 1940, #1711, 10"h, drilled, one with line 450-650
June 5, 1999 Sold for $140

1615. Rookwood vase, drip glaze, 1932, #6314, 7"h, mint 350-450
June 5, 1999 Sold for $230

1616. Rookwood vase, coromandel glaze, 1932, #6317F, 4"h, mint 300-400
June 5, 1999 Sold for $375

1617. Rookwood vase, goldstone glaze, 1930, #6142, 4.5"h, mint 450-650
June 5, 1999 Sold for $270

1618. Rookwood vase, drip glaze, 1932, #6317C, 7"h, mint 550-750
June 5, 1999 Sold for $450

1619. Rookwood vase, aventurine glaze, #H2052, 1936, #6503, 4.25"h, mint 250-350
June 5, 1999 Sold for $160

1620. Rookwood vase, matt glaze, iris, A.R. Valentien, 1901, #7BZ, 11"h, mint 10,000-15,000
June 5, 1999 Sold for $11,000

1621. Rookwood vase, Black Opal glaze, water lily design, H.E. Wilcox, 1926, #2984, 16"h, mint 5000-7000
June 5, 1999 Sold for $8000

1622. Rookwood vase, standard glaze, clover, C. Hickman, 1899, #748D, 6"h, mint 500-700
June 5, 1999 Sold for $350

1623. Rookwood vase, standard glaze, flowers and leaves, C. Steinle, 1900, #735D, 7.5"h, mint 350-450
June 5, 1999 Sold for $425

1624. Rookwood ewer, standard glaze, flowers, A.R. Valentien, 1886, #308, 19"h, mint 2000-3000
June 5, 1999 Sold for $1100

1625. Rookwood tray, standard glaze, mums, E.D. Foertmeyer, 1894, #591, 11"l, repaired 250-350
June 5, 1999 Sold for $250

1626. Rookwood ewer, standard glaze, wild roses, E.N. Lincoln, 1897, #495C, 5.5"w, glaze loss 200-300
June 5, 1999 Sold for $200

1627. Rookwood vase, standard glaze, wild rose, K. Matchette, 1892, #584C, 5.5"h, mint 450-650
June 5, 1999 Sold for $425

1628. Rookwood vase, vellum, landscape, S.E. Coyne, 1920, #1358C, 11"h, mint 3500-4500 June 5, 1999 Sold for $1000

1629. Rookwood vase, vellum, landscape, F. Rothenbusch, 1926, #2551, 14.5"h, mint 10,000-15,000 June 5, 1999 Sold for $9500

1630. Rookwood vase, standard glaze, tulips, M. Nourse, 1902, #856C, 13"h, glaze flaws 700-900 June 5, 1999 Sold for $550

1631. Rookwood ewer, standard glaze, flowers, S. Markland, 1892, #657D, 6.5"h, mint 400-600 June 5, 1999 Sold for $375

1632. Rookwood three-handled vessel, standard glaze, corn, M. Daly, 1893, 8"h, restored 450-650 June 5, 1999 Sold for $650

1633. Rookwood vase, standard glaze, portrait, S. Laurence, 1896, #798, 7"h, minute chip 800-1100 June 5, 1999 Sold for $650

1634. Rookwood ewer, standard glaze, floral design, J. Zettel, 1898, #715D, 7"h, mint 550-750 June 5, 1999 Sold for $425

1635. Rookwood vase, standard glaze, tulips, E.N. Lincoln, 1901, #903C, 8"h, mint 300-400 June 5, 1999 Sold for $375

1636. **Rookwood** vase, vellum, land-scape, E.F. McDermott, 1917, #939D, 8"h, mint 1500-2000
June 5, 1999 Sold for $900

1637. **Rookwood** vase, vellum, moun-tain scene, E. Diers, 1908, #1369D, 9"h, ground X, mint 1200-1700
June 5, 1999 Sold for $1400

1638. **Rookwood** vase, vellum, land-scape, E. Diers, 1921, #913E, 6.5"h, mint 1000-1500
June 5, 1999 Sold for $1100

1639. **Rookwood** blue ship dinnerware, vegetable dish, #M-24, 10.75"l, mint 200-300
June 5, 1999 Sold for $350

1640. **Rookwood** blue ship dinnerware, serving dish, #M-5, 13.5"l, mint 250-350
June 5, 1999 Sold for $300

1641. **Rookwood** blue ship dinnerware, platter, #M-3, 14", mint 250-350
June 5, 1999 Sold for $350

1642. **Rookwood** blue ship dinnerware, cups and saucers, 12 pieces, #M-1 and M-2, 2"h, mint 500-700
June 5, 1999 Sold for $650

1643. **Rookwood** blue ship dinnerware, teapot, creamer, sugar bowl, #M-15, #M-20 and #M-19, teapot 4.5"h, all mint 300-400
June 5, 1999 Sold for $375

1644. **Rookwood** blue ship dinnerware, broth/consommé cups, set of six, #M-27, 3"h, mint 500-700
June 5, 1999 Sold for $800

1645. **Rookwood** blue ship dinnerware, cups and saucers, 14 pieces, #M-9 and #M-10, 2.5"h, mint 550-700
June 5, 1999 Sold for $500

1646. **Rookwood** blue ship dinnerware, salad plates, set of 14, #M-6, 8"dia., minor wear, mint 600-800
June 5, 1999 Sold for $400

1647. **Rookwood** blue ship dinnerware, dinner plates, set of nine, #M-4, 10"dia., minor wear, mint 500-700
June 5, 1999 Sold for $700

1648. **Rookwood** blue ship dinnerware, cereal bowls, set of 13, #M-26, 6"dia., mint 600-800
June 5, 1999 Sold for $1000

1649. Rookwood vase, vellum, landscape, F. Rothenbusch, 1923, #356E, 6.5"h, mint 1500-2500
June 5, 1999 Sold for $2600

1650. Rookwood vase, vellum, landscape, C.J. McLaughlin, 1915, #925E, 7.5"h, mint 1500-2500
June 5, 1999 Sold for $4500

1651. Rookwood vase, vellum, landscape, E.T. Hurley, 1940, #6730, 5.5"h, mint 1500-2000
June 5, 1999 Sold for $2200

1652. Rookwood vase, matt glaze, hanging vegetation, A.B. Sprague, 1901, #4EZ, 6.5"h, mint 1200-1700
June 5, 1999 Sold for $1200

1653. Rookwood vase, matt glaze, birds, S. Toohey, 1915, #2204, 9.5"h, mint 800-1100
June 5, 1999 Sold for $900

1654. Rookwood vase, matt glaze, incised design, 1913, #918E, 6"h, mint 400-600
June 5, 1999 Sold for $550

1655. Rookwood tray, matt glaze, orchid, Valentien, 1904, #372AZ, 14.5"dia., minor chip repair 900-1200
June 5, 1999 Sold for $1800

1656. Rookwood handled vessel, matt glaze, Arts & Crafts design, A. Pons, 1907, #259D, 5"h, mint 500-700
June 5, 1999 Sold for $260

1657. Rookwood vase, matt glaze, geometric design, J.D. Wareham, 1910, #1805, 9.5"h, mint 700-900
June 5, 1999 Sold for $700

1658. Rookwood vase, butterfat glaze, flowers, M. Daly, 1900, #878, 14"h, restored 6500-8500
June 5, 1999 Sold for $3500

1659. Rookwood vase, butterfat glaze, flowers, 1927, L. Epply, #2581, 12"h, mint 3500-4500
June 5, 1999 Sold for $4500

1660. Rookwood vase, vellum, flowers, F. Rothenbusch, 1922, #357F, 6.5"h, crack 200-300
June 5, 1999 Sold for $210

1661. Rookwood vase, vellum, wisteria, E.T. Hurley, 1927, #2032E, 8"h, cracked 300-400
June 5, 1999 Sold for $425

1662. Rookwood vase, vellum, floral design, L. Asbury, 1923, #1326F, impressed P, 6"h, mint 700-900
June 5, 1999 Sold for $750

1663. Rookwood vase, matt glaze, rooks, 1920s, #2322, 7.5"h, mint 350-450
June 5, 1999 Sold for $650

1664. Rookwood vase, vellum glaze, morning glories, S. Sax, 1908, #1369D, 9"h, mint 1200-1700
June 5, 1999 Sold for $950

1665. Rookwood vase, matt glaze, floral, Shirayamadani, 1943, #6823, 8"h, glaze flaws, repaired 600-800
June 5, 1999 Sold for $600

1666. Rookwood vase, vellum glaze, floral design at top, M.H. McDonald, 1914, #551, 7"h, mint 350-450
June 5, 1999 Sold for $375

1667. Rookwood vase, vellum, wisteria, 1926, E.T. Hurley, #424, 14"h, mint 5500-7500
June 5, 1999 Sold for $7000

1668. Rookwood vase, vellum glaze, songbird, P. Conant, 1918, #2441, 14.5"h, mint 4000-6000
June 5, 1999 Sold for $3000

1669. Rookwood vase, matt glaze, berries, 1932, #6217, 4.5"h, mint 200-300
June 5, 1999 Sold for $325

1670. Rookwood vase, hi-glaze, geometric design, S. Sax, 1930, #962, 5.5"w, mint 1000-1500
June 5, 1999 Sold for $1400

1671. Rookwood vase, hi-glaze, flowers, Shirayamadani, 1944, #6869, 9"h, mint 2000-3000
June 5, 1999 Sold for $1800

1672. Rookwood vase, hi-glaze, bird, F. King, 1946, #922D, 7.5"h, mint 1700-2700
June 5, 1999 Sold for $1500

1673. Rookwood vase, hi-glaze, floral design, Shirayamadani, 1937, #6659F, 4.5"h, mint 1200-1700
June 5, 1999 Sold for $1100

1674. Rookwood covered vessel, hi-glaze, stylized grapes, A. Conant, 1919, #16, 7"w, mint 1500-2000
June 5, 1999 Sold for $4500

1675. Rookwood vase, mahogany glaze, carp, Shiraya-madani, 1899, #589E, 8.5"h, mint 3500-4500
June 5, 1999 Sold for $2800

1676. Rookwood vase, standard glaze, walnuts, M. Daly, 1888, #459A, 11"w x 11"h, mint 2500-3500
June 5, 1999 Sold for $4000

1677. Rookwood vase, standard glaze, pansies, C. Steinle, 1896, #8923, 4"w, mint 150-250
June 5, 1999 Sold for $350

1678. Rookwood vase, standard glaze, nasturtiums, A.D. Sehon, 1900, #733C, 7"h, mint 550-750
June 5, 1999 Sold for $475

1679. Rookwood vase, standard glaze, fruit, F. Rothenbusch, 1896, #381C, 7"h, minor scratches, mint 450-650
June 5, 1999 Sold for $425

1680. Rookwood vase, standard glaze, poppies, L. Asbury, 1903, #927D, 8"h, mint 800-1100
June 5, 1999 Sold for $1200

1681. Rookwood ewer, standard glaze, floral design, 1898, A.M. Valentien, #725C, 7.5"h, mint 500-700
June 5, 1999 Sold for $500

1682. Rookwood stein, standard glaze, embossed design, M. Nourse, 1897, #783, 7"h, restored 800-1100
June 5, 1999 Sold for $375

1683. Rookwood vase, standard glaze, clover, C. Lindeman, 1904, #923E, 7.5"h, mint 300-400
June 5, 1999 Sold for $325

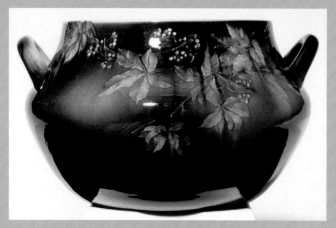

1684. Rookwood vase, standard glaze, berries, A.R. Valentien, 1889, #514, 16"w, mint 3500-5500
June 5, 1999 Sold for $4500

1685. Rookwood vessel, standard glaze, irises, silver overlay, Wilcox, 1893, #564B, 10.5"h, mint 6500-8500
June 5, 1999 Sold for $7000

1686. Rookwood vase, hi-glaze, flowers, M. Foglesong, 1946, #6432, 4"h, mint 250-350
June 5, 1999 Sold for $400

1687. Rookwood vase, hi-glaze, wheat, M.H. McDonald, 1936, 7.5"h, mint 550-750
June 5, 1999 Sold for $500

1688. Rookwood vase, hi-glaze, flowers, 1927, L. Epply, #2441, 13.5"h, mint 1000-1500
June 5, 1999 Sold for $800

1689. Rookwood vase, hi-glaze, floral decoration, L. Epply, 1929, #6111, 9"h, partial label, mint 800-1100
June 5, 1999 Sold for $600

1690. Rookwood vase, hi-glaze, wheat, M.H. McDonald, 1936, 7.5"h, mint 550-750
June 5, 1999 Sold for $400

1691. Rookwood vase, hi-glaze, flowers, M.H. McDonald, 1942, 7.5"h, minor glaze loss 400-600
June 5, 1999 Sold for $325

1692. Rookwood vase, vellum, landscape, F. Rothenbusch, 1909, #614B, 14"h, mint 4500-6500
June 5, 1999 Sold for $4000

1693. Rookwood vase, black iris glaze, crocus and stems, M. Daly, 1900, #S1614F, 4"w, mint 3500-4500
June 5, 1999 Sold for $4250

1694. Rookwood vase, matt glaze, molded tree, Shirayamadani, 1914, #1895, 7"h, mint 250-350
June 5, 1999 Sold for $350

1695. Rookwood vase, matt glaze, molded tulips, Shirayamadani, 1924, #1711, 10"h, mint 350-550
June 5, 1999 Sold for $550

1696. Rookwood tile, matt glaze, ship, 12"h, excellent condition 2500-3500
June 5, 1999 Sold for $2800

1697. Rookwood vase, matt glaze, rook, L. Asbury, 1923, #2154, 2.5"h, mint 200-250
June 5, 1999 Sold for $220

1698. Rookwood vase, matt glaze, floral design, 1900 but ca.1940s, #6893, 9"h, mint 350-450
June 5, 1999 Sold for $500

1699. Rookwood covered footed jar, matt glaze, Shirayamadani, 1910, #2004, 6"h, mint 350-450
June 5, 1999 Sold for $400

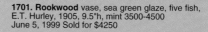

1700. Rookwood vase, iris glaze, geese, Shi-rayamadani, 1911, #907E, 9.5"h, line 4000-6000
June 5, 1999 Sold for $7000

1701. Rookwood vase, sea green glaze, five fish, E.T. Hurley, 1905, 9.5"h, mint 3500-4500
June 5, 1999 Sold for $4250

1702. Rookwood vase, matt glaze, rooks, five-sided form, 1925, #1795, 4.75"h, mint 300-400
June 5, 1999 Sold for $650

1703. Rookwood vase, matt glaze, geometric, 1905, #942B, 7.5"h, mint 450-650
June 5, 1999 Sold for $950

1704. Rookwood candleholder, matt glaze, English roses, S. Toohey, 1919, #1760, 8.5"l, repair 400-600
June 5, 1999 Sold for $800

1705. Rookwood vase, vellum, exotic bird, S. Sax, 1918, #1055B, 11"h, repaired 2500-3500
June 5, 1999 Sold for $1200

1706. Rookwood tile, matt glaze, ship, c.1905, 5.5"sq., mint 500-700
June 5, 1999 Sold for $475

1707. Rookwood tray, matt glaze, bird, 1906, #1210, 5"w, mint 400-600
June 5, 1999 Sold for $260

1708. Rookwood vase, matt glaze, trees, Shirayamadani, 1911, #1870, 7"h, mint 450-650
June 5, 1999 Sold for $550

1709. Rookwood vase, matt glaze, dragonfly, 1921, #1894, 6.5"h, mint 350-450
June 5, 1999 Sold for $400

1710. Rookwood plaque, matt glaze, landscape, 12"sq., excellent condition 3000-4000
June 3, 2000 Sold for $2600

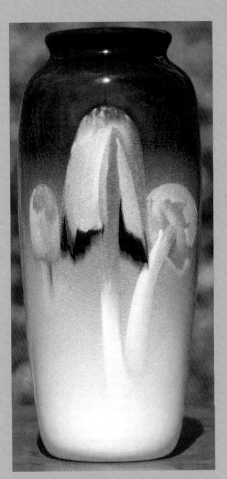

1711. Rookwood vase, iris glaze, mushrooms, 1902, C. Schmidt, #904D, 8"h, mint 3500-4500
June 3, 2000 Sold for $3250

1712. Rookwood vase, vellum, cyclamen, F. Rothenbusch, 1908, #614E, 8.5"h, mint 1000-1500
June 3, 2000 Sold for $1300

1713. Rookwood vase, vellum, cherry blossoms, E.T. Hurley, 1925, #389, 3.5"h, mint 600-800
June 3, 2000 Sold for $500

1714. Rookwood vase, vellum, flowers, M.H. McDonald, 1920, #913E, 6.5"h, mint 900-1200
June 3, 2000 Sold for $1100

1715. Rookwood vase, vellum, cherry blossom, E.T. Hurley, 1925, #1110, 4"h, mint 700-900
June 3, 2000 Sold for $850

1716. Rookwood vase, vellum, cherry blossoms, L. Epply, 1908, #949D, 9"h, mint 1000-1500
June 3, 2000 Sold for $1400

1717. Rookwood plaque, vellum, landscape, 1917, L. Epply, 11" x 9", mint 6000-8000
June 3, 2000 Sold for $6500

1718. Rookwood vase, iris glaze, poppies, C. Schmidt, 1908, #1358B, 13"h, mint 5500-7500
June 3, 2000 Sold for $4750

1719. Rookwood vase, vellum, dogwood, L. Asbury, 1904, #911E, 4.5"h, factory flaw on rim 700-900
June 3, 2000 Sold for $550

1720. Rookwood vase, vellum, daisies, M.H. McDonald, 1913, #1655F, 6.5"h, mint 900-1200
June 3, 2000 Sold for $950

1721. Rookwood covered vessel, vellum, flowers, C.J. McLaughlin, 1915, #1708, 7"h, mint 1200-1700
June 3, 2000 Sold for $800

1722. Rookwood vase, vellum, poppy, S. Sax, 1904, #30F, 6"h, mint 1000-1500
June 3, 2000 Sold for $1100

1723. Rookwood vase, vellum, stylized flowers and leaves, C. Klinger, 1917, #919D, 5"h, hairline 800-1100
June 3, 2000 Sold for $650

1725. Rookwood vase, standard glaze, portrait, 1901, A. Sehon, #902C, 9"h, mint 7000-9000
June 3, 2000 Sold for $7000

1724. Rookwood vase, standard glaze, portrait, 1900, M. Daly, #S1577, 20"h, mint 10,000-15,000
June 3, 2000 Sold for $12,000

1726. Rookwood vase, standard glaze, cherries, S.E. Coyne, 1900, #459C, 7.25"h, mint 550-750
June 3, 2000 Sold for $500

1727. Rookwood pitcher, standard glaze, violets, C.A. Baker, 1902, #547, 3.5"h, mint 200-300
June 3, 2000 Sold for $350

1728. Rookwood vase, standard glaze, grapes, L. Asbury, 1902, #905C, 10"h, mint 800-1100
June 3, 2000 Sold for $550

1729. Rookwood handled vessel, standard glaze, corn, S.E. Coyne, 1896, #76I, 4.75"h, scratches 350-450
June 3, 2000 Sold for $300

1730. Rookwood vase, standard glaze, narcissus, E.N. Lincoln, 1903, #900, 6.75"h, mint 450-650
June 3, 2000 Sold for $500

1731. Rookwood vase, standard glaze, geese in flight, M. Daly, 1898, #664B, 10.5"h, mint 5000-7000
June 3, 2000 Sold for $3750

1732. Rookwood lamp, matt glaze, geometric, Tiffany Studios shade, 12"dia., 1910, #131, overall height 15", excellent original condition 10,000-15,000
June 3, 2000 Sold for $12,000

1733. Rookwood vase, standard glaze, roses, M. Mitchell, 1902, #625, 6"h, mint 350-550
June 3, 2000 Sold for $475

1734. Rookwood vase, standard glaze, cherry blossoms, 1906, E. Noonan, #73C, 6.5"h, mint 450-650
June 3, 2000 Sold for $450

1735. Rookwood handled vessel, standard glaze, water lilies, A. Sprague, 1898, #495, 10"h, mint 900-1200
June 3, 2000 Sold for $900

1736. Rookwood vase, standard glaze, maple leaves, 1900, I. Bishop, #568E, 4.5"h, mint 350-550
June 3, 2000 Sold for $500

1737. Rookwood vase, standard glaze, clover, A. Marie Valentien, 1892, #517D, 5.5"h, mint 350-550
June 3, 2000 Sold for $550

1740. Rookwood vase, vellum, landscape, E.T. Hurley, 1927, #545C, 10"h, mint 2500-3500 June 3, 2000 Sold for $3750

1739. Rookwood vase, vellum, landscape, Rothenbusch, 1921, #907C, 15"h, mint 4000-6000 June 3, 2000 Sold for $4250

1738. Rookwood vase, vellum, snow scene, McDermott, 1917, #939D, 8"h, mint 1700-2200 June 3, 2000 Sold for $1600

1741. Rookwood vase, standard glaze, pansies, M. Perkins, 1893, #352, 6.5"h, mint 500-700 June 3, 2000 Sold for $500

1742. Rookwood handled vessel, standard glaze, daisies, Shirayamadani, 1887, #328, 6"h, mint 650-850 June 3, 2000 Sold for $1100

1743. Rookwood vase, standard glaze, jonquils, M. Nourse, 1897, #568B, 9"h, mint 800-1200 June 3, 2000 Sold for $800

1744. Rookwood chamberstick, standard glaze, berries, L. Lindeman, 1901, #635, 3"h, mint 250-450 June 3, 2000 Sold for $350

1745. Rookwood vase, standard glaze, narcissus, E.N. Lincoln, 1905, #941E, 6.5"h, flaw 450-650 June 3, 2000 Sold for $550

1746. **Rookwood** vase, vellum, landscape,
E.T. Hurley, 1942, #6823, 8"h,
mint 1500-2000
June 3, 2000 Sold for $1800

1747. **Rookwood** vase, vellum, landscape,
L. Asbury, 1913, #1121, 12"h,
mint 3500-4500
June 3, 2000 Sold for $2000

1748. **Rookwood** vase, vellum, landscape,
C.J. McLaughlin, 1914, #614, 9"h,
restoration 1500-2000
June 3, 2000 Sold for $1200

1749. **Rookwood** vase, standard glaze, flowers, E.N.
Lincoln, 1903, #937, 9"h, mint 800-1000
June 3, 2000 Sold for $800

1750. **Rookwood** vase, standard glaze, zephyr lilies, H.
Wilcox, 1886, #76G, 2.75"h, mint 350-450
June 3, 2000 Sold for $325

1751. **Rookwood** vase, standard glaze, blossoms, A.R.
Valentien, 1891, #610C, 10"h, mint 1500-2000
June 3, 2000 Sold for $2100

1752. **Rookwood** vase, standard glaze, Ginko, E.N.
Lincoln, 1893, #949, 3.5"h, mint 550-750
June 3, 2000 Sold for $950

1753. **Rookwood** vase, standard glaze, tulips, L. Van
Briggle, 1904, #925E, 6.5"h, mint 550-750
June 3, 2000 Sold for $650

1754. Rookwood vase, Black Opal glaze, lilies, H.E. Wilcox, 1928, #2785, 13"h, mint 5500-7500
June 3, 2000 Sold for $7500

1755. Rookwood vase, Black Opal glaze, floral, S. Sax, 1933, #2918B, 11"h, mint 4000-6000
June 3, 2000 Sold for $4500

1756. Rookwood vase, matt glaze, tulips, Shirayamadani, 1932, #6306, 7"h, cracked 150-250
June 3, 2000 Sold for $375

1757. Rookwood vase, porcelain, lilies, 1946, #6431, 3.5"h, mint 250-350
June 3, 2000 Sold for $260

1758. Rookwood vase, porcelain, magnolia, L. Holtkamp, 1950, #2984A, 16"h, mint 1000-2000
June 3, 2000 Sold for $700

1759. Rookwood vase, porcelain, bell flowers and hearts, S. Sax, 1925, 6.5"h, crack 200-300
June 3, 2000 Sold for $400

1760. Rookwood vase, matt glaze, tulips, 1938, signature not visible, 11.5"h, crazing, mint 1000-1500
June 3, 2000 Sold for $1000

1761. Rookwood vase, porcelain, owls, Toohey, 1930, #614E, 8.5"h, mint 1500-2000
June 3, 2000 Sold for $2600

1762. Rookwood vase, porcelain, Macaw, Hurley, 1922, #1667, 11"h, mint 3500-4500
June 3, 2000 Sold for $3750

1763. Rookwood vase, porcelain, berries, 1945, #6375, 5.5"h, mint 250-350
June 3, 2000 Sold for $250

1764. Rookwood vase, tulips, aventurine glaze, Shiraya-madani, 1940, #1711, 10"h, mint 250-350
June 3, 2000 Sold for $350

1765. Rookwood tray, lily, matt glaze, A. Valentien, 1904, #705Z, 9.5"l, mint 450-650
June 3, 2000 Sold for $700

1766. Rookwood vase, porcelain, maple leaves, 1940, #S2163, 12"h, drilled hole 1200-1500
June 3, 2000 Sold for $475

1767. Rookwood vase, sea green glaze, fish, E.T. Hurley, 1903, 9"h, #901, cracked 500-700
June 3, 2000 Sold for $650

1768. Rookwood vase, matt glaze, flowers, O.G. Reed, 1906, #969E, 3.75"h, cracked 250-350
June 3, 2000 Sold for $240

1769. Rookwood plaque, matt glaze, geese, S. Toohey, 9" x 4.5"h, mint 2000-3000
June 3, 2000 Sold for $3250

1770. Rookwood vase, iris glaze, coreopsis, S. Sax, 1906,
#913C, 8.5"h, mint 3500-4500
June 3, 2000 Sold for $3500

1771. Rookwood vase, vellum, wisteria, E.
Diers, 1925, #2720, 6.5"h, mint 1200-1700
June 3, 2000 Sold for $2400

1772. Rookwood vase, vellum, narcissus,
E.T. Hurley, 1928, #913D, 8"h,
mint 2500-3500
June 3, 2000 Sold for $3250

1773. Rookwood vase, vellum, iris, S. Sax,
1904, #169F, 4.5" h, mint 1000-1500
June 3, 2000 Sold for $1300

1774. Rookwood vase, vellum, swans, C.
Schmidt, 1915, #907C, 14"h,
mint 15,000-25,000
June 3, 2000 Sold for $20,000

1775. Rookwood plaque, landscape, vellum, L. Epply, 1917, 11" x 9", mint 4000-6000
June 3, 2000 Sold for $6000

1776. Rookwood vase, vellum, landscape, S.E. Coyne, 1914, #950, 7.5"h,
mint 1200-1700
June 3, 2000 Sold for $1300

1777. Rookwood vase, vellum, ducks,
Shirayamadani, 1909, #1658D, 9.5"h,
restored 1500-2500
June 3, 2000 Sold for $2300

1778. Rookwood vase, vellum, landscape, S.E. Coyne, 1921, #30E, 9"h,
mint 2500-3500
June 3, 2000 Sold for $2300

1779. Rookwood vase, standard glaze, Native American, S. Laurence, 1900, #907D, 11"h, mint 7000-9000
June 3, 2000 Sold for $5500

1780. Rookwood Faience jardineres, pair, relief design, 17.5" x 13.5" minor roughness 1500-2500
June 3, 2000 Sold for $3250

1781. Rookwood vase, porcelain, flowers and leaves, W.E. Hentschel, 1914, #S1904, 11"h, mint 900-1200
June 3, 2000 Sold for $1200

1782. Rookwood vase, porcelain, wheat shocks, M.H. McDonald, 1936, 7.5"h, mint 800-1100
June 3, 2000 Sold for $950

1783. Rookwood vase, porcelain, magnolia, L. Holtkamp, 1948, #2984A, 16"h, mint 800-1200
June 3, 2000 Sold for $750

1784. Rookwood vase, porcelain, stylized flowers and leaves, W. Rehm, 1945, #2917E, 6.5"h, mint 600-800
June 3, 2000 Sold for $850

1785. Rookwood vase, porcelain, stylized flowers, W.E. Hentschel, 1922, #1667, 11"h, mint 1200-1700
June 3, 2000 Sold for $1800

1786. Rookwood vase, sea green glaze, leaves, S. Laurence, 1901, #904C, 12"h, mint 6000-8000
June 3, 2000 Sold for $6000

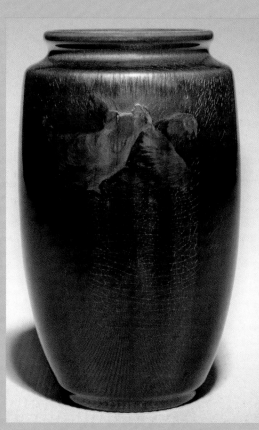

1787. Rookwood vase, Tiger Eye glaze, roosters, M. Daly, 1894, #734D, 7"h, mint 3000-4000
June 3, 2000 Sold for $2100

1788. Rookwood vase, Black Opal glaze, cherry blossoms, H.E. Wilcox, 1925, #1358E, 7"h, mint 1500-2000
June 3, 2000 Sold for $1800

1789. Rookwood vase, porcelain, floral design, A. Conant, 1919, #214E, 2.5"h, mint 500-700
June 3, 2000 Sold for $450

1790. Rookwood vase, Black Opal glaze, roses, H.E. Wilcox, 1924, #2789, 11"h, mint 200-300
June 3, 2000 Sold for $1500

1791. Rookwood vase, hi-glaze, floral design, H. Wilcox, 1898, 4.5"h, mint 700-900
June 3, 2000 Sold for $450

1792. Rookwood vase, porcelain, flowers, S. Sax, 1917, #2237, 5.5"h, repair to lip 700-900
June 3, 2000 Sold for $900

1793. Rookwood vase, matt glaze, thistles, K. Shirayamadani, 1904, #299AZ, 15"h, restored flaw at
lip 6500-8500
June 3, 2000 Sold for $7000

1794. Rookwood plaque, vellum, landscape, F. Rothenbusch, 1915, 7" x 9",
mint 3500-4500
June 3, 2000 Sold for $3750

1795. Rookwood handled vessel, Limoges style glaze,
beetle, A.R. Valentien, 1883, 10"h, mint 1500-2000
June 3, 2000 Sold for $1400

1796. Rookwood handled jug, dull finish glaze, flowers,
1883, H. Wenderoth, 5"h, incised initials, mint 300-400
June 3, 2000 Sold for $300

1797. Rookwood vase, dull smear glaze, goose, 1884, M.
Daly #162B, 11"h, minor flake at top rim 1200-1700
June 3, 2000 Sold for $1200

1798. Rookwood plate, Limoges style glaze, flowers and
leaves, 1887, #87, 6.5"l, mint 200-300
June 3, 2000 Sold for $220

1799. Rookwood vase, limoges style glaze, birds, M. Rettig, 1883, #90, 8"h, mint 900-1200
June 3, 2000 Sold for $850

1800. Rookwood vessel, hi-glaze, die impressed design,
1887, #262B, 10.5"h, mint 550-750
June 3, 2000 Sold for $325

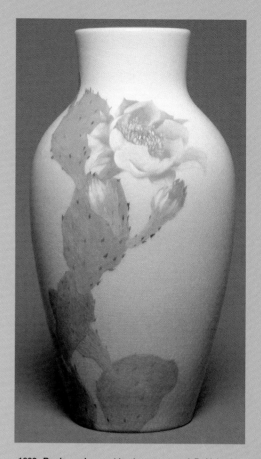

1801. Rookwood plaque, vellum, landscape, C. Schmidt, 1917, 5" x 8", mint 3000-4000
June 3, 2000 Sold for $3750

1802. Rookwood vase, iris glaze, cactus, A.R. Valentien, 1902, #926A, 13"h, mint 12,000-17,000
June 3, 2000 Sold for $11,000

1803. Rookwood vase, attribution, Limoges style, butterfly, M. Daly, 8"h, mint 1000-1500
June 3, 2000 Sold for $800

1804. Rookwood vase, dull finish glaze, flowers, G. Young, 1887, #355, 5"h, mint 500-700
June 3, 2000 Sold for $400

1805. Rookwood vase, Limoges style glaze, bats and spiders, M.L. Nichols, 1882, 14"h, hairline 2500-3500
June 3, 2000 Sold for $1900

1806. Rookwood handled vessel, dull finish glaze, die impressed design, 1883, 5"h, repair 250-350
June 3, 2000 Sold for $350

1807. Rookwood handled vessel, smear glaze, flowers, 1888, L.A. Fry, 11"h, mint 1000-1500
June 3, 2000 Sold for $1100

1808. Rookwood vessel, standard glaze, cyclamen, silver overlay, 1893, S. Toohey, #527, 4.5"l, mint 2000-3000
June 3, 2000 Sold for $1900

1809. Rookwood vessel, standard glaze, berries, silver overlay, P.H. Stuntz, 1892, 5.5"h, #584C, mint 2200-2700
June 3, 2000 Sold for $2200

1810. Rookwood vase, standard glaze, tulips, silver overlay, C. Lindeman, 1905, #914F, 5"h, hairline 900-1200
June 3, 2000 Sold for $600

1811. Rookwood vase, standard glaze, poppies, C. Lindeman, 1900, #604E, 6"h, mint 450-650
June 3, 2000 Sold for $550

1812. Rookwood vase, standard glaze, grapes, E. Diers, 1900, #734DD, 6.5"h, mint 450-650
June 3, 2000 Sold for $550

1813. Rookwood vase, standard glaze, magnolias, S. Laurence, 1902, #886C, 11.5"h, restored 1200-1700
June 3, 2000 Sold for $850

1814. Rookwood vase, hi-glaze, daisies, Shiraya-madani, 1888, #401, 4"h, mint 450-650
June 3, 2000 Sold for $350

1815. Rookwood vase, standard glaze, flowers, 1890, #402, G. Young, factory flaw 400-600
June 3, 2000 Sold for $700

1816. Rookwood vase, iris glaze, berries and leaves, S. Sax, 1902, #901D, 7.5"h, mint 1700-2500
June 3, 2000 Sold for $2800

1817. Rookwood vase, iris glaze, crocus, 1901, C. Schmidt, #765D, 8"h, mint 2000-3000
June 3, 2000 Sold for $2400

1818. Rookwood vase, iris glaze, thistle, S.E. Coyne, 1904, #904E, 6.5"h, mint 1200-1700
June 3, 2000 Sold for $1000

1819. Rookwood vase, standard glaze, poppies, H. Altman, 1902, #901D, 7.5"h, mint 500-750
June 3, 2000 Sold for $600

1820. Rookwood vase, standard glaze, bleeding hearts, F. Vreeland, 1901, #913, 6"h, mint 450-550
June 3, 2000 Sold for $700

1821. Rookwood vessel, standard glaze, oak leaves and acorns, L. Asbury, 1898, #X240X, 10"h, mint 900-1200
June 3, 2000 Sold for $800

1822. Rookwood bowl, flowers and circles, reminiscent Haviland, M.L. Perkins, 9.5"dia x 3"h, mint 500-700
June 3, 2000 Sold for $600

1823. Rookwood vase, standard glaze, cherries and leaves, C. Schmidt, 1900, #667, 6.5"h, mint 400-600
June 3, 2000 Sold for $500

1824. Rookwood vase, matt glaze, magnolias, M.H. McDonald, 1936, #6211, 10"h, mint 2000-3000
June 3, 2000 Sold for $3500

1825. Rookwood plaque, vellum, landscape, E.T. Hurley, 9"h x 11"w, mint 4000-6000
June 3, 2000 Sold for $4000

1826. Rookwood vase, vellum, flowers and leaves, L.E. Lindeman, 1904, #4, 6"h, mint 550-750
June 3, 2000 Sold for $650

1827. Rookwood vase, vellum, clover, L. Lindeman, 1906, #905E, 7"h, mint 700-900
June 3, 2000 Sold for $750

1828. Rookwood vase ,vellum, dogwood, E.N. Lincoln, 1908, #933D, 6.5"h, mint 800-1100
June 3, 2000 Sold for $900

1829. Rookwood vase, vellum, pansies, C. Steinle, 1910, #1343, 5"h, mint 700-900
June 3, 2000 Sold for $850

1830. Rookwood vase, vellum, cyclamen, 1901, C. Steinle, #1357E, 7"h, mint 800-1100
June 3, 2000 Sold for $900

1831. Rookwood plaque, vellum, harbor scene, C. Schmidt, 1921, #X7976X, 4" x 8", mint 3500-4500
June 3, 2000 Sold for $3750

1832. Rookwood vase, iris glaze, poppies, 1907, Shirayamadani, 16"h, mint 40,000-60,000
June 3, 2000 Sold for $32,500

1833. Rookwood vase, vellum, clematis, A. Craven, 1917, #838D, 8.5"h, minute repair to lip 700-900
June 3, 2000 Sold for $550

1834. Rookwood vase, vellum, Queen Anne's lace, E.N. Lincoln, 1909, #939D, 7.75"h, mint 800-1100
June 3, 2000 Sold for $1000

1835. Rookwood vase, vellum, tulips, S. Sax, 1904, #192D, 8"h, hairline 700-900
June 3, 2000 Sold for $750

1836. Rookwood vase, vellum, lily of the valley, E.N. Lincoln, 1909, #1655F, 6.5"h, repair to lip 450-650
June 3, 2000 Sold for $550

1837. Rookwood vase, vellum, flowers, 1916, C. Steinle, #939D, 8"h, mint 900-1200
June 3, 2000 Sold for $1100

1838. Rookwood vase, iris glaze, irises, C. Schmidt, 1903, #901C, 9"h, mint 3500-4500
June 3, 2000 Sold for $3500

1839. Rookwood plaque, vellum, landscape, E. Diers, c.1920, 12" x 9", original frame, mint 4000-6000
June 3, 2000 Sold for $6000

1840. Rookwood vase, iris glaze, morning glories, O. Reed, 1902, #922, 7"h, repair to rim 800-1100
June 3, 2000 Sold for $900

1841. Rookwood vase, iris glaze, berries and leaves, S. Sax, 1901, #860, 6.5"h, small bruise to side 300-400
June 3, 2000 Sold for $400

1842. Rookwood vase, iris glaze, cherry blossoms, L. Asbury, 1909, #80E, 8"h, hairline 900-1200
June 3, 2000 Sold for $550

1843. Rookwood vase, iris glaze, holly berries, S. Sax, 1904, #922D, 7"h, hairline to rim 700-900
June 3, 2000 Sold for $500

1844. Rookwood vase, dull finish, frogs, boy, bats, moon and spider, Nichols, 1883, 26"h, restoration 6000-8000
June 3, 2000 Sold for $3500

1845. Rookwood plaque, birds, A.R. Valentien, sea green glaze, 8" x 10", mint 25,000-35,000
June 3, 2000 Sold for $45,000

1846. Rookwood vase, iris glaze, lilies of the valley, L. Lindeman, 1906, #952F, 6"h, mint 800-1100
June 3, 2000 Sold for $550

1847. Rookwood vase, iris glaze, flower, I. Bishop, 1907, #842D, 5.5"h, mint 750-950
June 3, 2000 Sold for $700

1848. Rookwood vase, iris glaze, roses and buds, S.E. Coyne, 1907, #922, 8"h, mint 1500-2000
June 3, 2000 Sold for $1200

1849. Rookwood vase, iris glaze, leaves, S. Sax, 1901, #927E, 7"h, faint line inside lip, mint 1200-1700
June 3, 2000 Sold for $1200

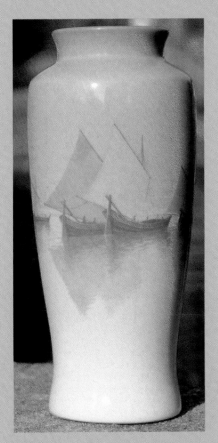

1850. Rookwood lamp, matt glaze, Arts & Crafts design, Tiffany Studios shade, 16"dia, overall height 22", 1911, #1118, restoration, excellent condition 8,000-11,000
June 3, 2000 Sold for $6500

1851. Rookwood vase, hi-glaze, harbor scene, C. Schmidt, 1923, #1664C, 13"h, mint 10,000-15,000
June 3, 2000 Sold for $12,000

1852. Rookwood vase, iris glaze, pinecones, R. Fechheimer, 1901, #913, 6"h, mint 1200-1700
June 3, 2000 Sold for $1100

1853. Rookwood vase, iris glaze, carnations, F. Rothenbusch, 1903, #3922C, 8.5"h, mint 1500-2000
June 3, 2000 Sold for $1400

1854. Rookwood vase, iris glaze, cyclamen, C. Todd, 1910, #1343, 4.5"h, mint 900-1200
June 3, 2000 Sold for $2500

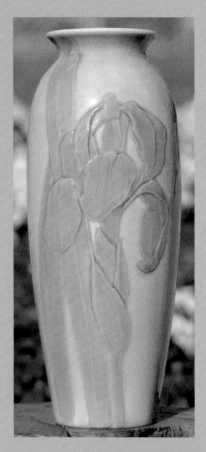

1855. Rookwood vase, sea green glaze, irises, S. Toohey, 1898, #829, 9.5"h, mint 5500-7500
June 3, 2000 Sold for $4750

1856. Rookwood vase, standard glaze, palm leaves, A.R. Valentien, 1889, 29"h, reglued chip 3500-4500
June 3, 2000 Sold for $5000

1857. Rookwood vase, black iris glaze, poppies, S.E. Coyne, 1910, #1278, 8"h, harmless lines 2000-3000
June 3, 2000 Sold for $2600

1858. Rookwood vase, iris glaze, sailboats, C. Schmidt, 1904, #901C, 8.5"h, mint 2500-3500
June 3, 2000 Sold for $2700

1859. Rookwood vase, iris glaze, fish, S.E. Coyne, 1911, #1369E, 7"h, mint 1500-2500
June 3, 2000 Sold for $2200

1860. Rookwood vase, Tiger Eye glaze, shellfish, 1885, indistinct initials, #117C, 8.5"h, mint 1000-1500
June 5, 1999 Sold for $850

1861. Rookwood vase, mahogany and Tiger Eye, water bird, A. Van Briggle, 1896, 7.5"h, mint 2000-3000
June 5, 1999 Sold for $3250

1862. Rookwood vase, Tiger Eye glaze, bird on tree branch, M. Rettig, 1885, #117, 8"h, mint 1500-2000
June 5, 1999 Sold for $1600

1863. Rookwood vase, Tiger Eye glaze, floral design, A.M. Valentien, 1889, 6"h, mint 1000-1500
June 5, 1999 Sold for $850

1864. Rookwood vase, standard glaze, clover, C. Lindeman, 1904, glaze flaws, mint 300-400
June 3, 2000 Sold for $350

1865. Rookwood ewer, standard glaze, cherries, E. Felten, 1900, #401, 4"h, restored handle 200-300
June 3, 2000 Sold for $220

1866. Rookwood vase, standard glaze, maple leaves, O.G. Reed, 1897, #827, 11"h, mint 650-850
June 3, 2000 Sold for $600

1867. Rookwood vase, standard glaze, flowers, C.F. Bonsall, 1903, #614F, 6"h, glaze flaw 300-400
June 3, 2000 Sold for $375

1868. Rookwood vase, standard glaze, berries and leaves, O.G. Reed, 1897, #798, 7"h, repaired 350-450
June 3, 2000 Sold for $270

1869. Rookwood vase, standard glaze, flowers, silver overlay, A. Sprague, 1892, #481, 9"h, mint 2000-3000
June 3, 2000 Sold for $2200

1870. Rookwood vase, standard glaze, day lilies, silver overlay, E.N. Lincoln, 1898, #482, 9.5"h, hairline 2000-3000
June 3, 2000 Sold for $1500

1871. Rookwood vase, vellum, landscape, M. Perkins, 1917, #534D, 8"h, mint 2500-3500
June 3, 2000 Sold for $2900

1872. Rookwood vase, vellum, snow scene, E. Diers, 1913, #1356D, 9"h, mint 2000-2500
June 3, 2000 Sold for $2400

1873. Rookwood vessel, standard glaze, cherries, C. Steinle, 1907, #830D, 6.5"h, repaired 650-850
June 3, 2000 Sold for $230

1874. Rookwood bowl, floral design, cameo glaze, 1890, 8"dia, #485, mint 350-550
June 3, 2000 Sold for $400

1875. Rookwood vase, standard glaze, iris, M. Daly, 1902, #907B, 17"h, cracks 800-1100
June 3, 2000 Sold for $700

1876. Rookwood candlestick, standard glaze, dogwood, A.M. Bookprinter, 1885, 8.5"h, mint 700-900
June 3, 2000 Sold for $700

1877. Rookwood covered vessel, standard glaze, floral, A.M. Bookprinter, 1885, #44A, 6.5"l, chips 400-600
June 3, 2000 Sold for $325

1878. Rookwood vase, matt glaze, stylized floral, L. Abel, 1922, #2101, 6.75"h, mint 1200-1700
June 2, 2001 Sold for $1200

1879. Rookwood vase, matt glaze, flowers, E.N. Lincoln, 1922, #819, 6.5"h, mint 1000-1500
June 2, 2001 Sold for $1000

1880. Rookwood vase, matt glaze, iris design, A.R. Valentien, 1901, #7BZ, 11"h, mint 10,000-15,000
June 3, 2000 Sold for $12,000

1881. Rookwood vase, matt glaze, W. Hentschel, 1930, #6010C, 12"h, mint 1200-1700
June 2, 2001 Sold for $1200

1882. Rookwood vase, hi-glaze, animals, E. Barrett, 1944, #2193, 4.5"h, mint 1000-1500
June 2, 2001 Sold for $950

1883. Rookwood vase, hi-glaze porcelain, deer, J. Jensen, 1931, #900C, 8.5"h, mint 4000-6000
June 3, 2000 Sold for $4000

1884. Rookwood vase, hi-glaze porcelain, deer, J. Jensen, 1931, #900C, 8.5"h, mint 4000-6000
June 3, 2000 Sold for $3500

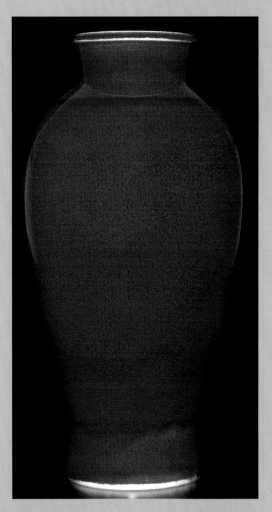

1885. Rookwood vase, sang-de-beouff glaze, Chinese inspired, 1928, #6079, 18"h, mint 2000-3000
June 3, 2000 Sold for $5000

1886. Rookwood vase, hi-glaze porcelain, stylized fruit, E. Barrett, 1945, #6891, 10"h, mint 2000-3000
June 3, 2000 Sold for $1500

1887. Rookwood vase, hi-glaze porcelain, animal figures, E. Barrett, 1944, #2193, 4.5"h, mint 1200-1700
June 3, 2000 Sold for $950

1888. Rookwood vase, standard glaze, holly,
J. Zettel, 1892, #614F, 5"h, mint 3000-4000
June 3, 2000 Sold for $2800

1889. Rookwood vase, standard glaze, floral
design, silver overlay, 1894, #724D, 5.5"h,
mint 2700-3700
June 3, 2000 Sold for $2100

1890. Rookwood vase, Tiger Eye glaze, egret and reeds,
A. Van Briggle, 1896, 7.5"h, mint 2000-3000
June 3, 2000 Sold for $1600

1891. Rookwood handle vessel, hi-glaze, portrait,
1894, #512, 9"h, glaze flaws, mint 800-1100
June 3, 2000 Sold for $450

1892. Matt Morgan vase, matt glaze, floral design,
signed, 3.5"h, minor chips to bottom 150-250
June 3, 2000 Sold for $180

1893. Rookwood bowl, cameo glaze, morning glories,
1887, 13"dia., #228, mint 600-800
June 3, 2000 Sold for $600

1894. Rookwood vessel, hi-glaze, fish, A.R. Valentien,
1897, #3564C, 10"h, repaired 700-900
June 3, 2000 Sold for $800

1895. Rookwood vase, crystalline glaze, stylized floral design, C. Todd, 1917, #270, 12"h, mint 2000-3000
June 3, 2000 Sold for $4000

1896. Rookwood vase, vellum, Roman style, E. Diers, 1910, #1663D, 9"h, mint 2500-3500
June 3, 2000 Sold for $2500

1897. Rookwood vase, vellum, Mt. Fugiyama, P. Conant, 1916, #900C, 9"h, mint 3000-4000
June 3, 2000 Sold for $3250

1898. Rookwood handled vessel, standard glaze, Native American, J. Swing, 1900, #837, 5"h, mint 1700-2700
June 3, 2000 Sold for $2300

1899. Rookwood vessel, standard glaze, portrait, 1898, H.R. Strafer, #564C, 10"h, mint 2750-3750
June 3, 2000 Sold for $3250

1900. Rookwood vessel, standard glaze, Native American, E.W. Brain, 1899, #656, 5"h, mint 1500-2500
June 3, 2000 Sold for $1300

1901. Rookwood plaque, vellum, harbor scene, C. Schmidt, c.1920, 4" x 8", original frame, mint 3500-4500
June 3, 2000 Sold for $3750

1902. Rookwood plaque, vellum, harbor scene, C. Schmidt, c.1920, 4" x 8", original frame, mint 3500-4500
June 3, 2000 Sold for $3750

1903. Rookwood vase, matt glaze, berries and leaves, F. Rothenbusch, 1905, #969C, 6"h, mint 900-1200
June 3, 2000 Sold for $850

1904. Rookwood vase, matt glaze, berries and leaves, K. Jones, 1925, #2191, 5"h, mint 550-750
June 3, 2000 Sold for $800

1905. Rookwood vase, matt glaze, geometric designs, C.S. Todd, 1919, 9"h, mint 900-1200
June 3, 2000 Sold for $950

1906. Rookwood handled vessel, matt glaze, mistletoe, A. Pons, 1907, #259D, 5"h, minor flaw 450-650
June 3, 2000 Sold for $350

1907. Rookwood vase, matt glaze, trumpet flowers, Shirayamadani, 1939, #2969, 8"h, mint 1500-2500
June 3, 2000 Sold for $2100

1908. Rookwood lamp, matt glaze, floral design, C.S. Todd, c. 1910, leaded glass shade is 16"dia., overall height 22", excellent condition 3500-4500
June 3, 2000 Sold for $2500

1909. Rookwood plaque, vellum, landscape, F. Rothenbusch, 1924, 7.5" x 5.5", mint 2500-3500
June 3, 2000 Sold for $3750

1910. Rookwood vase, matt glaze, peacock feather, W.E. Hentschel, 1914, #77A8, 5"h, mint 1000-1500
June 3, 2000 Sold for $950

1911. Rookwood vase, matt glaze, flowers and leaves, R. Fechheimer, 1903, #3D, 7"h, mint 1500-2000
June 3, 2000 Sold for $1900

1912. Rookwood vase, matt glaze, wild roses, H.E. Wilcox, 1901, #175CZ, 8.5"h, mint 2000-3000
June 3, 2000 Sold for $2700

1913. Rookwood vase, matt glaze, leaves, H.E. Wilcox, 1906, #30E, 8"h, mint 1500-2000
June 3, 2000 Sold for $1600

1914. Rookwood vase, matt glaze, berries and leaves, S. Sax, 1903, #4DZ, 7.5"h, line to body 900-1200
June 3, 2000 Sold for $600

1915. Rookwood vase, hi-glaze drip, 1950, #6644, 7"h, mint 250-350
June 3, 2000 Sold for $300

1916. Rookwood vase, hi-glaze, 1948, #6098, 5"h, mint 100-200
June 3, 2000 Sold for $290

1917. Rookwood vase, hi-glaze drip, 1932, #6320, 8.5"h, mint 350-450
June 3, 2000 Sold for $450

1918. Rookwood vase, hi-glaze drip, 1950, 5"w, no #, mint 150-250
June 3, 2000 Sold for $120

1919. Rookwood vase, aventurine hi-glaze, 1945, 9"h, mint 300-400
June 3, 2000 Sold for $325

1920. Rookwood vase, hi-glaze, 1933, 6"h, mint 250-350
June 3, 2000 Sold for $500

1921. Rookwood vase, matt glaze, irises and poppies, V. Tischler, 1921, #2189, 7"h, mint 800-1100
June 3, 2000 Sold for $950

1922. Rookwood vase, matt glaze, stylized flowers, W.J. Pullman, 1928, #2182, 5.5"h, repaired 300-400
June 3, 2000 Sold for $375

1923. Rookwood vase, matt glaze, stylized leaves and fruit, C.S. Todd, 1919, #2033C, 12"h, mint 1200-1700
June 3, 2000 Sold for $1400

1924. Rookwood vase, matt glaze, dots and drip affect, 1920, C.S. Todd, #604E, 6.5"h, mint 650-850
June 3, 2000 Sold for $850

1925. Rookwood handled vessel, matt glaze, cherries, J. Jensen, 1929, #2974, 7.5"h, mint 1200-1700
June 3, 2000 Sold for $1500

1926. Rookwood vase, aventurine glaze, 1944, 4.5"h, mint 200-300
June 3, 2000 Sold for $350

1927. Rookwood vase, hi-glaze, 1933, #6361, 7"h, mint 250-350
June 3, 2000 Sold for $350

1928. Rookwood vase, hi-glaze, 1922, #2545-C, 11"h, mint 200-300
June 3, 2000 Sold for $375

1929. Rookwood vase, aventurine glaze, 1932, #6316, 4"h, mint 250-350
June 3, 2000 Sold for $325

1930. Rookwood vase, drip hi-glaze, 1933, #6369, 5"h, mint 250-350
June 3, 2000 Sold for $300

1931. Rookwood vase, drip glaze, 1949, #6644E, 6.5"h, mint 300-400
June 3, 2000 Sold for $375

1932. Rookwood vase, vellum, daisies, S.E. Coyne, 1919, #1091D, 7"h, mint 1000-1500
June 3, 2000 Sold for $1000

1933. Rookwood vase, vellum, roses, K. Van Horne, 1915, #1278B, 9"h, mint 1000-1500
June 3, 2000 Sold for $1000

1934. Rookwood vase, vellum, chrysanthemum, E. Diers, 1914, #1342, 8.5"h, mint 1700-2700
June 3, 2000 Sold for $2000

1935. Rookwood covered vessel, vellum, stylized flowers, E.N. Lincoln, 1919, #2005, 4.5"h, mint 800-1100
June 3, 2000 Sold for $950

1936. Rookwood vase, vellum, stylized flowers, M.H. McDonald, 1920, #1055C, 9"h, mint 2500-3500
June 3, 2000 Sold for $1600

1937. Rookwood vase, vellum, lake and tree, F. Rothenbusch, 1918, #907B, 17.5"h, mint 8000-11,000
June 2, 2001 Sold for $7500

1938. Rookwood plaque, vellum, nocturnal scene, K. Van Horne, 1912, 4" x 8", minor line 2500-3000
June 2, 2001 Sold for $2700

1939. Rookwood vase, matt glaze, flowers and leaves, unknown artist, 1925, #1779, 7.5"h, mint 700-900
June 3, 2000 Sold for $500

1940. Rookwood vase, matt glaze, stylized flowers, V. Tischler, 1924, #927D, 9"h, mint 900-1200
June 3, 2000 Sold for $1200

1941. Rookwood bowl, matt glaze, blossoms, J. Jensen, 1928, #957B, 9"dia., mint 700-900
June 3, 2000 Sold for $550

1942. Rookwood vase, vellum, leaf and berry design, L. Epply, 1916, #1369D, 9"h, mint 700-900
June 3, 2000 Sold for $850

1943. Rookwood vase, vellum, flowers and buds, K. Van Horne, 1915, #1369E, 7.5"h, repair 550-750
June 3, 2000 Sold for $650

1944. Rookwood plaque, sea green glaze, songbird, A.R. Valentien, 8"w x 10"h, mint 10,000-20,000
June 2, 2001 Sold for $17,000

1945. Rookwood vase, vellum, landscape, E.T. Hurley, 1912, #1660A, 16"h, mint 8000-11,000
June 2, 2001 Sold for $7500

1946. Rookwood vase, porcelain, floral design, J. Jensen, 1946, #8593, 4.5"h, mint 800-1100
June 3, 2000 Sold for $1300

1947. Rookwood vase, porcelain, stylized design, L. Epply, 1934, 5"h, mint 600-800
June 3, 2000 Sold for $600

1948. Rookwood vase, butterfat glaze, stylized leaves, J. Harris, 1930, #6204C, 7.5"h, mint 900-1200
June 3, 2000 Sold for $1000

1949. Rookwood vase, porcelain, nude, W. Rehm, 1940s, #6292C, 7.5"h, mint 550-750
June 3, 2000 Sold for $375

1950. Rookwood vase, butterfat glaze, circles, E. Barrett, 1944, #6183F, 4.75"h, mint 600-800
June 3, 2000 Sold for $500

1951. Rookwood ewer, standard glaze, pansies, A.R. Valentien, 1891, #498B, 5.5"h, mint 550-750
June 2, 2001 Sold for $750

1952. Rookwood vase, standard glaze, floral design, Shirayamadani, 1894, #469W, 11"h, minor scratches, mint 1500-2000
June 2, 2001 Sold for $1100

1953. Rookwood vase, standard glaze, floral design, C.J. Dibowski, 1894, #32W, 4"dia., mint 300-400
June 2, 2001 Sold for $280

1954. Rookwood vase, vellum, flowers, V. Tischler, 1921, #357F, 6"h, hairlines and chip 150-250
June 2, 2001 Sold for $160

1955. Rookwood vase, vellum, cherry blossoms, L. Asbury, 1914, #581E, 9"h, mint 1200-1700
June 2, 2001 Sold for $800

1956. Rookwood vase, vellum, wisteria, E. Diers, 1912, #950D, 9"h, mint 1200-1700
June 2, 2001 Sold for $1100

1957. Rookwood vase, standard glaze, floral design, K. Hickman, 1899, #565, 8"h, mint 700-900
June 2, 2001 Sold for $450

1958. Rookwood vase, standard glaze, floral, Shirayamadani, 1891, #292BW, 14"h, firing lines 900-1200
June 2, 2001 Sold for $1100

1959. Rookwood vase, standard glaze, oak leaf and acorn, S. Toohey, 1895, #483, 6"h, mint 550-750
June 2, 2001 Sold for $550

1960. Rookwood vase, standard glaze, floral design, C. Steinle, 1907, #900, 7.75"h, mint 700-900
June 2, 2001 Sold for $1100

1961. Rookwood vase, standard glaze, daffodils, M. Daly, 1902, #901B, 11.5"h, insignificant line 550-650
June 2, 2001 Sold for $550

1962. Rookwood handled vessel, standard glaze, grapes, L. Lindeman, 1908, #1071, 5"h, mint 250-350
June 2, 2001 Sold for $190

1963. Rookwood vase, matt glaze, iris, J. Jensen, 1934, 5"h, mint 700-900
June 2, 2001 Sold for $1100

1964. Rookwood vase, matt glaze, floral design, M. McDonald, 1933, 8"h, mint 800-1100
June 2, 2001 Sold for $650

1965. Rookwood vase, matt glaze, floral design, K. Jones, 1928, #914E, 5.5"h, mint 550-750
June 2, 2001 Sold for $600

1966. Rookwood handled vessel, standard glaze, floral design, B. Cranch, 1895, #657C, 8.5"h, line 350-450
June 2, 2001 Sold for $190

1967. Rookwood vase, standard glaze, carnations, Shirayamadani, 1892, #496AW, 13"h, restored 900-1200
June 2, 2001 Sold for $900

1968. Rookwood vase, mahogany glaze, floral design, not signed, 5"h, mint 400-600
June 2, 2001 Sold for $325

1969. Rookwood demitasse cup and saucer, mahogany glaze, floral design, H. Wilcox, 1886, #291R, minor glaze chips 200-300
June 2, 2001 Sold for $160

1970. Rookwood vase, dull finish, songbird, M. Daly, 1885, #141, 10.5"h, mint 1000-1500
June 2, 2001 Sold for $850

1971. Rookwood ewer, mahogany glaze, floral design, S. Toohey, 1890, 7"h, mint 650-850
June 2, 2001 Sold for $800

1972. Rookwood vase, matt glaze, ferns fronds, Fechheimer, 1905, #969D, 4.5"h, mint 550-750
June 2, 2001 Sold for $500

1973. Rookwood vase, matt glaze, apples, A. Pons, 1907, #935D, 7.25"h, mint 800-1100
June 2, 2001 Sold for $1600

1974. Rookwood vase, matt glaze, swirl design, 1909, #1120, 5"h, mint 400-600
June 2, 2001 Sold for $500

1975. Rookwood vase, standard glaze, turtle, A.R. Valentien, 1885, #141, 11"h, small chip 500-700
June 2, 2001 Sold for $750

1976. Rookwood vase, standard glaze, floral design, A.R. Valentien, 1900, #216G, 12"h, minor flake 500-700
June 2, 2001 Sold for $350

1977. Rookwood jug, dull finish, flowers, 1883, Wenderoth, 5"h, mint 300-400
June 2, 2001 Sold for $260

1978. Rookwood vase, vellum, roses, E. Diers, 1905, #952EV, 6.25"h, mint 800-1100
June 2, 2001 Sold for $750

1979. Rookwood vase, vellum, floral design, L. Epply, 1908, #949D, 9"h, mint 1200-1700
June 2, 2001 Sold for $1200

1980. Rookwood vase, vellum, floral design, C. Steinle, 1916, #995E, 5.5"h, mint 900-1200
June 2, 2001 Sold for $800

1981. Rookwood handled vessel, standard glaze, holly, S. Markland, #259EW, 4.5"h, repaired 200-300
June 2, 2001 Sold for $90

1982. Rookwood vase, standard glaze, water lily, L. Asbury, 1901, #906B, 7"h, mint 700-900
June 2, 2001 Sold for $800

1983. Rookwood vessel, standard glaze, butterfly handle, holly, E.N. Lincoln, 1896, #329, 2"h, mint 200-300
June 2, 2001 Sold for $300

1984. Rookwood vase, vellum, floral design, M.G. Denzler, 1914, #1873, 6"h, mint 500-700
June 2, 2001 Sold for $450

1985. Rookwood vase, vellum, roses, E. Diers, 1914, #1842, 8"h, mint 1200-1700
June 2, 2001 Sold for $1800

1986. Rookwood vase, vellum, daffodils, L. Epply, 1907, #952E, 7.5"h, mint 900-1200
June 2, 2001 Sold for $1800

1988. Rookwood tile, matt glaze, ship, in a Arts & Crafts oak frame 12" x 12", minor repairs 1000-1500
June 2, 2001 Sold for $1700

1987. Rookwood vase, hi-glaze, violets, C.A. Baker, 1903, #916C, 7.5"h, mint 3000-4000
June 7, 1997 Sold for $6000

1989. Rookwood vase, porcelain glaze, stylized roses, E.T. Hurley, 1925, #2825A, 16.25"h, mint 3000-4000
June 2, 2001 Sold for $2600

1990. Rookwood vase, porcelain glaze, hemlock, E.T. Hurley, 1934, 5"h, mint 1500-2500
June 2, 2001 Sold for $2100

1991. Rookwood vase, matt glaze, flowers and vines, H. Wilcox, 1902, #3DZ, 7"h, mint 2500-3500
June 2, 2001 Sold for $7500

1992. Rookwood Faience tile frieze, group of sixteen, matt glaze, floral design, each is 6"sq. and impressed with Faience numbers, a few chips, framed, excellent condition 2500-3500
June 2, 2001 Sold for $2200

1993. Rookwood vase, sea green glaze, frogs, A.R. Valentien, 1896, #786D, 8"h, mint 2500-3500
June 3, 2000 Sold for $1600

1994. Rookwood vase, sea green glaze, leaves and iris buds, M. Daly, 1897, #562, 9"h, mint 2500-3500
June 3, 2000 Sold for $3000

1995. Rookwood vase, matt glaze, three-footed form, 1910, #11, 6"h, mint 550-750
June 2, 2001 Sold for $600

1996. Rookwood vase, matt glaze, 1921, #2301B, 13"h, minor flakes 450-650
June 2, 2001 Sold for $375

1997. Rookwood vase, matt glaze, leaf design, 1920, #2181, 8"dia., mint 450-650
June 2, 2001 Sold for $360

1998. Rookwood vase, matt glaze, 1953, #950D, X'd, mint 450-550
June 2, 2001 Sold for $325

1999. Rookwood vase, matt glaze, berries, 1919, #2485, 9.5"h, chips 400-600
June 2, 2001 Sold for $400

2000. Rookwood vase, matt glaze, 1906, #950D, 9"h, mint 400-600
June 2, 2001 Sold for $550

2001. Rookwood vase, matt glaze, 1904, #1911E, 4.5"h, mint 200-300
June 2, 2001 Sold for $250

2002. Rookwood vase, matt glaze, geometric, 1913, #1358D, 8.5"h, mint 650-850
June 2, 2001 Sold for $750

2003. Rookwood vase, matt glaze, incised, 1907, #919D, 4.5"h, mint 400-600
June 2, 2001 Sold for $375

2004. Rookwood vase, iris glaze, holly, S. Sax, 1904, #922D, 7"h, hairline 700-900
June 2, 2001 Sold for $550

2005. Rookwood vase, iris glaze, pansies, C.A. Baker, 1902, #927E, 6.5"h, mint 1200-1700
June 2, 2001 Sold for $1800

2006. Rookwood vase, iris glaze, blossoms, C.A. Baker, 1904, #30E, 8"h, chip repair 550-750
June 2, 2001 Sold for $375

2007. Rookwood compote, matt glaze, 1905, #1215, 7"h, mint 350-550
June 2, 2001 Sold for $425

2008. Rookwood vase, matt glaze, roses, 1917, #2013, 8"h, mint 400-600
June 2, 2001 Sold for $375

2009. Rookwood vase, matt glaze, geometric, 1937, #1912, 6"h, mint 250-350
June 2, 2001 Sold for $250

2010. Rookwood vase, iris glaze, floral, I. Bishop, 1906, #1120, 4"h, mint 800-1100
June 2, 2001 Sold for $1100

2011. Rookwood vase, iris glaze, Rothenbusch, 1903, #925CC, 8"h, mint 1700-2200
June 2, 2001 Sold for $1600

2012. Rookwood vase, iris glaze, lily, I. Bishop, 1906, #950E, 6.75"h, hairlines 400-600
June 2, 2001 Sold for $300

2013. Rookwood vase, vellum, landscape, A. Conant, 1922, #900D, 7"h, drilled hole restored 1000-1500
June 2, 2001 Sold for $950

2014. Rookwood vase, vellum, landscape, E. Diers, 1918, #907C, 15"h, deteriorating repair 1500-2500
June 2, 2001 Sold for $750

2015. Rookwood vase, vellum, harbor scene, C. Schmidt, 1920, #1667, 11"h, repaired chip 2500-3500
June 2, 2001 Sold for $2500

2016. Rookwood vase, vellum, floral design, M.G. Denzler, 1914, #2040, 7.5"h, mint 900-1100
June 2, 2001 Sold for $1000

2017. Rookwood jar, floral, McLaughlin, 1915, #1708, 6.5"dia., mint 2500-3500
June 2, 2001 Sold for $1000

2018. Rookwood vase, vellum, tulips, S. Sax, 1907, #932E, 7.5"h, mint 1200-1700
June 2, 2001 Sold for $1200

2019. Rookwood vase, vellum, floral design, K. Van Horne, 1915, #1358D, 9"h, mint 900-1200
June 2, 2001 Sold for $950

2020. Rookwood vase, matt, floral design, C. Covalenco, 1925, #2247C, 14"h, mint 2500-3500
June 2, 2001 Sold for $2900

2021. Rookwood vase, matt glaze, floral design, Shirayamadani, 1937, #6644E, 6"h, mint 1000-1500
June 2, 2001 Sold for $1200

2022. Rookwood vase, vellum, cherry blossoms, E.T. Hurley, 1948, #922D, 7"h, mint 1700-2200
June 2, 2001 Sold for $1300

2023. Rookwood vase, vellum, dogwood, S.E. Coyne, 1905, #943D, 8"h, mint 1200-1700
June 2, 2001 Sold for $1200

2024. Rookwood vase, vellum, 1925, L. Asbury, #2719, 6"h, mint 1200-1700
June 2, 2001 Sold for $1100

2025. Rookwood vase, vellum, daisies, L. Epply, 1902, #950F, 5.75"h, mint 450-650
June 2, 2001 Sold for $650

2026. Rookwood vase, vellum, dogwood, L. Asbury, 1911, #1353D, 9"h, restoration 550-750
June 2, 2001 Sold for $260

2027. Rookwood vase, vellum, cherry blossoms, S.E. Coyne, 1909, #1321, 5"h, mint 500-700
June 2, 2001 Sold for $450

2028. Rookwood vase, vellum, dogwood, E. Noonan, 1909, #1358E, 6.25"h, mint 900-1200
June 2, 2001 Sold for $800

2029. Rookwood vase, matt glaze, cherry blossoms, S.E. Coyne, 1917, #932D, 9.5"h, mint 1200-1700
June 2, 2001 Sold for $1100

2030. Rookwood vase, vellum, cherry blossoms, E.N. Lincoln, 1909, #1321, 5"h, mint 600-800
June 2, 2001 Sold for $600

2031. Rookwood plaque, vellum, seascape, F. Rothenbusch, 1928, 8"w x 6"h, mint 4000-5000 June 2, 2001 Sold for $3750

2032. Rookwood plaque, vellum, landscape, E.T. Hurley, 1914, 10"w x 12"h, mint 6500-7500 June 2, 2001 Sold for $9000

2033. Rookwood plaque, vellum, landscape, E.T. Hurley, 1939, 7" x 12"h, mint 4750-5750 June 2, 2001 Sold for $5000

2034. Rookwood plaque, vellum, landscape, McDermott, 1914, 8" x 5.5", mint 2500-3500
June 3, 2000 Sold for $3500

2035. Rookwood plaque, vellum, landscape, Diers, 1935, 8" x 10"h, mint 4000-5000
June 2, 2001 Sold for $4000

2036. Rookwood plaque, vellum, landscape, Hurley, 1920, 6" x 4", mint 2000-3000
June 3, 2000 Sold for $3500

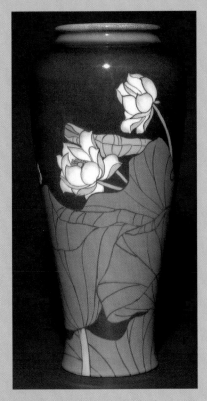

2037. Rookwood vase, porcelain glaze, water
lily, S.E. Coyne, 1924, #2551, 13.5"h,
repaired 2500-3500
June 2, 2001 Sold for $4500

2038. Rookwood vase, iris glaze, irises, C. Schmidt,
1908, #732B, 10.5"h, minor bruise to lip 3500-5500
June 2, 2001 Sold for $4500

2039. Rookwood vase, Black Opal glaze, roses, H.E. Wilcox,
1924, #2789, 11"h, mint 2500-3500
June 2, 2001 Sold for $2100

2040. Rookwood vase, iris glaze, poppies, C. Schmidt,
1908, #940DW, 9.5"h, mint 4500-6500
June 2, 2001 Sold for $6500

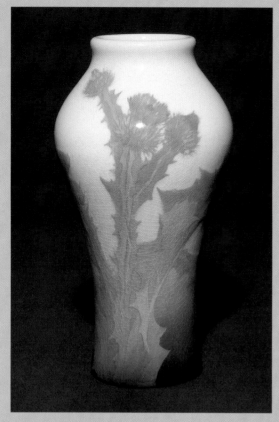

2041. Rookwood vase, iris glaze, thistles, S. Sax, 1906, #909G, 8.5"h, mint 2500-3500
June 2, 2001 Sold for $2600

2042. Rookwood vase, iris glaze, floral design, S. Sax, 1901, #786C, 10"h, mint 2500-3500
June 2, 2001 Sold for $3500

2044. Rookwood vase, iris glaze, magnolias, L. Asbury, 1906, #915C, 7"h, mint 2500-3500
June 2, 2001 Sold for $3750

2043. Rookwood vase, iris glaze, roses, E. Diers, 1903, #932D, 8.5"h, mint 2500-3500
June 2, 2001 Sold for $3500

2045. Rookwood vase, porcelain glaze, geese and ducks, A. Conant, 1920, #905A, 19"h, mint 5500-7500
June 2, 2001 Sold for $5000

2046. Rookwood lamp, Arts & Crafts style, 1903, R. Fechheimer, never electrified, shade by Handel which is signed, #2325, 14"dia. x 20.5"h, mint 6500-8500
June 2, 2001 Sold for $7000

2047. Rookwood vase, dull finish, frogs and spiders, Asian man resting among tall grasses, attributed to M.L. Nichols, 1883, 26"h, minor restoration 4500-6500
June 2, 2001 Sold for $3750

2048. Rookwood vase, vellum, floral design, L. Epply, 1920, #907A, 21"h, circular lines to base 3500-4500
June 2, 2001 Sold for $4500

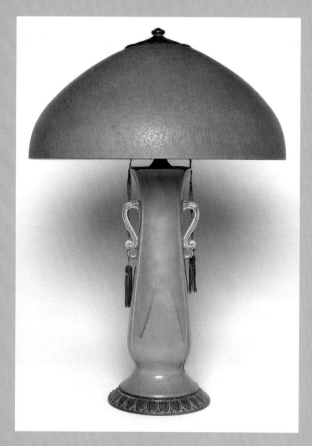

2049. Rookwood lamp, matt glaze, etched Handel shade, all original, 25.5"h x 18"dia., mint 4500-6500
June 2, 2001 Sold for $5500

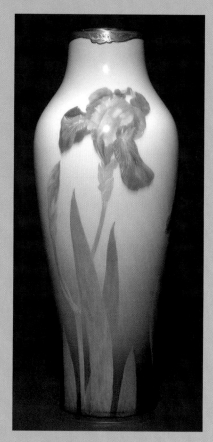

2050. Rookwood vase, iris glaze, irises, silver overlay, A.R. Valentien, 1904, #879C, 14.5"h, repaired 8,000-11,000
June 2, 2001 Sold for $11,000

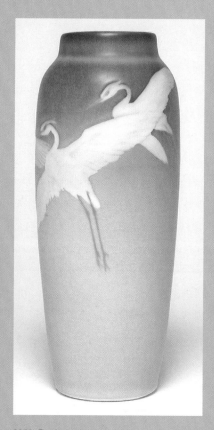

2051. Rookwood vase, vellum, cranes, Shiraya-madani, 1906, #907DD, 10"h, repaired 2000-3000
June 2, 2001 Sold for $3750

2052. Rookwood vase, dull finish, floral, die impressed bands, A.R. Valentien, 1886, #162, 24"h, mint 4500-6500
June 2, 2001 Sold for $4500

2053. Rookwood vase, vellum, floral, L. Asbury, 1927, #63, 4.5"h, mint 700-900
June 2, 2001 Sold for $1000

2054. Rookwood vase, vellum, roses, E. Diers, 1926, #917D, 7"h, mint 1000-1500
June 2, 2001 Sold for $1700

2055. Rookwood vase, vellum, daffodils, Hurley, 1942, #890E, 3.5"h, mint 800-1100
June 2, 2001 Sold for $1100

2056. Rookwood plaque, vellum, landscape, C. Schmidt, 7" x 9"h, mint 5500-7500
June 2, 2001 Sold for $5500

2057. Rookwood vase, matt, floral design, Shirayamadani, 1939, #2996, 8"h, mint 1700-2700
June 2, 2001 Sold for $1900

2058. Rookwood vase, matt, floral design, Shirayamadani, 1944, #6357, 6.5"h, mint 1200-1700
June 2, 2001 Sold for $1200

2059. Rookwood vase, standard glaze, floral design, M. Nourse, 1894, #535EW, 7"h, mint 600-800
June 2, 2001 Sold for $500

2060. Rookwood vase, standard glaze, catfish, Shirayamadani, 1896, #825, 10.5"h, repair 700-900
June 2, 2001 Sold for $700

2061. Rookwood vase, standard glaze, floral design, C.J. Dibowski, 1895, #712, 4.5"h, tight hairline 300-500
June 2, 2001 Sold for $230

2062. Rookwood plaque, vellum, landscape, E.T. Hurley, 1941, 6" x 8"h, framed, mint 3750-4750
June 2, 2001 Sold for $3500

2063. Rookwood vase, standard glaze, cherries, L. Van Briggle, 1900, #304C, 7.5"h, mint 550-750
June 2, 2001 Sold for $850

2064. Rookwood vase, standard glaze, magnolias, S. Laurence, 1902, #886C, 11"h, repair 800-1100
June 2, 2001 Sold for $800

2065. Rookwood vase, standard glaze, holly, E.N. Lincoln, #40, 1899, 5.5"h, mint 450-650
June 2, 2001 Sold for $550

2067. Rookwood bowl, Black Opal glaze, magnolias, S. Sax, 1926, #2258, 13"dia., mint 1500-2500
June 2, 2001 Sold for $1200

2066. Rookwood plaque, vellum, landscape, F. Rothenbusch, 1917, 9.5" x 11"h, mint 7000-8000
June 2, 2001 Sold for $6500

2068. Rookwood plaque, vellum, seascape, no signature, 1911, 8"w x 4"h, harmless chips 3500-4500
June 2, 2001 Sold for $4500

2069. Rookwood vase, standard glaze, bird, Shirayamadani, 1895, #30D, 9"h, mint 2500-3500
June 2, 2001 Sold for $3750

2070. Rookwood vase, matt glaze, floral design, W. Rehm, 1944, #6877, 8"h, mint 1500-2500
June 2, 2001 Sold for $1200

2071. Rookwood plaque, vellum, Venetian scene, E.T. Hurley, 1916, 10" x 8"h, mint 5500-7500
June 2, 2001 Sold for $5000

2072. Rookwood vase, vellum, irises, C. Schmidt, 1913, #614B, 14.5"h, minor flake, hairline 4000-6000
June 2, 2001 Sold for $4000

2073. Rookwood plaque, vellum, landscape, E.T. Hurley, 1948, 10" x 12"h, mint 5500-7500
June 2, 2001 Sold for $5000

2074. Rookwood vase, matt glaze, mistletoe design, M. Daly, 1901, #14Z, 2.5"h, mint 500-700
June 2, 2001 Sold for $500

2075. Rookwood vase, matt glaze, rose design, H. Wilcox, 1901, #175CZ, 8"h, repaired 800-1100
June 2, 2001 Sold for $1500

2076. Rookwood vase, matt glaze, leaf design, O.G. Reed, 1904, #316EZ, 2.5"h, mint 900-1200
June 2, 2001 Sold for $1100

2077. Rookwood vase, matt glaze, floral design, S.E. Coyne, 1929, #929, 4.5"h, mint 600-800
June 2, 2001 Sold for $650

2078. Rookwood vase, matt glaze, floral design, S.E. Coyne, 1925, #2040D, 9"h, mint 700-900
June 2, 2001 Sold for $850

2079. Rookwood vase, matt glaze, floral design, L. Lincoln, 1921, #2191, 5"h, mint 400-500
June 2, 2001 Sold for $450

2080. Rookwood vase, matt glaze, leaf design, S. Toohey, 1909, #111EZ, 5"h, mint 450-650
June 2, 2001 Sold for $500

2081. Rookwood vase, matt, feather design, W. Hentschel, 1914, #77A, 8.5"h, mint 1000-1500
June 2, 2001 Sold for $1500

2082. Rookwood vase, matt glaze, stylized design, W. Hentschel, 1914, #568, 4"h, mint 550-750
June 2, 2001 Sold for $500

2083. Rookwood vase, stylized design, 1925, #2903, 10"h, mint 650-850
June 2, 2001 Sold for $700

2084. Rookwood vase, stylized leaves, 1931, #6233, 5"h, mint 250-350
June 2, 2001 Sold for $190

2085. Rookwood vase, floral design, 1925, #2904, 9"h, mint 700-900
June 2, 2001 Sold for $700

2086. Rookwood vase, crystalline matt glaze, 1927, #1807, 4"h, mint 200-300
June 2, 2001 Sold for $230

2087. Rookwood vase, molded design, 1927, #2911, 8"h, mint 800-1100
June 2, 2001 Sold for $700

2088. Rookwood vase, Arts & Crafts design, 1913, #931, 4.5"h, mint 400-500
June 2, 2001 Sold for $450

2089. Rookwood bowl, blossoms, J. Jensen, 1928, #957B, 9"dia., mint 550-750
June 2, 2001 Sold for $450

2090. Rookwood vase, roses, E.N. Lincoln, 1925, #2246C, 14.5"h, minor 2000-3000
June 2, 2001 Sold for $1400

2091. Rookwood bowl, floral design, E.N. Lincoln, 1921, #9570, 3"h, mint 500-700
June 2, 2001 Sold for $325

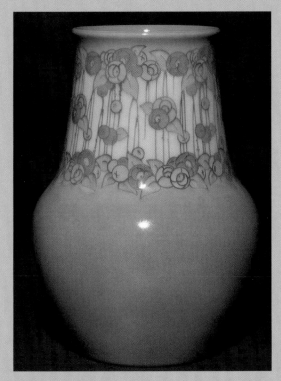

2092. Rookwood vase, porcelain, rose design, S. Sax, 1918, #975BT, 9"h, mint 3500-4500
June 2, 2001 Sold for $3750

2093. Rookwood vase, vellum, berries, E.N. Lincoln, 1910, #905E, 6.5"h, mint 1500-2500
June 2, 2001 Sold for $1800

2094. Rookwood plaque, vellum, landscape, L. Asbury, 1926, 14.5" x 9.25"h, mint 8500-9500
June 2, 2001 Sold for $9000

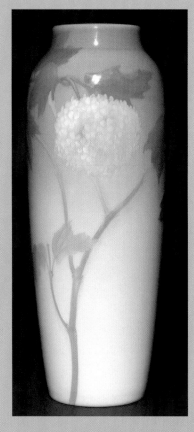

2095. Rookwood vase, Iris glaze, hydrangea, A.R. Valentien, 1902, #907C, 14"h, mint 7000-9000
June 2, 2001 Sold for $7000

2096. Rookwood sculpture, carved and painted woman, A.M. Valentien, 1903, #313Z, 6"l, mint 1500-2500
June 2, 2001 Sold for $2700

2097. Rookwood plaque, vellum, landscape, L. Asbury, 1926, 16" x 14"h, mint 17,500-22,500
June 2, 2001 Sold for $17,000

226

2098. Rookwood vase, stylized floral, J. Jensen, 1934, #S, 6"h, cracked 200-300
June 2, 2001 Sold for $160

2099. Rookwood vase, stylized floral, S. Sax, 1930, #6115, 10"h, mint 1200-1700
June 2, 2001 Sold for $1000

2100. Rookwood vase, leaf design, K. Ley, 1946, #6914, 5.5"h, mint 700-900
June 2, 2001 Sold for $850

2101. Rookwood vase, porcelain glaze, J. Jensen, 1931, #356F, 5.5"h, mint 450-550
June 2, 2001 Sold for $375

2102. Rookwood vase, figure, W. Rehm, 1940s, #6292C, 7.5"h, mint 550-750
June 2, 2001 Sold for $375

2103. Rookwood smoking set, birds, J. Harris, 1946, #6922A, 5"h, mint 550-750
June 2, 2001 Sold for $350

2104. Rookwood vase, dogwood, C. Lindeman, 1908, #904, 8"h, mint 1700-2200
June 2, 2001 Sold for $1700

2105. Rookwood vase, iris, S. Sax, 1900, #914A, 4"h, mint 1200-1700
June 2, 2001 Sold for $1200

2106. Rookwood vase, poppy, S.E. Coyne, 1906, #904D, 7.25"h, mint 2000-2500
June 2, 2001 Sold for $1800

2107. Rookwood vase, poppy, C. Schmidt, 1901, #905E, 6.25"h, mint 1200-1700
June 2, 2001 Sold for $1100

2108. Rookwood vase, thistle, L. Asbury, 1904, #907E, 8.25"h, hairlines 500-700
June 2, 2001 Sold for $475

2109. Rookwood vase, leaf, C. Lindeman, 1903, #915F, 4.25"h, mint 900-1200
June 2, 2001 Sold for $1100

2110. Rookwood vase, stylized deer, E. Barrett, 1934, 7"h, mint 1000-1500
June 2, 2001 Sold for $1300

2111. Rookwood vase, head, 1930, Hentschel, #6122, 8"h, mint 2500-3500
June 2, 2001 Sold for $8000

2112. Rookwood vase, antelope, Hentschel, 1931, #6203E, 5"h, mint 900-1200
June 2, 2001 Sold for $950

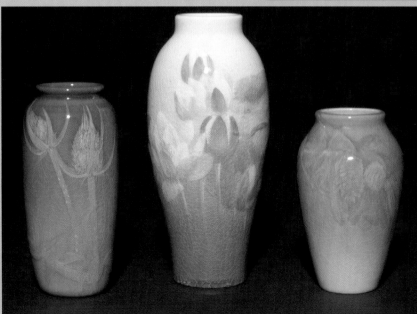

2113. Rookwood vase, thistles, S.E. Coyne, 1904, #904E, 6.5"h, mint 1200-1700
June 2, 2001 Sold for $1200

2114. Rookwood vase, water lily, C. Baker, 1905, #901C, 9"h, mint 1200-1700
June 2, 2001 Sold for $1200

2115. Rookwood vase, pinecones, R. Fechheimer, 1901, #913, 6"h, mint 1200-1700
June 2, 2001 Sold for $1100

2116. Rookwood vessel, standard glaze, Native American, 1896, C.M. Zanetta, #512, 7"h, mint 4000-6000
June 2, 2001 Sold for $5500

2117. Rookwood vase, vellum, daisies, E. Diers, 1927, #1369E, 7"h, mint 1500-2000
June 2, 2001 Sold for $1800

2118. Rookwood vase, vellum, landscape, F. Rothenbusch, 1926, #2251, 14"h, mint 9,000-12,000
June 2, 2001 Sold for $9000

2119. Rookwood vase, poinsettia, C. Todd, 1914, #1654C, 11"h, mint 3500-4500
June 2, 2001 Sold for $3250

2121. Rookwood humidor, standard glaze, Native American, G. Young, 1901, #683, 6"h, mint 3500-4500
June 2, 2001 Sold for $3750

2120. Rookwood vase, vellum, berries, L. Epply, 1923, #2102, 6.5"h, mint 2500-3500
June 2, 2001 Sold for $3750

2122. Rookwood vase, vellum, wisteria, E.T. Hurley, 1928, #614E, 8"h, mint 1500-2500
June 2, 2001 Sold for $1800

2123. Rookwood vase, matt glaze, orchids, Shiraya-madani, 1942, #904D, mint 3000-4000
June 2, 2001 Sold for $3500

2124. Rookwood vase, vellum, landscape, L. Epply, 1912, #951D, 9"h, mint 1200-1700
June 2, 2001 Sold for $1800

2125. Rookwood vase, vellum, landscape, Asbury, 1916, #1126, 9"h, repair 1500-2000
June 2, 2001 Sold for $2200

2126. Rookwood vase, vellum, Rothenbusch, 1921, #901, 8"h, mint 1500-2000
June 2, 2001 Sold for $1700

2127. Rookwood vase, matt glaze, flowers, K. Jones, 1929, #2078, 5"h, mint 500-700
June 2, 2001 Sold for $550

2128. Rookwood vase, matt glaze, leaves, C. Todd, 1911, #497, 7.75"h, mint 700-900
June 2, 2001 Sold for $850

2129. Rookwood vase, matt glaze, flowers, K. Jones, 1926, #654D, 5"h, mint 450-650
June 2, 2001 Sold for $550

2130. Rookwood vase, vellum, landscape, McDermott, 1919, #614F, 6.5"h, mint 1000-1500
June 2, 2001 Sold for $1500

2131. Rookwood vase, vellum, landscape, K. Van Horne, 1914, #1667, 11"h, mint 1200-1700
June 2, 2001 Sold for $1300

2132. Rookwood vase, vellum, landscape, L. Asbury, 1913, #901C, 9.5"h, mint 1700-2200
June 2, 2001 Sold for $2300

2133. Rookwood vase, standard glaze, silver overlay, J. Zettel, 1892, #614FW, 4.5"h, mint 3000-4000
June 2, 2001 Sold for $2600

2134. Rookwood vase, standard glaze, silver overlay, A. Sprague, 1892, #481W, 9"h, break to silver 3000-4000
June 2, 2001 Sold for $2100

2135. Rookwood vase, standard glaze, silver overlay, unknown artist, 1894, #724DW, 5"h, repair 1500-2500
June 2, 2001 Sold for $2000

2136. Rookwood vessel, dull finish glaze, floral, A.M. Bookprinter, 1887, #282C, 7.5"h, mint 1000-1500
June 2, 2001 Sold for $950

2137. Rookwood ewer, standard and Tiger Eye glaze, flowers, M. Daly, #267W3, 10.25"h, mint 800-1100
June 2, 2001 Sold for $650

2138. Rookwood handled vessel, brown glaze, fish, M.A. Daly, 1885, #54C, 5.5"h, mint 800-1100
June 2, 2001 Sold for $1200

2139. Rookwood vase, standard glaze, silver overlay, K. Hickman, 1898, #809E, 6"h, mint 2500-3500
June 2, 2001 Sold for $2100

2140. Rookwood vase, standard glaze, silver overlay, S.E. Coyne, 1897, #304, 8"h, mint 2500-3500
June 2, 2001 Sold for $2600

2141. Rookwood ewer, standard glaze, silver overlay, unsigned, 1893, #509, 5.25"h, mint 2000-3000
June 2, 2001 Sold for $2000

2142. Rookwood plaque, rook, early matt glaze, S. Toohey, 1904, 5" x 9", mint 5500-7500 June 2, 2001 Sold for $5500

2143. Rookwood tile frieze, matt glaze, three tiles, houses, 12"h x 36"l, repaired 5500-7500 June 2, 2001 Sold for $5000

2144. Rookwood plaque, hi-glaze, classical figures, high relief, 18" x 8", mint 800-1200 June 2, 2001 Sold for $1200

2145. Rookwood tray, leaf and mushrooms, sea green glaze, Shirayamadani, 1901, #308Z, 7"dia., minor flaws 1500-2500
June 2, 2001 Sold for $1600

2146. Rookwood tile frieze, matt glaze, three tiles, ships, 12"h x 36"l, repaired 3500-5500
June 2, 2001 Sold for $4000

2147. Rookwood mug, standard glaze, bee, A.M. Valentien, 1889, #328D, 6"h, mint 1000-1500
June 1, 1996 Sold for $600

2148. Rookwood mug, standard glaze, walking figure, S. Toohey, 1892, #259C, 6"h, mint 1200-1700
June 1, 1996 Sold for $850

2149. Rookwood mug, standard glaze, frog in skirt dancing, M.A. Daly, 1890, #328B, 6"h, mint 1200-1700
June 1, 1996 Sold for $800

2151. Rookwood miniature vessel, Aerial Blue, maiden, B. Horsfall, 1895, #769, 3"h, mint 1500-2500
June 2, 2001 Sold for $1300

2150. Rookwood vase, vellum, landscape, S.E. Coyne, 1924, #904C, 12"h, mint 4000-6000
June 2, 2001 Sold for $6500

2152. Rookwood plaque, vellum, landscape, S.E. Coyne, 1924, 8"w x 5"h, mint 3500-4500
June 2, 2001 Sold for $4000

2153. Rookwood vase, drip glaze, five-footed form, S. Toohey, 1920, #S2009, 16"h, mint 3500-5500
June 6, 1998 Sold for $3750

2154. Rookwood vase, vellum, landscape, E.T. Hurley, 1931, #904C, 12"h, mint 4500-5500
June 2, 2001 Sold for $4500

2155. Rookwood plaque, vellum, landscape, S.E. Coyne, 9" x 5"h, mint 3250-4250
June 2, 2001 Sold for $4000

2156. Rookwood vase, vellum, floral, E.N. Lincoln, 1908, #907F, 7.5"h, mint 700-900
June 2, 2001 Sold for $750

2157. Rookwood vase, vellum, roses, Diers, 1927, #927D, 9"h, chips, hairline 450-650
June 2, 2001 Sold for $425

2158. Rookwood vase, vellum, clover, C. Steinle, 1909, #1857E, 7"h, mint 700-900
June 2, 2001 Sold for $800

2159. Rookwood vase, matt glaze, floral, C. Todd, 1920, #951F, 6"h, repaired 350-550
June 2, 2001 Sold for $300

2160. Rookwood vase, matt glaze, leaves, C. Todd, 1913, #1872, 7.5"h, mint 700-900
June 2, 2001 Sold for $650

2161. Rookwood vase, matt glaze, floral, C. Todd, 1916, #939D, 7"h, mint 700-900
June 2, 2001 Sold for $900

2162. Rookwood vase, matt glaze, floral, J. Jensen, 1930, #604F, 6.5"h, mint 450-650
June 2, 2001 Sold for $650

2163. Rookwood vase, matt glaze, floral, Lincoln, 1920, #1356, 11"h, mint 1200-1700
June 2, 2001 Sold for $1200

2164. Rookwood vase, matt glaze, grapes, Barrett, 1924, #2639E, 8.5"h, mint 700-900
June 2, 2001 Sold for $750

2165. Rookwood bowl, hi-glaze, apples, A. Conant, 1919, #2287, 3.5"h, mint 600-800
June 2, 2001 Sold for $500

2166. Rookwood box, hi-glaze, floral, W. Hentschel, 1924, #2793, 5.5"dia., crack 250-350
June 2, 2001 Sold for $110

2167. Rookwood bowl, hi-glaze, floral, E. Barrett, 1944, #6313, 8"dia., mint 500-700
June 2, 2001 Sold for $375

2168. Rookwood vase, standard glaze, dogwood, Van Briggle, 1889, #464, 8"h, mint 700-900
June 2, 2001 Sold for $850

2169. Rookwood vase, standard glaze, floral design, H. Wilcox, 1895, #566B, 12"h, mint 800-1100
June 2, 2001 Sold for $950

2170. Rookwood ewer, standard glaze, floral design, I. Bishop, 1899, #304D, 5.5"h, mint 400-600
June 2, 2001 Sold for $375

2171. Rookwood vase, hi-glaze, flowers, artist H.F., 1945, #6432, 3.5"h, mint 250-350
June 2, 2001 Sold for $220

2172. Rookwood vase, hi-glaze, magnolia, L. Holtkamp, 1950, #2984A, 16"h, mint 1000-1500
June 2, 2001 Sold for $650

2173. Rookwood vase, hi-glaze, berries, 1945, #6375, 5.5"h, mint 250-350
June 2, 2001 Sold for $140

2174. Rookwood tile, matt glaze, landscape, Arts & Crafts style, 12"sq., excellent condition 2500-3500
June 2, 2001 Sold for $1900

2175. Rookwood tile, matt glaze, landscape, Arts & Crafts style, 12"sq., excellent condition 2500-3500
June 2, 2001 Sold for $2000

2176. Rookwood tile, matt glaze, landscape, Arts & Crafts style, 12"sq., excellent condition 2500-3500
June 2, 2001 Sold for $2700

2177. Rookwood vase, matt glaze, blossoms, C. Covalenco, 1925, #2831, 5.25"h, mint 600-800
June 2, 2001 Sold for $650

2178. Rookwood vase, matt glaze, flowers, E.N. Lincoln, 1927, #1918, 9"h, mint 1200-1700
June 2, 2001 Sold for $1200

2179. Rookwood vase, matt glaze, flowers, C. Covalenco, 1925, #2671, 4.5"h, mint 550-750
June 2, 2001 Sold for $425

2180. Rookwood vase, matt glaze, floral design, 1931, #6034, 7.5"h, mint 200-300
June 2, 2001 Sold for $400

2181. Rookwood vase, matt glaze, poppies, 1922, #1710, 10.5"h, mint 450-650
June 2, 2001 Sold for $700

2182. Rookwood vase, rare crystalline glaze, 1936, #6319D, 5"h, mint 150-250
June 2, 2001 Sold for $450

2183. Rookwood vase, vellum, poppies, Lyons, 1914, #951E, 7.5"h, hairline 500-700
June 2, 2001 Sold for $325

2184. Rookwood vase, vellum, floral design, F. Rothenbusch, 1917, #951D, 9"h, mint 800-1100
June 2, 2001 Sold for $1000

2185. Rookwood vase, vellum, floral design, McLaughlin, 1915, #2103, 5.5"h, mint 500-700
June 2, 2001 Sold for $600

2186. Rookwood match holder, standard glaze, L.V.B., 1902, #855, 2"h, mint 300-500
June 2, 2001 Sold for $240

2187. Rookwood ewer, standard glaze, berries, E. Felten, 1899, #510, 7"h, mint 500-700
June 2, 2001 Sold for $475

2188. Rookwood vase, standard glaze, floral design, Pons, 1906, #943F, 4"h, minute flake 250-350
June 2, 2001 Sold for $350

2189. Rookwood vessel, standard glaze, playing cards, McDonald, 1895, #830B, 7"h, mint 1500-2500
June 2, 2001 Sold for $1200

2190. Rookwood vase, standard glaze, frog, A.R. Valentien, 1898, #806D, 6.25"h, mint 1500-2500
June 2, 2001 Sold for $600

2191. Rookwood vessel, standard glaze, pansies, E.N. Lincoln, 1900, #234, 5.5"h, mint 800-1100
June 2, 2001 Sold for $650

2192. Rookwood vase, standard glaze, water lilies, Valentien, 1897, #537B, 18"h, restored 1500-2500
June 2, 2001 Sold for $700

2193. Rookwood vase, standard glaze, lily, silver overlay, Lincoln, 1898, #482, 9.5"h, lines 1500-2500
June 2, 2001 Sold for $1600

2194. Rookwood ewer, standard glaze, cherries, Valentien, 1891, #504, 18"h, mint 2000-3000
June 2, 2001 Sold for $1900

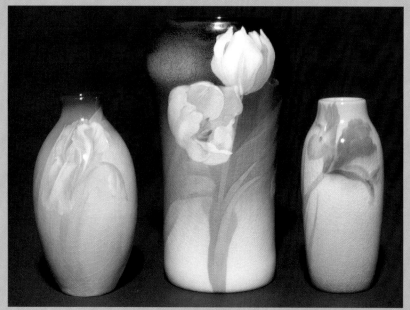

2195. Rookwood vase, iris glaze, irises, C. Schmidt, 1900, #732C, 6"h, mint 1500-2000
June 2, 2001 Sold for $1300

2196. Rookwood vase, iris glaze, tulips, S. Sax, 1906, #935C, 8.5"h, mint 2000-3000
June 2, 2001 Sold for $2800

2197. Rookwood vase, iris glaze, irises, C. Schmidt, 1904, #932F, 6"h, mint 1200-1700
June 2, 2001 Sold for $1300

2198. Rookwood vase, matt glaze, geometric, E. Barrett, 1919, #2254D, 5"h, mint 700-900
June 2, 2001 Sold for $950

2199. Rookwood vase, hi-glaze, geometric, 1951, #7069, 11.5"h, mint 1000-1500
June 2, 2001 Sold for $750

2200. Rookwood vase, hi-glaze, floral, S. Sax, 1930, #6180, 6"h, mint 2500-3500
June 2, 2001 Sold for $4000

2201. Rookwood vase, iris glaze, birds, Wareham, 1900, 8"h, minor crack 600-800
June 2, 2001 Sold for $425

2202. Rookwood vase, floral, Valentien, 1898, #S1366BB, 14.5"h, mint 2000-3000
June 2, 2001 Sold for $1500

2203. Rookwood vase, iris glaze, geese, C. Schmidt, 1900, #917, 9"h, restored hole 2000-3000
June 2, 2001 Sold for $3500

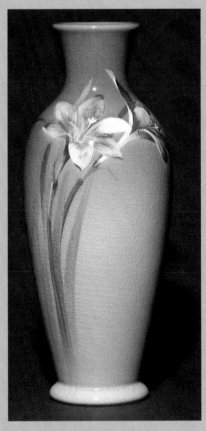

2204. Rookwood vase, iris glaze, star lily decoration,
C. Schmidt, 1902, #562, 9.5"h, mint 2500-3500
June 2, 2001 Sold for $3750

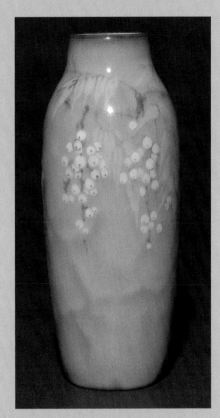

2205. Rookwood vase, porcelain glaze, bayberry, L.
Epply, 1921, #932B, 9.5"h, mint 3000-4000
June 2, 2001 Sold for $3750

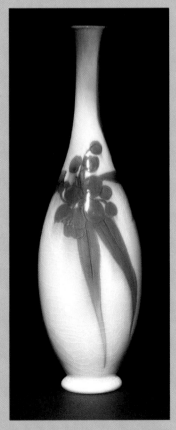

2206. Rookwood vase, iris glaze, flowers
and leaves, R. Fechheimer, 1900, #742D,
12.5"h, mint 2500-3500
June 2, 2001 Sold for $2200

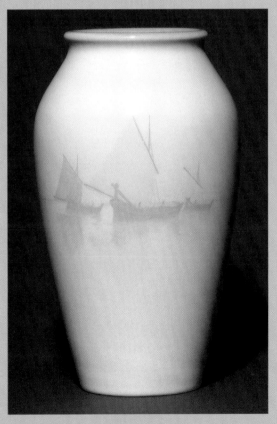

2207. Rookwood vase, porcelain glaze, sailboat, C. Schmidt, 1923,
#913D, 7.5"h, mint 3500-5500
June 2, 2001 Sold for $4500

2208. Rookwood vase, sea green glaze, leaf design, M. Daly, 1894, #749CW, 6.5"h, mint 2500-3500
June 2, 2001 Sold for $2200

2209. Rookwood vase, sea green glaze, rook, M. Daly, 1899, #904C, mint 4500-6500
June 2, 2001 Sold for $8500

2210. Rookwood tankard, standard glaze, character, applied copper, H. Wilcox , 1899, 9"h, mint 8000-11,000
June 2, 2001 Sold for $8000

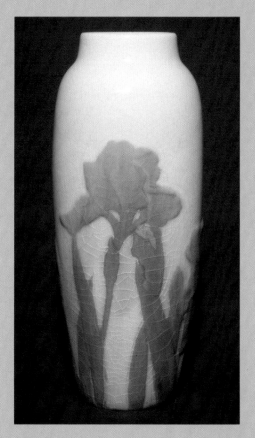

2211. Rookwood vase, iris glaze, iris design, M. Daly, 1900, #907D, 10.25"h, mint 3000-4000
June 2, 2001 Sold for $3250

2212. Rookwood plaque, ombroso glaze, 1915, #2031, 7.5" x 3.5", minor flakes 3000-5000
June 1, 2002 Sold for $6000

2213. Rookwood vase, grape design, matt glaze, C.S.
Todd, 1915, #218B, 10.5"h, mint 1500-2000
June 1, 2002 Sold for $1900

2214. Rookwood vase, vellum, sailboats and tugboat, E.T. Hurley, 1912,
#938D, 7"h, mint 3000-4000
June 1, 2002 Sold for $3500

2215. Rookwood plaque, vellum, landscape, L. Asbury, 1920, original frame, 7.5" x 5", mint 2500-3500
June 1, 2002 Sold for $4000

2216. Rookwood vase, jewel porcelain, floral design, C. McLaughlin, 1919, #999C, 9.5"h, mint 3000-4000
June 1, 2002 Sold for $2750

2217. Rookwood vase, Tiger Eye Empire green, sea horse, E.T. Hurley, 1923, #295D, 9.25"h, mint 2500-3500
June 1, 2002 Sold for $3500

2218. Rookwood vase, viola, standard glaze, #90C-3W, H.E. Wilcox, 4"h, mint 300-400
June 1, 2002 Sold for $300

2219. Rookwood ewer, sugar maple, standard glaze, #646, C. Steinle, 4.5"h, minute flake 200-300
June 1, 2002 Sold for $150

2220. Rookwood vase, standard glaze, Japanese quince, L. Asbury, 1903, #905D, 7.5"h, mint 650-750
June 1, 2002 Sold for $750

2221. Rookwood vase, standard glaze, persimmon, Van Briggle, 1889, uncrazed, #534C, 6.75"h, mint 650-850
June 1, 2002 Sold for $550

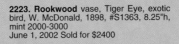

2222. Rookwood floor vase, standard glaze, magnolia, Shirayamadani, 24.5"h, repair 2500-3500
June 1, 2002 Sold for $2250

2223. Rookwood vase, Tiger Eye, exotic bird, W. McDonald, 1898, #S1363, 8.25"h, mint 2000-3000
June 1, 2002 Sold for $2400

2224. Rookwood vase, Tiger Eye, swan, W. McDonald, 1892, #562, R for red clay, 9.5"h, minor repair 600-800
June 1, 2002 Sold for $500

2225. Rookwood handled vessel, standard glaze, corn, J. Zettel, 1896, 4.5"h, mint 250-350
June 1, 2002 Sold for $200

2226. Rookwood handled vessel, standard glaze, grapes, L. Lindeman, 1908, #1071, 5"h, mint 250-350
June 1, 2002 Sold for $250

2227. Rookwood vase, standard glaze, clover, #452, A.M. Valentien, 1892, 7.5"dia., mint 1000-2000
June 1, 2002 Sold for $900

2228. Rookwood inkwell, standard glaze, violets, #418A, R. Fechheimer, 1899, 6"dia., minute flake 600-800
June 1, 2002 Sold for $750

2229. Rookwood vase, standard glaze, English ivy, J. Zettel, 1893, #571W, 7.5"h, mint 650-850
June 1, 2002 Sold for $750

2230. Rookwood vase, standard glaze, apple blossoms, #720, C.A. Baker, 1895, 6"dia., mint 500-700
June 1, 2002 Sold for $450

2231. Rookwood ewer, standard glaze, water lily, E.N. Lincoln, 1902, #611B, 10"h, mint 700-900
June 1, 2002 Sold for $850

2232. Rookwood ewer, standard glaze, floral design, #497, A.R. Valentien, 1892, 7.5"h, line 300-400
June 1, 2002 Sold for $190

2233. Rookwood vase, mahogany glaze, butterfly, impressed Rookwood, M. Rettig, 1885, 3"h, mint 300-400
June 1, 2002 Sold for $425

2234. Rookwood vase, standard glaze, pansies, #698E, S.E. Coyne, 1899, 4"h, mint 300-400
June 1, 2002 Sold for $400

2235. Rookwood plaque, landscape, L. Asbury, 1922,
9.5" x 12", original frame, mint 6500-8500
June 1, 2002 Sold for $8000

2236. Rookwood plaque, vellum, sailboat,
C. Schmidt, 1912, 4" x 7.5", mint 3500-4500
June 1, 2002 Sold for $3750

2237. Rookwood plaque, vellum, landscape,
F. Rothenbusch, 1935, 9" x 12", mint 6500-8500
June 1, 2002 Sold for $7000

2238. Rookwood plaque, titled "Winter Twilight," snow laden landscape, E. McDermott, 1910, 9" x 11.5", mint 7000-9000
June 1, 2002 Sold for $7500

2239. Rookwood plaque, vellum, landscape, E.T. Hurley, 1912, 5.5" x 7.5", mint 3000-4000
June 1, 2002 Sold for $4250

2240. Rookwood plaque, vellum, landscape, E. Diers, 1916, signed, 8.5" x 11", mint 5500-7500
June 1, 2002 Sold for $6500

2241. Rookwood vase, vellum, daisies, M.G. Denzler, 1914, #1278F, 7.5"h, mint 650-850
June 1, 2002 Sold for $500

2242. Rookwood vase, vellum, apple blossoms, K. Van Horne, 1911, #1655F, 6.5"h, mint 650-850
June 1, 2002 Sold for $550

2243. Rookwood vase, floral design, E.N. Lincoln, 1925, #2066, 8"h, hairline 300-400
June 1, 2002 Sold for $375

2244. Rookwood vase, matt glaze, floral design, E.N. Lincoln, 1922, #900D, 7"h, mint 600-800
June 1, 2002 Sold for $550

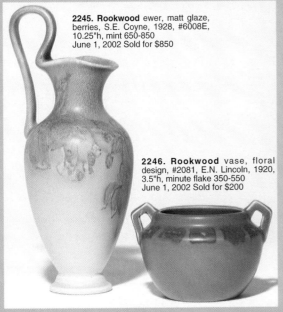

2245. Rookwood ewer, matt glaze, berries, S.E. Coyne, 1928, #6008E, 10.25"h, mint 650-850
June 1, 2002 Sold for $850

2246. Rookwood vase, floral design, #2081, E.N. Lincoln, 1920, 3.5"h, minute flake 350-550
June 1, 2002 Sold for $200

2247. Rookwood vase, matt glaze, floral design, marked, #939C, C.S. Todd, 1919, 9.5"h, flaw 550-750
June 1, 2002 Sold for $475

2248. Rookwood vase, matt glaze, grapes, C.S. Todd, 1921, #155F, 7"h, minor line 400-600
June 1, 2002 Sold for $300

2249. Rookwood vase, matt glaze, floral design, K. Jones, 1926, #952F, 6.5"h, mint 400-600
June 1, 2002 Sold for $500

2250. Rookwood vase, vellum, landscape, F. Rothenbusch, 1911, #952F, 6.25"h, hairline 400-600
June 1, 2002 Sold for $600

2251. **Rookwood** vase, hawthorn, L. Asbury, 1898, #749C, 6.5"h, mint 500-700
June 1, 2002 Sold for $400

2252. **Rookwood** vase, Japanese quince design, 1894, J. Zettel, 6"w, mint 450-650
June 1, 2002 Sold for $550

2253. **Rookwood** ewer, chrysanthemums, dull finish glaze, A. Valentien, #62W7, 1887, 7.5"h, mint 900-1200
June 1, 2002 Sold for $500

2254. **Rookwood** ewer, standard glaze, roses, #443, S. Toohey, 1889, 6.5"h, mint 600-800
June 1, 2002 Sold for $550

2255. **Rookwood** vase, Aerial blue, violets, L. Asbury, X158X, 5"h, mint 1500-2000
June 1, 2002 Sold for $1900

2256. **Rookwood** handled vessel, Aerial blue, woman and trees, B. Horsfall, 1895, #769, 3"h, mint 1500-2500
June 1, 2002 Sold for $1500

2257. **Rookwood** Turkish teapot, dull finish glaze, frog fishing and sandcrabs, M.L. Nichols, 1883, 11"h, mint 2000-3000
June 1, 2002 Sold for $1500

2258. **Rookwood** covered vessel, dull finish glaze, morning glories, A. Van Briggle, 1887, #326, 6.5"h, repair 1200-1700
June 1, 2002 Sold for $500

2259. **Rookwood** ewer, early brown glaze, apple blossoms, A.R. Valentien, 1888, #391, 12"h, minor scratches 1000-1500
June 1, 2002 Sold for $850

2260. **Rookwood** ewer, standard glaze, Japanese quince, M. Nourse, 1896, #684, 8"h, minor scratches 650-850
June 1, 2002 Sold for $500

2261. Rookwood vase, black iris glaze, cherry blossoms, Shiraya-madani, 1906, #951C, 10"h, mint 7500-10,000
June 1, 2002 Sold for $7500

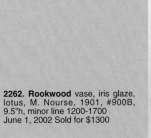

2262. Rookwood vase, iris glaze, lotus, M. Nourse, 1901, #900B, 9.5"h, minor line 1200-1700
June 1, 2002 Sold for $1300

2263. Rookwood vase, standard glaze, nasturtium, silver overlay, E.N. Lincoln, 1896, #565, 8"h, mint 5000-7000
June 1, 2002 Sold for $5750

2264. Rookwood vase, Magnolia soulangeana, L. Asbury, 1924, #900A, 13"h, mint 8000-11,000
June 1, 2002 Sold for $8500

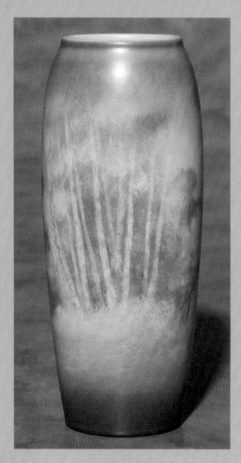

2265. Rookwood vase, landscape,
#951E, 1940, E.T. Hurley, 1940,
#951, 7.5"h, mint 2500-3500
June 1, 2002 Sold for $3500

2266. Rookwood vase, landscape,
1912, #1660A, E.T. Hurley, 16"h,
mint 7000-9000
June 1, 2002 Sold for $8000

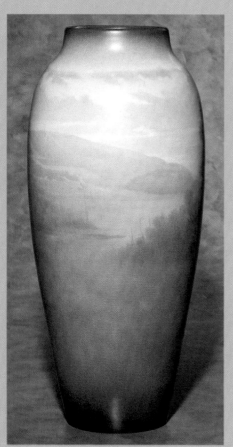

2267. Rookwood vase, landscape,
vellum, #907B, C. Schmidt, 1918,
17.5"h, minor line 6500-8500
June 1, 2002 Sold for $4500

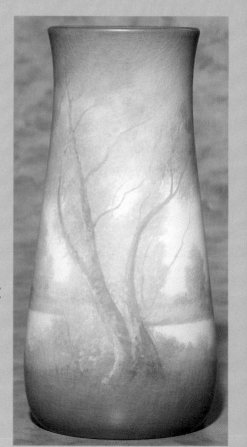

2268. Rookwood vase, landscape,
vellum, 1923, #7023C, E. Diers,
10.5"h, mint 3000-4000
June 1, 2002 Sold for $3750

2269. Rookwood vase, poppy pod design, ombroso glaze, #130, C.S. Todd, 1915, 6.5"w, mint 1500-2500
June 1, 2002 Sold for $2200

2270. Rookwood vase, matt glaze, C.S. Todd, 1915, #966, 3.5"h, mint 700-900
June 1, 2002 Sold for $1000

2271. Rookwood tray, feather, matt glaze, 1905, #1048D, 5"w, mint 150-250
June 1, 2002 Sold for $200

2272. Rookwood vase, ombroso glaze, #515, C.S. Todd in 1915, 14"h, repair to hairline at rim 1200-1700
June 1, 2002 Sold for $1600

2273. Rookwood vase, double vellum, anemones, Shirayamadani, 1936, #6601, 9.5"h, mint 2000-3000
June 1, 2002 Sold for $1600

2274. Rookwood vase, double vellum, anemones, Shirayamadani, 1936, #6601, 9.5"h, mint 2000-3000
June 1, 2002 Sold for $1700

2275. Rookwood vase, landscape, vellum, E. Diers, 1918, #30E, 8.5"h, mint 2500-3500
June 1, 2002 Sold for $3250

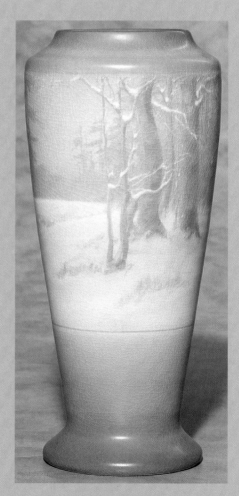

2276. Rookwood vase, landscape, vellum, E. Diers, 1909, #1856B, 13.5"h, drilled, mint 1500-2500
June 1, 2002 Sold for $1900

2277. Rookwood vase, geometric design, E. Barrett, 9"h, no shape number and date 350-450
June 1, 2002 Sold for $400

2278. Rookwood vase, Mat Moderne glaze, geometric design, #6201D, E. Barrett, 1931, 6.75"h, mint 800-1100
June 1, 2002 Sold for $950

2279. Rookwood vase, geometric design, matt glaze, E. Barrett, 1944, #6306, 7"h, mint 450-650
June 1, 2002 Sold for $400

2280. Rookwood vase, jewel orcelain, blueberries, L. Epply, 1943, #5194F, 5"h, mint 400-600
June 1, 2002 Sold for $475

2281. Rookwood vase, floral design, matt glaze, W. Rehm, 1931, #2077, 6.5"h, mint 550-750
June 1, 2002 Sold for $950

2282. Rookwood vase, modernist design, matt glaze, #6196E, J. Jensen, 1930, 6.25"h, mint 450-650
June 1, 2002 Sold for $650

2283. Rookwood vase, leaf design, jewel porcelain, S. Sax, 1930, #2996, 8.5"h, repaired 800-1100
June 1, 2002 Sold for $500

2284. Rookwood vase, geometric design, jewel porcelain, #6194D, J. Harris, 1931, 6.5"h, minor line 450-650
June 1, 2002 Sold for $425

2285. Rookwood vase, squeezebag design, Mat Moderne glaze, W.E. Hentschel, 1927, #614C, 13"h, mint 2500-3500
June 1, 2002 Sold for $2200

2286. Rookwood vase, Mat Moderne glaze, leaf and berry design, E. Barrett, 1929, #2914, 8.5"h, mint 1000-1500
June 1, 2002 Sold for $700

2287. Rookwood vase, poppies, double vellum, Shirayamadani, 1936, #6578, 8.25"h, mint 1700-2200 June 1, 2002 Sold for $1700

2288. Rookwood vase, vellum, mariposa lily, #2831, 1926, Shirayamadani, 5.5"h, mint 1500-2000 June 1, 2002 Sold for $1500

2289. Rookwood vase, vellum, roses, E. Diers, 1906, #1126C, 9"h, chips 350-550 June 1, 2002 Sold for $250

2290. Rookwood vase, vellum, landscape, E. Diers, 1917, #940D, 10.5"h, bruise 2000-2500 June 1, 2002 Sold for $1200

2291. Rookwood vase, jewel porcelain, irises, C. Schmidt, 1923, #356F, 5.5"h, mint 2500-3500 June 1, 2002 Sold for $2500

2292. Rookwood vase, jewel porcelain, peonies, 1920, #356F, A. Conant, 5.5"h, mint 2200-2700 June 1, 2002 Sold for $3500

2293. Rookwood vase, vellum, mistletoe, H. Lyons, 1913, #918E, 6"h, mint 700-900 June 1, 2002 Sold for $700

2294. Rookwood vase, matt glaze, dogwood, M. McDonald, 1936, 5.5"h, mint 650-850 June 1, 2002 Sold for $550

2296. Rookwood ewer, standard glaze, leaf design, #754, E.N. Lincoln, 1900, 6.5"h, mint 500-750
June 1, 2002 Sold for $350

2295. Rookwood ewer, standard glaze, maple leaves, #584C, R. Fechheimer, 1898, 5.5"h, mint 350-550
June 1, 2002 Sold for $300

2298. Rookwood vase, standard glaze, tulips, #909, J. Zettel, 1901, 9"h, drilled 350-450
June 1, 2002 Sold for $650

2297. Rookwood vase, standard glaze, holly, #744C, J.D. Wareham, 1895, 7.75"h, minute bruise 350-450
June 1, 2002 Sold for $375

2299. Rookwood ewer, standard glaze, roses, #578C, E.T. Hurley, 1903, original label, 13"h, mint 800-1100
June 1, 2002 Sold for $700

2300. Rookwood vase, standard glaze, leaf and berry design, O.G. Reed, 1893, 9.5"h, mint 650-750
June 1, 2002 Sold for $550

2301. Rookwood vase, standard glaze, water lily, L. Asbury, 1902, #913C, 8.5"h, mint 600-800
June 1, 2002 Sold for $800

2302. Rookwood vase, standard glaze, flowering plum, #424C, Shirayamadani, 1890, 10"h, cracked 350-450
June 1, 2002 Sold for $500

2303. Rookwood ewer, early hi-glaze, irises, #101A, A.R. Valentien, 1885, 11.5"h, repaired 350-450
June 1, 2002 Sold for $550

2304. Rookwood ewer, standard glaze bachelor buttons, marked, #471, 1893, 11"h, breaks to handle 300-400
June 1, 2002 Sold for $190

2305. Rookwood vase, daisies, matt glaze, M.H. McDonald, 1916, #1358F, 6"h, mint 700-900
June 1, 2002 Sold for $450

2306. Rookwood vase, stylized floral design, matt glaze, C.S. Todd, 1919, #2103, 5.5"h, mint 550-750
June 1, 2002 Sold for $500

2307. Rookwood vase, iris glaze, fish, S.E. Coyne, 1911, #918E, 6"h, mint 900-1200
June 1, 2002 Sold for $1200

2308. Rookwood vase, vellum, fish, E.T. Hurley, 1904, #162D, 5.5"h, mint 1000-1500
June 1, 2002 Sold for $1100

2309. Rookwood vase, magnolia design, hi-glaze, W. Rehm, 1945, #2917E, 6.5"h, mint 700-900
June 1, 2002 Sold for $450

2310. Rookwood vase, fish and flowers, J. Jensen, 1946, #6569, mint 800-1100
June 1, 2002 Sold for $650

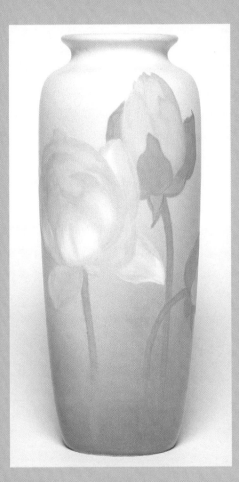

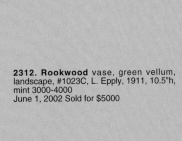

2311. Rookwood vase, vellum, peonies, S. Sax, 1905, #904C, 11.75"h, mint 3000-3500
June 1, 2002 Sold for $4250

2312. Rookwood vase, green vellum, landscape, #1023C, L. Epply, 1911, 10.5"h, mint 3000-4000
June 1, 2002 Sold for $5000

2313. Rookwood vase, Hercules parsnip, sea green, A.R. Valentien, 1895, #578, 14.5"h, mint 6500-7500
June 1, 2002 Sold for $5500

2314. Rookwood vase, vellum, landscape, F. Rothenbusch, 1919, #1660D, 9"h, mint 2500-3500
June 1, 2002 Sold for $3000

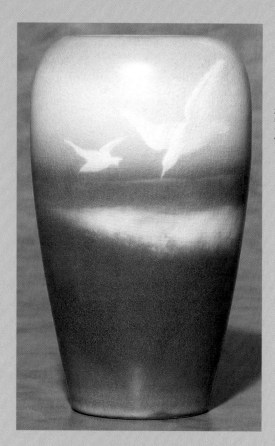

2315. Rookwood vase, vellum, seagulls, E.T. Hurley, 1907, #1126C, 9"h, mint 3000-4000
June 1, 2002 Sold for $3500

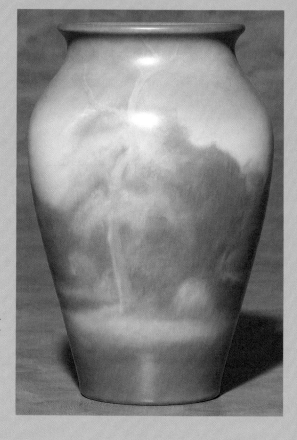

2316. Rookwood vase, vellum, landscape, F. Rothenbush, 1931, #2996, 8.5"h, mint 2750-3250
June 1, 2002 Sold for $3000

2317. Rookwood vase, black iris glaze, grasses, Shirayamadani, 1900, #900B, 9.5"h, hairline 2500-3500
June 1, 2002 Sold for $5000

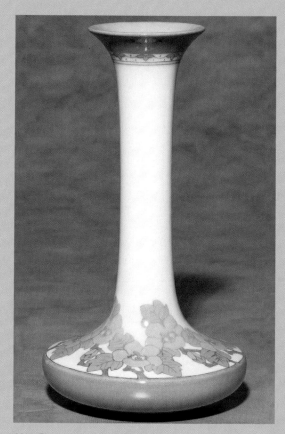

2318. Rookwood vase, jewel porcelain, floral design, S. Sax, 1918, #553C, 10"h, mint 2750-3250
June 1, 2002 Sold for $2000

2319. Rookwood vase, iris glaze, Virginia creeper, F. Rothenbusch, 1902, #902D, 7"h, mint 1200-1700
June 1, 2002 Sold for $1700

2320. Rookwood vase, iris glaze, hawthorn, L.E. Lindeman, 1903, #9265, 6"h, mint 800-1100
June 1, 2002 Sold for $850

2321. Rookwood vase, matt glaze, floral design, #1124E, O.G. Reed, 7"h, mint 1000-1500
June 1, 2002 Sold for $1000

2322. Rookwood vase, vellum, irises, K. Van Horne, 1905, #1655F, 6.5"h, mint 900-1200
June 1, 2002 Sold for $1000

2323. Rookwood vase, iris glaze, pansies, S. Sax, 1911, #905E, 6.75"h, mint 900-1200
June 1, 2002 Sold for $1500

2324. Rookwood vase, iris glaze, clover, O.G. Reed, 1900, #917, 5.5"h, mint 800-1100
June 1, 2002 Sold for $800

2325. Rookwood vase, vellum, landscape, #952, L. Asbury, 1915, 7.75"h, mint 1000-1500
June 1, 2002 Sold for $1300

2326. Rookwood vase, vellum, landscape, L. Epply, 1913, #1930, 7"h, mint 900-1200
June 1, 2002 Sold for $1100

2327. Rookwood plaque, vellum, landscape, E. Diers, 1919, 14.5" x 9.25", mint 8,000-11,000
June 1, 2002 Sold for $10,000

2328. Rookwood plaque, vellum, waterfall, F. Rothenbusch, 1927, 7" x 9", mint 7000-9000
June 1, 2002 Sold for $9000

2329. Rookwood vase, bird, matt glaze, W. Hentschel, 1912, #1342, 8.5"h, repaired 1200-1700
June 1, 2002 Sold for $900

2330. Rookwood vase, matt glaze, apple blossoms, C. Covalenco, 1925, #2831, 5.25"h, mint 600-800
June 1, 2002 Sold for $750

2331. Rookwood vase, matt glaze, floral design, S.E. Coyne, 1924, #2722, 6.25"h, mint 400-500
June 1, 2002 Sold for $375

2332. Rookwood vase, matt glaze, berries, #1925, 1916, 5.5"h, mint 550-750
June 1, 2002 Sold for $450

2333. Rookwood vase, double vellum, poppies, Shiraya-madani, 1944, #6357, 6.5"h, mint 1200-1700
June 1, 2002 Sold for $1100

2334. Rookwood vase, vellum, roses, H. Wilcox, 1926, #363, 6"h, mint 1200-1700
June 1, 2002 Sold for $1100

2335. Rookwood plaque, vellum, landscape, titled "Across the Lake," F. Rothenbusch, 8" x 6", mint 4000-5000
June 1, 2002 Sold for $5500

2336. Rookwood plaque, vellum, sailboats, titled "The Morning Hour," C. Schmidt, 9.5" x 11.5", mint 6000-8000
June 1, 2002 Sold for $6500

Index
Numbers listed are plate numbers.

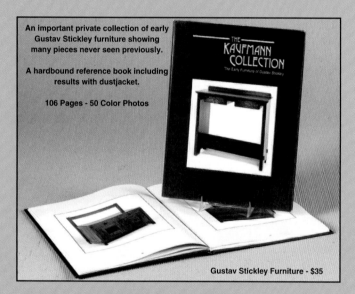
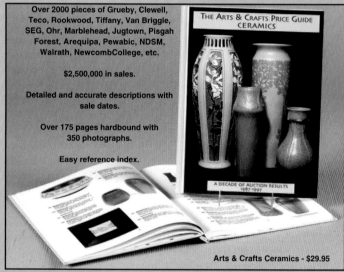

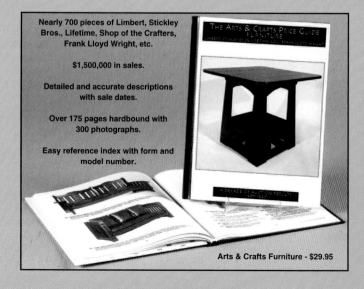

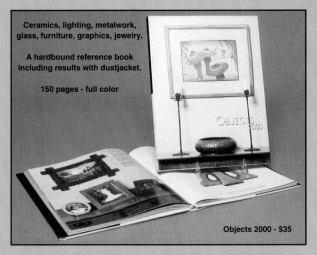

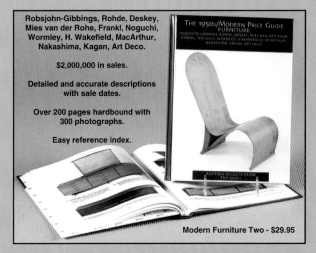
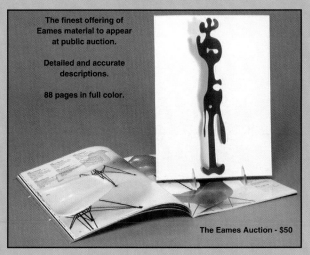
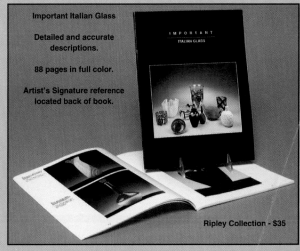